MOON POWER STARGUIDE 1998

UNIVERSAL GUIDANCE AND PREDICTIONS

Louis Turi, M.D.S.

MOON POWER STARGUIDE 1998

UNIVERSAL GUIDANCE AND PREDICTIONS

Louis Turi, M.D.S.

NOT FOR SALE
ORDER 1999 MOON POWER SEND $28.00
ORDER POWER OF THE DRAGON 525 PAGES SEND $35.00
S/H INCLUDED TO: DR. TURI P.O. BOX
81529 SAN DIEGO, CA 92110 (619) 275-5853

KENDALL/HUNT PUBLISHING COMPANY
4050 Westmark Drive   Dubuque, Iowa 52002

Copyright © 1997 by Dr. Louis Turi

All rights reserved. No part of this publication may be reproduced or transmitted in any form or by any means, electronic or mechanical, including photocopy, recording, or any information storage and retrieval system, without permission in writing from the publisher.

ISBN 0-7872-4426-0

Published by
Truth Seeker Co., Inc.
P. O. Box 28550
San Diego, California 92198

Special Issue — Limited Edition
August 1997

Printed in the United States of America

10 9 8 7 6 5 4 3 2 1

Starguide 1998

Table of Contents

	Acknowledgments	1
	My Story	5
	Letter From the Author	11
1.	Starguide's Purpose	19
2.	Predictions for the Century	21
3.	1998 Slow-Moving Planets Predictions	25
4.	Pluto's Impact on Generations	33
5.	The Universal Law	39
6.	Your Personal Horoscopes for 1998	49
7.	Your 1998 Starguide Day-to-Day Guidance	85
8.	Solar and Lunar Eclipses	289
9.	Supernova Windows for 1998	293
10.	Back in Time	297
11.	Earthquake Predictions	303
12.	Celebrity Predictions	309
13.	1998 World Predictions	311
14.	Dragon's Head and Tail Universal Predictions	315
15.	Astro-Profile of Marshall Applewhite	331
16.	Interviews with Dr. Turi	341
17.	In the News	359
18.	Closing Thoughts	361
19.	About Dr. Turi's Practice	362
20.	Dr. Turi — Services Offered	365

Acknowledgments

I am infinitely grateful for the love, support, respect and insight of my sweet Brigitte. A special thanks to Bonnie, Nancy, Owen, Annie, Eddie, Alice, Jon, Jean, Ron, Jordan, David, Paul and all the staff from the Truth Seeker Co., Inc. To all my great friends, family, faithful clients, students, subscribers and readers from all over the world.

A special thanks to: California Publisher & Editor, *Perceptions Magazine*; Minnesota Publisher & Editor, *Fate Magazine*; Washington Publisher & Editor, *The Missing Link*; Arizona Publisher & Editor *Association Of Astrologers*; California Publisher & Editor *Lightsource*; Canada Publisher & Editor, *Insight Magazine;* California Publisher & Editor *Light News;* Colorado Publisher & Editor *International Tesla Society, Inc.*; Michigan Publisher & Editor *Connecting Link*; Publisher & Editor *Planetary Connections*; Argentina Publisher & Editor *Oculto Magazine*; Mexico Publisher & Editor *OVNI Magazine*; Dr. Nakamura, President, Scripps Clinic Medical Group; Dr. William Watkins; Dr. David Jungclaus.

Exceptional Friends: Colonel Wendelle C. Stevens; Randolph Winters; Robert O. Dean, Dr. Frank E. Stranges; Bill Cooper Veritas, John Gray, *Men are from Mars, Women from Venus;* John Hogue, *Nostradamus: The Complete Prophecies*; Richard J. Boylan, *Project Epiphany;* Randolph Winters, *Mind and Spirit*; Michel Malecot, Owner *French Gourmet*; Stan Kozak, *Polka Family;* Publisher G. Cope Schellhorn, Horus House Press, Inc.; German Publisher & Editor, *Magazine 2000;* Michael Heseman; Gary Miller, telephone engineer; Skylar Dodd, handwriting analyst; R. Rev. Helga Morrow, *The Morrow Chronicles*; Dr. D. L. Lucas, *The Mini Metaphysical Manual*; Producer, Carlsbad,

Daniels CableVision; Rob Baldwin, Shawn Atlantic Director San Diego UFO Society; A. J. Gevaerd, Director, UFO Brazilian Center DBPDV; James Aramat, President UFO West; Tim Bekley, President Global Communications; Penny Harper, Director, Aquarius Ranch Communication; Dr. Frederika L. Gold; Stebbins F. Deans, Executive Director, Fresno Chamber of Commerce.

A special thanks to the numerous open-minded journalists and hosts of radio and television programs. I am grateful to all of those spiritual men and women who have helped me to enlighten their audiences with the stars. I appreciate all those souls who have guided and supported my work. In their common efforts to further the truth they all are vital participants in the understanding of the human experience. All of you have been invaluable in furthering the truth, and I am infinitely grateful for allowing me to pass on my celestial message to the world.

Radio:

Host: Jeff Rence – *End of the Line* Premiere Radio Network
Host: Rob McConnel – *The X Chronicles* – IPBN – Int Radio Network
Host: Jon Rappoport – KLAV 1230 AM – Las Vegas
Host: Dave Allan – KSCO 1080 AM – Monterey, CA
Host: Sandra Marshall – KGLV 1340 AM – San Luis Obispo CA
Host: Roger Hedgecock – KSDO 1130 AM – San Diego, CA
Host: Dr. Frederika L. Gold – KCIN – Apple Valley, CA
Host: Dave Berg – KGMG AM 1320 – Oceanside, CA
Host: Austin Vali – KULA 96.3 FM/AM Honolulu, HI
Host: John Van Zante – KCEO 1000 AM – Vista, CA
Host: Dave Burger – 91X AM/FM – San Diego, CA
Host: Joyce Isaacs – KVET 1300 AM – Austin, TX
Host: Rob McConnel – Internet *X Chronicles* World Wide, Canada
Host: Art Bell – *Dreamland* – Nationwide Syndication
Hosts: Steve Ryan & Ross Ford – KILO 94.3 FM – CO
Host: Pat McMahon – KTAR 620 AM – Phoenix, AZ
Host: Jan Ross – KFYI 910 AM – Phoenix, AZ

Host: Paxton Quigley – KMPC AM 70 – CA
Host: Lou Epton – KNXP 840 AM – Las Vegas, NV Nationwide Syndication
Host: Randy Ranshow – KSCJ 1360 AM – Iowa

Television:

Host: Dave Balsiger – Sun Int. Pictures – CBS/NBC – *Ancient Mysteries of the World*
Host: Kathryn A. Kaycoff – *Sightings* – Fox Television .
Host: Kim and Tom Reese Executive Director, Channel 37 – KOCT – Oceanside, CA
Host: Ted Loman – UFOAZ – Tucson AZ.
Host: Charlotte Evans – Channel 8 News – KLAS – Las Vegas, NV
Host: Sylvia DiPietro – WNYX – New York, NY
Host: Laura Buxton – Channel 10 News – KGTV – San Diego, CA
Host: Pat McMahon – Channel 10 News – Phoenix, AZ
Host: Russ Estes – Crystal Sky Productions – Victorville, CA
Host: Kim Rettberg – KOCT Television – Oceanside, CA
Host: Jason Walker – Daniels CableVision – Carlsbad, CA
Host: Penny Harper – A.R.C. TV – Los Angeles, CA
Host: Mitch Battros – Channel 29 Live TV – Seattle, WA

He is wise who understands that the stars are luminaries, created as signs. He who will conquer the stars will hold the golden keys to God's mysterious universe.

— Nostradamus

My Story

Dreamer, Slacker, Head in the Clouds, Stargazer, I am sure that we have all heard those terms, but none rang so clear in my head as "Stargazer." I am not in the strictest sense of the word a Stargazer but I do read the messages that they have left indelibly across all men's souls. Now, I did not start out in life with this intent. No way, I was gonna be a big rock-and-roll star. That's right. I went to the Royal School of Music in London, applied and was accepted to my immense amazement. My piano teacher said that I would be, but you never believe that kind of thing until it actually happens. I still had to work to pay for my studies, and I worked hard as a barman for a prestigious hotel. This job suited me well; I got to meet new girls all the time, make just enough money to pay for my studies and a pint of lager at the end of the day. But when I wasn't working, I practiced my piano until my fingers bled. All the while wishing I still had my guitar, but that had been broken by a gang that hung out in the Victoria Station metro after dark.

Before I was able to get a job and a piano teacher, I had to survive in a new country where I did not speak the language, being a Frenchman; English is a real twist. So, I started out in the tubes singing French songs and making a few pence a day; so that I would be able to eat something later on. Incidentally, my first English words came to me as I went shopping for my first dinner. I scanned the shelves in the store until I found the cheapest thing that I could. It came out of a can and was cold and crunchy but it filled my belly. After eating, I got out my little French-to-English dictionary and looked up to words, "Dog" and "Food." You can imagine my disgust when I found out what this meant, but I was lucky and got to eat that day. When there was a lull in the metro I would run up the steps and be right at Victoria Station, and huge and busy place with a whole bank of telephones. I would run up and down, listening for someone who spoke my native tongue. I finally found a Swiss man who spoke both English and French who gave me a job in the hotel. I started out as a janitor and moved up to dishwasher and finally to barman after much work. I was to stay in England for almost ten years as I worked and studied my music. Finally, I graduated at the top of my class earning the prized "Distinction Cup" and commendation from some faraway Royal family members. This led me to a deal, not a good deal but still a deal with Phillips Phonogram records. I produced several records and then went back to France to promote them for awhile, glad to leave the harsh English weather behind, especially in November.

My brother owned a discotheque at the time called L'Interdit or The Forbidden, it was quite the hot spot, and he asked me to come and do my songs there. I gladly accepted the invitation and we left his farmhouse about forty-five minutes away from his place about 9:00 p.m. While driving through the deserted roads by the vineyards I saw lights flashing out in the vineyards and remarked to my brother that there were people in the vineyards harvesting. He looked at like I had lost my mind, "Louis," he said, "It's November, all the grapes have been picked a long time ago!" I then watched the lights come closer and closer until our car was bathed in light so bright that we could not see, and my brother's brand-new Mercedes stalled right there in the middle of the road and would not restart. We both had our noses to the windscreen trying to see this thing in the air that was showering us in all this light, but it was still too bright, so I got out of the car, and then the lights dimmed down until the car, with my brother in it scared to death, and me outside were then bathed in a reddish pink light with a pleasing glow coming from none other than a Spaceship or UFO suspended about thirty feet above our heads for at least five minutes. It made a slight humming sound like a baby making the motorcycle noise to himself. It was beautiful with multi-colored lights all around it that couldn't be seen while its two main bright white headlights were on.

It just hung there in the sky for our viewing pleasure just out of reach. We stared in awe, me banging on the car, yelling and cursing for all I was worth for my brother to get out of the car, but he wouldn't. So much for being a big bad guy. Big brothers, what do you expect? Finally, it just flew away, careless as you please and we watched as it picked up speed and disappeared. When I got back into the car, my brother swore me to secrecy, that "We would never tell anyone about this ever!!!!" When we arrived at the disco that night everything was in full swing, which is very strange because we should have arrived with the crew who was opening; looking back I would say that we had a missing-in-time thing happen, but we didn't know anything about that back then, just that it was really strange. The next day, my mother called me up and asked if my brother was okay. I laughed, remembering the secrecy deal and assured my mom everything was fine. Which it was, but my soul had somehow changed and I began to think that there was more to life than gigging and making records. Maybe I could make a greater contribution, I didn't know what yet, but I wanted something. It didn't take me long to get the wanderlust again, and I was off to America. I had written a song about this great land, with a dream in my heart just a few short years before. Now I was going. I didn't know anybody, didn't have any money, because it turns out my contract had my music playing everywhere in Europe except my country and I couldn't collect my share.

Oh, the trials of youth! But I had high hopes and a business card from a man I met in London who said, "Come to America, I will help you start a new life!" I arrived in Los Angeles, the City of Angels, smoggy and yucky, caught a Greyhound bus to San Diego, gorgeous and green, got out my little wallet with fifty dollars and the business card searching for the business on Garnet Avenue in Pacific Beach, California. I am still searching for this man and his business. Disheartened, I took thirty of my precious dollars and paid for a motel for the night, and then went to a bar up the street. I ordered a drink and then went to the cigarette machine; weird thing, never saw one of those before, I couldn't figure out how to work it. So I asked a man at the end of the bar if he could help me out. He looked at me funny for a minute or two and then showed me how it worked. Later on he told me why he looked at me funny; he thought I was gay and that this was a come-on! Better not tell that to my wife, you know how wives are!!! This man's name is John Stewart and he became one of my best friends. We got drunk and told lies that night, I thought I might as well, didn't know what the future would hold, but I still held a shiny bit of enthusiasm in my soul.

I had begun to learn the ways of the great Cosmic Clock then and knew that I arrived on American soil during a great trend! When I awoke the next morning, I went up the street with my suitcase in one hand and a purse in the other. In France it is customary for men to carry purses. This may be another reason why John looked at me funny, as that is definitely not the custom here. I smelt the ocean and took off in that direction; the waves crashing against the shore was soothing to my nerves, but the girls all wearing tops was more culture shock for me. I spent another dollar or two of my precious money getting a cup of coffee and then grabbed a newspaper, *The La Jolla Light*. I needed a place to stay and found a section called "Roommates." There was a great ad for a beautiful house on the ocean in La Jolla with a telephone number and an address. I called the lady up and told her that I was on my way. When I arrived with my suitcase, she remarked how fast and eager I was, with a worried look on her face. She then explained that with two more guys like me, we would all be able to afford a beautiful home on the sea. Wow, new word for me, roommate. I explained my situation and she felt sorry for me, and said I could stay with her and tutor her daughter in French. Housing settled for the moment, I went to find a job.

Up the street, I ran into a little restaurant called, "The French Gourmet." Soon I had my first job in America, washing dishes, not glamorous, but a job. Nice guy, my boss, Michel Malecot. I worked for him for four years, working my way up to general manager. I also soon moved into my very own apartment, and in every spare minute I had I read and studied my new obsession: Astrology. I inhaled books and knowledge everywhere I went; I even painted the apartment that Michel gave me to oversee his catering department, with my own astrological chart, the human body and what sign rules each part as well as other pictures with UFOs prevalent in the bringing of knowledge. The more I read, the more I went back to the books I read about Nostradamus and his works, as well as the books that the great man himself had written. He had a particular way of interpreting the stars that echoed down the valleys of my soul. He made so much more sense than all the mathematical process in every other way. I dedicated myself to his method and learned and learned, and then seemed to channel knowledge from the universe itself. When Michel came to collect his rent for the first month and found his beautiful apartment all painted up, you can imagine his shock, but I sat him down and said, "I want to give you a reading."

He was my first client! He is still a client today. I began to tell people about my passion and people began to come for readings. I had stopped working for Michel; I couldn't take the stress any longer. I had gone back to working engineering, welding and heavy equipment, what I learned as a young boy with my stepfather. I would toil with a bulldozer all day and then come home tired, shower, grab a meal, and see the clients — at least one every night. It was hard, but my energy for this seemed inexhaustible.

One night, a brunette appeared at my door; she had a 7:00 p.m. appointment to see me, and her name was Brigitte. She recommended me to all her friends, even paying for their visits to see me. She is now my wife! I was not so great then that I knew that this would be my wife, or I might not have let her in the house! But I knew that she was special, and wounded but tougher than anything I had ever come across in my life. This might not sound like the greatest recipe for love to you, but for a man like me, it's a perfection unequaled by anything on this plane of existence.

Now, ten years later with thousands of satisfied clients in all walks of life, hundreds of successful predictions (such as: The Kobe earthquake, the O. J. Simpson dilemma, Bill Cosby's loss, the mass suicide in San Diego. I even get mail from President Clinton!) and four published books (*The Power of the Dragon, Starguide – Moon Power 1995, 1996 & 1997*) that contain all my predictions for each year behind me, I can say that I am not a Stargazer (this is just one who gazes at the stars); I am an Astrophile, a Lover of the Stars! Just as you would be if you understood their messages as I do; I believe that everyone, and I mean everyone, should be educated in this discipline. The mystery of life would be solved. Everyone has their own mystery to uncover, and the stars are all that covers that mystery; they were definitely placed in the heavens for more than the sake of beauty. All men are enslaved by the creator to understand their meaning one way or the other; you might as well take the easy way and ask someone who knows!

Letter From the Author
1998: Happy New Year to All

6/25/97

Dear Clients and Friends:

Well one thing is sure in life and that is changes. Yes, one more year went by and 1997, as predicted for Pisces, has been a year that I will never forget as long as I live. I thought to be above the stars and even able to control the outcome of my own destiny. Predicting one's own divorce is somehow unthinkable, and how much freewill we really have over the stars is now a new challenge for me. When I wrote the 1997 predictions, I laughingly told my wife Brigitte, "Hey, honey, we'd better be careful while the Dragon's Tail resides in Pisces; it will be right on me and the Head right in our seventh house of marriage!" She, at that time, did not know that just a few months away we were about to end nine years of wedlock.

The first victim of the Dragon was a Pisces friend who had to endure the dramatic end of a thirty-one-year marriage. This acquaintance of mine went literally through hell and, after many devastating grieving telephone calls, I began to question his very safety. He once said to me, "Well, your Moon Power book forecast for Pisces seems to be damned accurate!" I did all I could to help him through this terrible separation, not knowing that I was to be the next victim of the Dragon's Tail in Pisces. One thing is sure, now that I have "hands-on" experience involving a painful upcoming divorce, I will be much more compassionate in helping future unlucky clients. I am a firm believer of the "Power Within" or the future being simply the reincarnation of my own thoughts. I must admit that I always had a deep-seated fear inside of me, and that I would lose Brigitte either in an accident (in one of our many trips around the country), or from an incurable disease. If our common fate had imposed such a occurrence and ended with her death, I knew I could not have taken it. I would have rejoined her soon after her departure from this earth. This is to demonstrate the true love I have and will always have for her. They say that "time will heal all wounds," and for the first time in my life I wish I were a few months or a few years older.

The unfolding experience that I am going through right now feels like a loud raging train hitting me straight in the face; a form of wake-up call impossible to avoid. The changes imposed upon me are really hard, and adapting to my unexpected freedom seems to be a new challenge. Tons of support came from my very close astonished friends, and I thank them here again. This is where you really see and appreciate your real friends. The entire situation and her decision must have been quite difficult for her too, as I still believe she deeply feels something is dying between the both of us. But that was her choice and I must respect her decision. She is a brilliant brunette, competitive and also quite stubborn (Taurus, Moon in Aries) and she always wanted to be an actress. Somehow, she felt her wishes could not be granted because of her relationship and her environment. Thus I can only admire her decision to make the necessary changes to reach all her dreams. I wish her all the luck in the world and even though we are finished as a couple, I will always provide her with the best I can offer her.

In the late part of May we were in a Las Vegas television location, taping my infomercial. We all worked very hard to produce it and, completely exhausted after the taping, we drove back to San Diego in the early hours of May 29th, 1997. The Moon was waning (negative) and in the depressive sign of Pisces. Brigitte is by nature extremely sensitive and as expected she fell victim to both depressive Neptune and the accompanying waning Moon. As we were driving closer to home in San Diego, I proposed she spend a few days with her good friend, Cole, who lives a few miles away. She took me up on the idea, packed a couple of suitcases and left me, never to come back.

My lesson was a hard one, and that is to become responsible for all of my actions. The constant stress involving my work desensitized me from my caring partner. Especially when my job requires a twenty-four-hour on-call type of service. I used to blame her for many little things that did not go right in my daily life. I used hard language and my fiery temperament did not help at all. Brigitte (a Taurus) is very sophisticated and has a lot of class, while I am a self-made man, rough and extremely competitive. I must blame my militant, impatient, self-centered Aries Dragon's Head and my tough upbringing.

A mixture of anger, sadness, guilt and emotional distress took over my rational mind and I began to imagine that anyone who had been close to her had had an affair with my wife. A quick telephone call from her (today 6/25/97, 7:00 p.m.) cleared the situation as she heard from some friends of my doubts of her having an affair. I sincerely apologized and asked for her forgiveness. She knew I was a wreck and understood my insecurity. I am sure many of you have been in this awful situation and, under so much stress, our regular common sense seems to fly out of the window. I never nurtured such a feeling before as I know for a fact that she has never been unfaithful to me. As a matter of fact, I was proud of the incredibly loyal quality she possessed. In my mind, she loved me only because I was a great guy, well able to provide her with financial security.

Before the beginning of the end of our relationship we were at Sam's Town Casino in Las Vegas, a beautiful place that Brigitte booked for the second time, as she knew I liked the cascade show. It is important for me to mention this segment of our lives as it denotes the power of my subconscious trying in his own way to give an hint of what was ahead of me. The show is just incredible and takes place in a man-made wild environment where a mixture of wild birds, waterfall, rocks, a laser show and a wolf play a very important part in the clever display. The western-style music adds to the magic of duplicating the wilderness.

As the water rises with the music the laser show becomes very effective, even passionate. It seems to bring about some residue of many of our past lives where once upon a time man was one with nature. Those who carry many past lives (as Indians) seem to be very affected by the true wild environment. This display does reflect, even revives, a direct epilogue of long-gone experiences there and then. I could feel the magic involving my own previous lives and really enjoyed it all. Brigitte was also mesmerized as the show stirred some of her own wild past-life residues. Then it came, the crucial moment where my subconscious was interpreting my very own future. It happened when an old wolf came out of his den above the waterfall and began howling. The deep and desperate long howling sound went right trough my soul. Shortly after this day, the pain, sorrow and grief I am experiencing is reflected by my silent but constant deep howling!

The moral of this devastating experience is pretty clear: money and security are not all that she really needed. Love, respect and attention seemed to be more appropriate, and she felt that I could not provide it all; thus she is now gone. Freedom, experience, security and success are her aims, and may God reward her for what she has done for both of us. Even now that I lost the breath of my life, I must accept that I am the only one to blame for my failure and I will always love her. Is that the reason why she shared my life for nine years? If so, I've learned a painful but valuable lesson, that with God's will, it must be somehow indispensable for my future partner. Thank you Brigitte, thank you for being, thank you for steering the highest and lowest emotion in me. Well, I have lost a jewel, and no words have yet been invented to express not only my love but my respect for that woman.

Many of those experiences have brought all of us more knowledge and many new strengths. The firmament of 1999 is already upon us and with this new year, various opportunities and new tasks are ahead of all of us.

Whatever you have to go through in 1998, learn to promote only positive thoughts. There is no room for the past in your future, and with all the implication this involves, the job must be done. For every action, positive or negative, physical or spiritual, there will be an equal reaction. So, do not forget that your future is nothing else than the reincarnation of your thoughts. No matter what you've been through you must let go of the past, refine your thoughts, purify your spirit and keep working towards your goals.

Whether you realize it or not, progress was made towards some of your objectives. If, after all the hard work you completed, things got messed up, the universe may be trying to tell you something. Either you did not try hard enough, or the people you are working with do not have the same ethical aims you do. Possibly some of your wishes cannot be granted because of your limited working environment, lack of respect for the Universal Law or an inappropriate emotional relationship. Therefore, you were fired or dismissed first, allowing the universe to grant you with the freedom and the opportunity you need to go in the right direction. Now, knowing it was a blessing that you've lost your job, someone you loved, etc., you must accept the challenge to start all over again with a positive attitude. It might sound strange at first, but subconsciously you did set the stage to go through these dramatic experiences. Look back with an objective mind; you did it all so that you ultimately could do the right thing for yourself. You may also need to educate or trust yourself a little more, but are you willing to put your heart into it? If you do, the upcoming year will be a formidable year of accomplishment for you.

Offensive people may have mistreated you emotionally or financially, and left you in a distressing situation. No matter what you experienced, you must go on with your life. This world is a teaching ground and sometimes we learn lessons that may be harsh to deal with, where we must feel the result of all our negative words and actions through pain and suffering. Exacting experiences seem to be the only way for humankind to burn karma and gain real knowledge; a sort of inferno of passions and stress, well designed by God to refine all of us from ignorance and destruction to pure love and caring.

Before reincarnating yourself in this world, you chose a specific time in space. You also picked a set of stars (your natal chart), the country and city of your birth, as well as the souls who ultimately became your parents. You may not be aware of it just yet, but your karmic plan on this dense physical world was chosen by you. In the long run, the soul frees himself from this dimension and aims for his higher purpose. Simply explained, the idea is to further your consciousness, rise above all earthy vices and become a co-creator with God. Over the years, the experiences you suffered will consume some of that karmic debt and further awareness of your immortality. Some precious people that whom love have been called to the great beyond and are now performing in another reality much closer to God. They will act as Guardian Angels and will watch over you.

By interacting with the Dynamics of our universe and conforming to the dialogue of the stars, man's karmic journey could be easier. The *Moon Power Starguide* was created for the purpose of assisting you to live your life in harmony with the cosmic will. This book will provide you with a day-to-day celestial guidance and a genuine spiritual support. Its content is healing, informative, entertaining and useful. In times of trouble, this work will touch you directly and give you solid direction and a means of divine support.

The daily message of the stars will prepare you for your day and beyond. With patience and investigation, you will notice how much the planets affect you, others and your life in general. In this work, you will find cautionary and specific guidance for certain days. Just be aware of the dates and, most of all, listen and watch those around you. Like robots, your friends, parents, children, loved ones will respond to the tremendous pull of the stars.

To the learned man, the daily celestial energy released upon the earth is obvious, and it shapes our thoughts and actions, vices and virtues.

Teaching anyone to recognize and respect God's subtle tools is a large task. However, with education, time and observations, those who "ask, shall receive" cosmic knowledge. The stars do not pick favorites, not you, me or anyone else, but, much like everything in nature, they simply do a job. As imposed by the Creator in its sublime celestial design, their task is to affect us and make us discover. Learning to interpret the universal mind will be beneficial for us all. Curiosity will bring the Golden key of wisdom and further your cosmic consciousness. This fact changes lives, mostly because knowledge means power. The possibility of achieving the best, in promoting education, peace of mind, faith, love — a chance to experience genuine happiness. Over the years, *Starguide's* essence will help you to control the outcome of their destiny. Do not hesitate to offer *Starguide* to a loved one or a friend in need. You are not just giving a book, you become a contributor of hope and enlightenment. You are empowering someone with a piece of the Divine.

Once more, thank you for your patronage and trust in my work.

— Dr. Turi

Man is superior to the stars if he lives in the power of superior wisdom. Such a person, being the master over heaven and earth by means of his will, is a magus, and magic is not sorcery but supreme wisdom.

— Paracelcus

Chapter 1

Starguide's Purpose
1998 — Universal Guidance and Predictions

Starguide Universal Calendar of predictions is the result of over 20 years of strenuous research into the architecture of our Universe. My findings will help you to triumph over your daily challenges by identifying and obeying the Divine will of the cosmos. Starguide offers genuine guidance, positive growth and vital, daily information.

— Dr. Turi

Every year, *Starguide* offers the kind of support and direction you're looking for to achieve your goals. The easy-to-read suggestions for each day of the year will get you started with the right attitude and expectations. Each period of time is empowering you with the Herculean will of the cosmos, thus, the opportunity to synchronize with the creative forces of the universe. *Starguide* will encourage and guide you to take positive steps to improve your world, find love, a great career and financial secur-ity. This publication will correctly guide you each day of 1998. It will give you the opportunity to avoid costly emotional or financial mishaps. All you need to know about people's spiritual makeup and forecasts for 1998 is in *Starguide*. This work will accurately translate the implacable rules of the universe into daily guidance. This physical world could not exist without its spiritual counterpart. *Starguide's* purpose is to help you to understand God's universal laws.

You have been taught how to drive and respect the physical laws of the road to avoid an accident. Starguide will teach you the spiritual laws of the universe and will guide you safely, all along the wonderful road of your life. Realize that in life there is no room for ignorance; breaking man's physical law will bring heavy penalty to the offender! The same applies for God's celestial laws. Starguide is specifically designed to teach and remind you of these planetary rules. Ultimately, this publication will help you to manage your life in accordance with the Universal laws and harvest harmony in both the physical and spiritual plane.

When suffering is on all sides and man hungers for the unmanifested mystery in all phenomena: He seeks the reflection of the divine. God's higher truths are cloaked in his creation and the message is in the stars.

— Nostradamus

Chapter 2

Predictions for the Century

Approximately every two thousand years, our planet comes under the influence of a new zodiacal sign. January 12, 1996, marks the entrance of Uranus (the future) into his own sign of Aquarius (new age). We slowly began to explore the possibility of a New consciousness and uncover both the strength and the danger of this upcoming incredible age. This liberal sign follows nebulous Pisces. Over the last twenty years, Uranus (the awakener) has advocated more discoveries than have been made during the last 2000 years spent under the illusive power of Neptune (ruler of Pisces). Pisces is the last sign of the Zodiac, and traditionally, it rules the twelfth house. This area governs restriction, sorrow, imprisonment, psychological trouble and secret enemies as well as creativity, dance, high forms of music and works of art. Asylum, hospital, churches, prisons, movie theaters, concert halls and theme parks are Neptune's legacy. It is also a mute energy; it has no voice of its own. Submissive by nature, Neptune tends to make those born under its heavy influence pessimists and fatalists prone to addictions and fanaticism. It is a deceiving energy prone to suffering and acceptance. Nuns, evangelists, drug addicts are particularly loaded, for good or for bad, with Neptune's illusive power. Interestingly, the two thousand years that have elapsed during the rule of Pisces started around the time of the beginning of Christianity. For nearly 2000 years, the world has been largely under the influence of Judaeo-Christian theology, whose first early chosen symbol was the sign of the fish. Oriental and near-Oriental minds delight in fairy stories, and they are continually spinning such beautiful myths about the lives of religious and political heroes. In the absence of printing, when most human knowledge was passed by word of mouth, from one generation to the next, the illusive power of Pisces opened the doors for myths to become tradition and those traditions to eventually be accepted as fact.

Unmistakably, under the sign of Pisces, Jesus Christ suffered sorrow, imprisonment, restrictions and tortures at the hands of secret political enemies. Also, Christianity has been preaching the blind acceptance of suffering, repentance and sacrifice, if you are to proceed to the paradise of God. According to astrology, Neptune's energy (Pisces) is forcing the soul towards its opposite sign (Virgo) or the Virgin Mary and its purity principle. This indicates why Christians have subconsciously chosen the symbol of the fish to represent their religion and beliefs. The last 2000 years of Neptunian influence have produced over 875 different religions worldwide, and in the process, millions of people have died and still die in devastating holy wars.

It is well documented that many former civilizations simply worshipped God or gods with the stars, the moon and the sun. The Creator's Divine Manifestation throughout the Universe (Astrology) was well used and understood by the ancients. Whereas Pisces is mute and accepting, Aquarius has a voice. Aquarius rules curiosity, invention, electronics, the UFO phenomena and astrological investigation. Uranus rules the future, electronics, electricity, radio, television, airships and aeronautics. Among its metals are uranium, radium and all of the other radioactive elements.

Thus, we can look upon the Aquarian age as a bringer of hope, universal love, promotion of great technological advances and a vast increase in man's mental exploration. Uranus rules cosmic consciousness, psychic awareness and the genius quality of man. Uranus is also classified as the "sudden release of energy" and is responsible for nature's devastating forces such as earthquakes, tornadoes, hurricanes and typhoons. Wrongly used, Uranus can be the potential destroyer of the human race through the use of atomic weaponry and as yet undiscovered powers.

We must learn to understand the true message of Aquarius and the awesome power of Uranus. We must overcome the negative forces of this planet, for that is the lesson of the age of Aquarius, and enjoy an age of great spiritual awakening. We must learn to accept the values and workings of Uranus upon our thought processes, thus creating our own amazing future reality complete with ETs and UFOs. We must create a universal brotherhood, where love, progress and responsibility become the ultimate goals. If we fail to recognize the awesome power of Uranus, the Aquarian age may be the last age man will live on this planet.

Chapter 3

1998 Slow-Moving Planets Predictions

Jupiter in Aquarius: The giant planet cruised through Aquarius since January 22nd, 1997. Jupiter's expansive power has been felt all over the world of terms of education. Many people felt the urge to explore "The New Age" message and more and more people educated themselves with computers. Jupiter brought an expansion in both the metaphysical and computer world. Schools also benefited from his passage in Aquarius. Jupiter (ruler of all teachings) will also help in bringing the old science back to our colleges and universities within the next few years. My premonition in 1996 was accurate as President Clinton in 1997 passed a bill to the Senate pertaining to schools, homes and their availability to computers and the Internet.

Many dogmatic teachers and political leaders did resist the pull of Jupiter's desire to educate his children in 1997 and will try to stop the New Wave without much success. In this age of communication, with the increase in technology and computers, many students in different universities worldwide will be able to receive and exchange valuable information. Thus, burning questions (and answers) pertaining to the New Age, Astrology, predictions, UFOs etc., were available to them. These long-awaited moves of Jupiter (education) in the sign of Aquarius (New Age) did mark a time of great exploration and promotion for the young generation. With the passage of Great Jupiter in Aquarius, spiritual regeneration has been offered and made available for those children willing to ask some of those metaphysical questions. As mentioned in your 96 Starguide, the crashing of the comet on Jupiter in July, 1994 did mark the beginning of the restructure of education and theology being replaced by a new awareness. Spiritual leaders started to teach the world of God's manifestation throughout the Universe.

> **Note**: In 1997 Jupiter promoted great discoveries and a new wave of powerful computers and many programs were made available to all educational organizations. The legacy of Jupiter's impact in Aquarius in 1997 was a positive expansion (by house and sign) of many terrestrials' souls. Many did take electronic and astrology studies and others will have to travel far to enjoy their new careers.

Jupiter in Pisces: With the entrance of philosophical Jupiter in the religious sign of Pisces on February 4th, 1998, traditional education will get another boost until this planet moves into the sign of Aries on February 13th, 1999. Be ready for another wave of apocalyptic nonsense where we are all supposed to repent or die in the inferno promised by an infuriated God. Don't let this happen to you or your children; instead teach them love, respect and faith in the future. The Middle East (a Pisces area) may suffer unrest due to their fanatical conviction that their supreme deity wants to rule the world. Those souls have been deprived of education and controlled by their rulers for thousands of years and will find difficult to "rebirth" themselves with the rest of the world. On a positive note, much work will be done to help those in trouble with the compassion of both Pisces and Jupiter.

When Jupiter enters the sign of Aries (self-exploration) on February 13th, 1999 many souls will be allowed to further self-discovery and self-esteem. They will be then apt to make decisions of their own without fears.

Ignorance is evil: when you control someone's source of information or education, chances are that you will control that person's entire life.

— Dr. Turi

Saturn in Aries: Saturn, "the teacher," is still going through the fiery sign of Aries and will stay in this sign until June 9, 1998. Karmic Saturn is also called the "Great Malefic" and its gloomy power brings depression by the sign and house he resides in. In the sign of Aries, he may make one overly concerned with his past, produce guilt and generate a low self-esteem. In any case, if you are feeling Saturn's gloomy energy, you must use your will: the part of God in you is much stronger than any planet. Saturn in Aries rules personal fears and with Neptune, ruler of the Dragon's Tail presently in Pisces until October 20th, 1998, you are strongly advised to think twice before letting yourself fall down with depression by controlling your imagination. Saturn is cold and calculated, Mars is fast and aggressive. So, make solid plans, stick to them and respect the Universal Law in all your endeavors.

On a more positive note, the structural power of Saturn will provide Aries (Mars' enterprising spirit) objectivity, discipline and a reasonable approach to any business venture. Many people will feel the urge to "assert" the competitive side of themselves and much progress will be accomplished for those involved in competition, organization and structural endeavors. Some karmic souls born with an afflicted Saturn (caution) will take forever to act, while others with too much Mars (speed) will make hasty decisions and learn from their mistakes the hard way. Saturn rules politics while Mars rules war and violence. Thus, many political speeches will sound like "warriors" ready to "verbally" destroy their opponents. In some parts of the world barbarous "coups d'état" are to be expected. Force instead of diplomacy will be used to gain position and power. Expect the US taxpayers' money to be used for the construction of safer buildings such as prisons and hospitals, as well as roads, bridges and an overhaul of the face of the White House. With the passage of Saturn (re-structure) in Aries (war/destruction), nature's devastating forces may compel the rebuilding of many civilian buildings. In the long run, safer and more solid structures will be erected for the benefit of our society.

> **Note**: Mars rules the Army and the Navy, with structural Saturn involvement 1997 has been a year where many prominent Army and Navy officers were forced to impose new structures. (*Men are from Mars, Women are from Venus* is now a famous best-seller and the author John Gray is a student of mine!) Thus Mars also means sex, while women are Venusian and could only induce trouble as we are all just humans. Many restructures were imposed in 1997 as predicted in this area.
>
> June 7, 1997 WASHINGTON — Secretary of Defense William Cohen announced Saturday that three panels will be set up to review military training, privacy issues and the "clarity" of its policy on adultery. "Recent perceptions that our system is inconsistent damage the morale of our troops," Cohen said in a statement read at a briefing. "The actions I am taking today will assure that our training remains superb and that our rules are well understood at all levels of command."

On a more positive note for the US, due to some governmental (Saturn) unrest in some parts of the world, the Army and Navy (Mars) demand for more weaponry will provide the private sector with new contracts. This will bring also a form of financial rebirth for many people involved with Uncle Sam.

With practical Saturn still residing in their sign, Aries should work harder as 1998 is a year of serious progress for them. Expect some frustration at first, but success later, wherever Mars and Aries are located in your natal chart.

Saturn in Taurus: On June 9th, 1998, the structural power of Saturn will affect the world of Taurus (finances) and may put some stress on the general financial security of many nations. However, Saturn will bring painful but rewarding restructures. Saturn will also promote scientific research in many departments such as geology and until the "scientists" begin to show a good use of our tax dollars in their endeavors, financial support may be cut off or seriously diminished. Much investment has been made for unrewarding results as they are still unable to "predict" or come close to when or where an earthquake will take place. More tax money is spent on their living, expensive equipment and colleges/universities than anything else. Thus it became a bad habit which is growing year after year at the expense of all of us. Saturn will see to it and induce a serious cutdown in this area.

Saturn also rules the earth and everything involving mining and mineralogy. Some earth conservationists groups will pressure those wealthy organizations unwilling to spend on the clean up stage. The general attitude towards security and money at large will be quite depressive due to the impact of gloomy Saturn in Taurus. Switzerland is a Taurus country (Merrill Lynch Co. subconsciously selected the Bull?) and this sign regulates the second house of money and the banking industry. Thus this independent country is up for some explanations regarding secret financial transactions made with Germany (an Aries/war) country in both World War 1 & 2. The passage of Saturn in Aries in 1997 has already touched many financial organizations and more stress and explanations is in store for them in 1998.

Uranus in Aquarius: Uranus is the future; be ready to experience a taste of the unbelievable as we get closer to the year 2000. Uranus in Aquarius will force the masses to open up to the new age. What are now considered eccentric topics like: astrology, UFO, reincarnation, psychic power, etc., will be approached with an open mind, explored, and finally accepted by the majority. All this will take place before the end of this century. Some of the old sciences will be brought back to our colleges and universities and accepted as true and useful disciplines. Soon after this new consciousness, the human race will be prepared for the possibility of exploring the universe with friendly extraterrestrials.

> **Note**: The Dragon's Tail (negative) will enter the sign of Aquarius which controls the sudden release of energy such as earthquakes, explosions, volcanoes, atomic forces, uranium. Uranus will be still in Aquarius (his own sign) in 1998, but after entering the Dragon's Tail on October 20th, 1998 the worst of nature's forces will be experienced by mankind and especially in Hawaii, Japan and California. This does not mean the end of the world, but a reminder that old mother earth is still alive and needs now and then to reshape herself. Needless to say that as we are getting close to the end of the millennium, the uninformed, God-fearing mass will lose it. Again, do not fall for the "Apocalyptic times" as what will actually take place is a "Pass Over" or a change in the human race consciousness. The worst that can happen is the secret manipulation and sales of nuclear devices that could end in the hands of fanatical groups to further their specific religious or political agenda. Remember, our future is nothing else than the reincarnation of our common thought process. Thus participate in the restructuring of the human psyche by furthering education, love and faith in the very essence of life, the future and God.

The world is a big orchestra, where all men are competitors, all of us are acting some part in the drama of life harmony. Some wielding the bat and fired by the sympathy of onlookers; others feeling that they are only present but humbled by inferiority.

— Dr. Turi

Chapter 4

Pluto's Impact on Generations: Past — Present — Future

Indeed, Pluto is a dramatic planet and its impact on generations is obvious for those blessed with the knowledge of the stars. Hitler was born on April 20, 1889 and Pluto (power) was located in the sign of Gemini (communication) from 1883 until 1913. Wherever Pluto is located by sign and house in your chart, a sense of power and regeneration will be offered to you. Thus, using his well-known, inborn "hypnotic sound power," it was easy for Hitler, in his numerous "Plutonic" speeches, to persuade the German population to go to war against the rest of the world. The immediate generation to suffer his manipulation were the young German soldiers and everybody else around the world born between 1913 and 1937 with Pluto (death) in Cancer (family). Thus, the "invaders" and all of the war's victims were the result of an awful Pluto disturbing the basic security principle, homes, families and indeed can be associated with the First and Second World Wars, into the sad historically "Wasted Baby Generation." The entire world and its security (Cancer) were shattered between both deadly (Pluto) World Wars, and millions of children from many different ethnic groups met with their fate.

When Pluto moved from Cancer (security/home) to Leo (love/life) from 1938 to 1957, the world experienced a re-birth of its population. Responding subconsciously to the power of the stars, the unaware masses called the phenomenon "The Baby Boom Generation." Leo (Sun) rules love, the arts, freedom, and the 50's and 60's were good examples of the love and freedom-oriented attitudes with hippie music and drugs (Woodstock) that plagued this generation. Pluto rules sex, and Leo children became a free, sexually-oriented generation. Jimi

Hendrix's fate (sex, drugs, rock-and-roll), is a good example of a personal Pluto in Leo that ultimately got the best of him.

Pluto then moved to the puritanical sign of Virgo (health) from 1957 to 1976, and this generation is the next to take governmental power. This generation is fanatic about nature, perfection, work and health. Smokers have already suffered the impact of this "Baby Buster Generation," as this generation must upgrade health and perfection in our society. Unlike Leo (life) Virgo is dry and sterile, thus fewer babies were produced during this era. Since Pluto entered the sign of Virgo, facilities for health programs and exercises boomed to satisfy a generation that craved fitness. The health businesses (body/mind/tools) have started and are still booming with Pluto in Virgo. This generation is banning smokers from restaurants and public places (and they voted the 40¢ tobacco tax increase). On a more positive note, this age group will fight hard to preserve nature, animals and the remainder of the rain forest. Computers and microchips were developed by this generation and their "electronic war/Patriot Missiles" as seen in Operation Desert Storm are deadly accurate. Their ideal is very pure in thought and action, but this generation must guard against Pluto's (fanaticism) subtle power for "perfection." If the power of Pluto in Virgo is exaggerated, it becomes as deadly as the poison they try so hard to avoid.

Many of these souls will lose their lives by being too concerned with health (anorexia, hypochondria), turning rapidly to vegetarian diets, thus upsetting their naturally weak digestive tracts. They must understand that cats and dogs were born with strong claws and long, sharp teeth to tear apart raw flesh as intended by nature, while cows, horses, lambs, etc. are herbivores and were designed by God to eat only "salad." They are none of those. They are omnivorous and must eat meat as a vigilant balance for their sensitive metabolism. Some souls who are overwhelmed by Pluto are too crazy for carbohydrates. They are also protein paranoid. Some starve themselves after 6:00 p.m. Others take their heart rates much too seriously, some have a penchant for pain, and more are victims of the fat-burning syndrome. Worst of all for women is the weight lifting dilemma. It is, genetically speaking, impossible for a woman to take on a man's physical power, and no matter how hard they try, they will never look like Arnold Schwarzenegger. Because of the inborn critical attitude and a strong desire for health and perfection, those natural "puritans" won't find someone good enough for them, and many will end up alone in the game of love.

From October 5, 1971 until November 6, 1983, dramatic Pluto (death) moved into the sign of Libra (partnerships). Traditionally, Libra (7th house) rules associations, open enemies, partners and the day-to-day people entering your life. This nefarious combination has created a form of regular open death manifestation as shown by the infamous, daily drive-by shootings. Born with Pluto (death) in Libra (others), those children are willing to die for their inner Plutonic sense of justice (scales) imposed by their partners (gang members). Constantly influenced (bullied) by Pluto or more ferocious souls, they must give in to their high sense of justice for the group. This righteous "die for you/die for me" attitude is now in full operation in our present society and has created "The unbalanced Aggressive Gang Generation." If not for survival or money, respect, power and justice belong to the group (no matter what), and Pluto is the subtle force behind gang activity. The Plutonic rough initiation principle (beating) is a form of love/hate/submission, participation and respect found within the sign of Libra in the declaration of peace or war. Then, the ruthless test for security, love, hate, respect and deadly commitment to others (Libra) in the group (gang) has been established. Contrary to what is commonly believed, and to the amazement of psychologists, many children of the gang generation have had perfect upbringings and many are from middle and upper class families.

Early environment plays an important part in how these souls will react to others. If the upbringing happens to be rough and difficult, these Plutonic souls may become the imposing bullies. Negative members of this generation are in constant need of a dramatic regeneration principle taking place within a group constantly involved in war with others. To those born with Pluto in Libra, it is also a sure indication of a strong inner sense of justice owed to the group for good or for bad. This Pluto (death) generation in Libra (the law) will savagely fight their enemy (authority figures) and other gangs without any fear or regard for the deadly consequences. This problem with the police force has already started and will keep dangerously growing, making some parts of the cities unsafe for the common citizen. This sad situation will continue swelling to a dangerous size and will force the government to take drastic measures. The year 1998 will be a memorable year as strong efforts will be made to avoid the breaking down of our society. In the process, many youths and numerous police officers' lives will be wasted.

Pluto then inhabited, from 1983 until 1995, his own daredevil sign of Scorpio. Those very young and wild children have already made dramatic news by executing each other and murdering adults for any reason. Such as in Rachula, Missouri on December 28, 1994, an off-duty police officer had been shot to death by his girlfriend's 9-year-old grandson. The child was born with Pluto in Scorpio on his Dragon's Tail (negative). Many of those "kids" have been reported killing adults for money to buy drugs and guns at the tender age of 10 years. Again in May 1997 a brutal slaying follows a beer-drinking in Central Park, New York. Two teen-agers stabbed a real estate agent at least 30 times and tried to chop off his hands so police couldn't use fingerprints to identify him before dumping him in a lake in Central Park. Both perpetrators, Daphne Abdela, 15, and her boyfriend, 15-year-old Christopher Vasquez, "gutted the body so it would sink." Both of those young souls are from the dramatic Pluto generation, "The Death Wish Generation." More than previous degrading generations, these children need constant spiritual regeneration and a good reason to be alive.

Thus, our society is already witnessing "The Dramatic Death Wish Generation" in action. They are strong-willed, unwavering in thought and action, immensely emotional and totally fearless in front of death. Pluto (sex) is making them very active sexually at an early age, and they will also look for a mixture of sex, crime and drugs to survive their harsh young lives. At the tender age of 12 years many of those children have already experienced the use of drugs and sex and some others have committed repellent murders.

The passion for self-discovery is extreme and if left without legitimate spiritual food, the worst can only happen to many of these children. They will not react to dogma and common religious teachings as they "naturally" understand the motivation behind the manifestation. The miserably failing psychological field won't be of any help in the understanding and motivation behind the upcoming killer generation. Unless the old science of Astrology is reinstated, (Astropsychology) in our colleges and universities, there will be either no understanding or therapeutic healing measures available for these children. A few years from now, once in power, indeed, this unyielding generation has the awful potential to destroy the world with the use of irreversible atomic weapons. God's implacable Universal Rules have been broken and ignored for too long and a serious penalty is awaiting mankind. There is no room for ignorance at any level of consciousness or any other worlds above or below us.

Slowly but surely, mankind is witnessing the slow and painful suffocating end of another young generation. Hopefully, the "ridicule" will be cast aside by our scientists and solid investigation of "Divine Astrology" will bring it back into the traditional educational system. Only then, the real therapeutic deeds involving Astrology will begin to heal and regenerate the psyche of all of these unquiet spirits.

Life is not a game of chance; the Creator did not put us where we would be the sport of circumstances, to be tossed about by a cruel fate, regardless of our efforts to save our world.

— George B. Emerson

Chapter 5

The Universal Law

There is a tide in the affairs of man, when taken at its crest, leads on to fortune.
— Shakespeare

Every day that God has created sees the procession of stars across the vault of the sky; they have followed the same path through the heavens, tracing the immutability of the cosmos and its constellations, which have spoken to the wise since the beginning of time. This work will explain in detail the subtle energy produced by the Moon's passage through the twelve houses and signs of the Zodiac. These houses govern the twelve facets of our life, and the rhythms of our cycles, our emotions, finances, consciousness, home, children, career, friends, wishes, fears, love, personality and all that goes to make up our sorrows and joys. Depending on the mystical rhythm of the Moon and her relationship — harmonious or discordant — to the constellations and houses of the sky over which they rule, she will govern our human activity and give birth to our vices and virtues. The infinite and concealed dance of the Moon through the Zodiac is far from affecting only you, but all of us. You are a "microcosm" or a child of the Universe and there is reason for you to be. You are a part of this incredible physical and spiritual structure called a "macrocosm."

Sir Isaac Newton wrote "for every action there is an equal and opposite reaction." We are what we think, having become what we thought. This statement emphasizes that for every thought or action there will be an effect. This is what I call the "Universal Law," the causes and effects of the yin and yang recognized as the law of KARMA. The Moon is, by herself quite responsible for much of our and the world's fate. By the tracking of the

Universal Law and using Starguide, you will be allowed to see this lunar impact and reaction every day of your life. Obviously, the waxing and waning periods of our closest satellite will produce the daily process of tides. Thusly, women will have a spiritual and physical manifestation (menstruation), and all of us will be responding subconsciously to the words "lunatic/moody." Without opposite forces at work there would be no reaction thus no life possible on both the spiritual and physical plane.

Our so-called "dead" satellite is very much alive, and much more than a rock hanging above our heads. She is a vital part of a Divine celestial design, she is the beating heart of the earth. Vigilantly observing her whereabouts will aid in understanding the real psychology of man.

— Dr. Turi

The Changing face of the Moon was revered and understood by the ancients as an aspect of the feminine and idolized as the Lady of the Night who ruled over fertility and magic. Your awareness of the Moon's passage through the Zodiac will enable you to discover a basic structure of energy patterns that underlies the changes and circumstances of your life. This is, indeed, the purpose of a good astrologer, and his main objective is to reveal an order or meaning beneath or within what often appears to be a random or chaotic situation. The Moon's passage through the housing system is one expression of the archetypal structure we call a cycle. While many of the formally educated scientists have lost their cosmic consciousness, it has still remained hidden within astrological values and basic astrological foundations.

All of the signs of the Zodiac, the twelve houses, and the numerous astrological aspects are based upon God's higher order in the established, interstellar cycle. Their subtle meanings are derived from a particular place or function to each other, and all operate within the ordered cycle as a whole. Our lives unfold according to our specific cyclic pattern, interacting with the Universal cycle. Discerning the Universal Mind at work is difficult; those gifted at birth will naturally understand the cosmic mind, using their inborn, intuitional and objective mental tools. However, when properly educated, anyone can learn to further his cosmic consciousness and realize his close relationship with God and the Universe. It often starts with a willingness to expand the consciousness, and the simple realization that what can not be seen or touched doesn't mean it is non-existent. That's what makes a real scientist, respecting the essence of the word investigation! Sadly enough, the majority of these educated souls fear the ridicule or abandonment by their peers or churches. Those methodical scholars will never be able to penetrate the "cultivated" domain of my research. Those scholastically oriented souls are plagued at birth with a limited view and conception of the unknown. Usually, a weak Mercury (the mind), a phlegmatic Uranus (inquiry) in an unassuming sign (rationale) becomes the logical reason for the inability to reach a higher level of understanding. In a nutshell, they inherited a common astrological formation deprived of cosmic ability. To them, the moon is nothing else than a dead satellite orbiting around the earth with no more purpose than to produce the daily tides.

The obvious structure of the Moon's cycle is derived from the fact that it consists of a beginning, a middle and an end. Thus, the monthly lunar cycle suggests by observation that it is divided into two halves. During the first half, the movement is outward, as our close satellite travels away from the area of space occupied by the Sun. As this happens, the powerful light of the Sun increases, "waxing" (positive) on the white face of the Moon. The turning point is symbolized by the Full Moon; it reverses motion. The Moon begins to approach the Sun as the reflected light on its surface "wanes" (negative), until they meet again at the New Moon (new start). Halfway between the New Moon and the Full Moon, we notice another important division point where light and darkness are equal on the moon's surface. At the first waxing quarter, the light is increasing, while at the last waning quarter, it is decreasing. These simple astronomical observations can only provide the scientist's mind with knowledge for interpreting the physical lunar cycle's phase. Now if the positive cannot be without the negative, and knowing that it takes two for anything to be, then the scientist should be able to "investigate" this intuitional domain. There is so much behind this "lunar manifestation," I began to feed my own critical observations.

As a child, I always thought of the moon to be something much more than a frigid white globe orbiting around the earth. Many times in the darkness of the night, I found myself staring at her, wondering about her hidden power. She is the swiftest of the planets, passing through the 12 signs of the zodiac in about 28 days. I knew that sooner or later, I was to uncover her subtle way and find some of the answers. To me, all those stars in the night sky, shining above my head, were more than beautiful luminaries to light the way in the dark of the night. It does, however, take more than the five regular senses to tap into her subtle manifestation upon our psyche and life in general. Nothing happens randomly in the universe, and the timely return in full each month surely indicates an ultimate order. Month after month, I patiently watched her becoming New and Full, and I learned my first and one of the most important lessons in metaphysics: "The undiluted truth is not to be found inside my limited world, but in others and the Universal mind."

Being so close to the earth, the Moon's magnetic pull (gravitational force) is so great, that she is solely responsible for the daily process of the tides. Therefore, curiosity, observation and comparison became the key elements to promote my cosmic consciousness. As I met her, becoming full and new, month after month, I slowly began to understand her powers. By constantly watching my environment, friends and family members, she began to speak about her clearly visible impact and astute control over man's psyche. As the years went by, I realized her uncompromising role over the sea, and I became more aware of her powerful impact on our daily affairs. I made notes day after day, week after week and month after month, realizing the consequences of ignoring or adapting to her passage through the twelve signs of the Zodiac. Later on, I learned that the farmers of the past followed her fluctuations for the betterment of their crops.

Then I carefully put my observations to test in my life and the lives of those around me. I did not take long to realize that by respecting the Universal Law, my life became much more productive. Her positive and negative effect on man's emotions, actions and reactions became so obvious to me that I decided to make a full-time job telling others about her. As I watched the news in times of a full Moon, I understood why people became destructive, "lunatic," eccentric, moody and psychopathic. I then named it the Uncompromising Universal Law. Since then, as a professional Divine Astrologer, wherever I am needed, I am teaching the value of this simple and valuable knowledge.

When you first learned how to drive a car, you were carefully introduced to the rules of the road. You learned that you must stop at a red light or follow a road sign, as your very life depends on your doing so. These are the codes that you have learned, and they must be respected anywhere you happen to be in the world. Following established rules will take you safely wherever you have to go. Sadly enough, too many people do not respect these rules, and innocent people have died accidentally. Awareness, knowledge and respect of these rules are desperately needed. However, the spiritual rules established by God, written in the constellations, have been misplaced. Only a minority is aware of the impact produced by the moon, and the rest, the majority of us are completely ignorant of these Divine rules. The result is seen during a Full Moon and each time the moon is crossing a destructive sign. This lack of awareness turns into a formidable chaos, producing despair, drug addiction, depression, violence, criminal behavior . . . and the list goes on and on. Know that ignoring either the physical or spiritual rules will lead any one of us to pay a heavy penalty.

So-called "holy wars" have plagued man all through the ages. Ignorance and fear cast aside the real Universal message. To my mind, the millions of deaths produced by continuous religious wars all around the world were a good example of the destructive power of fanaticism. I realized that everyone's relationship to God or many gods was deeply personal and that no two people feel the same way about it. I myself was taught by my great mother that God is love, beauty, education, responsibility and knowledge, a belief I have steadfastly clung to. I have noticed the dualistic nature of life, man/woman, front/back, up/down, black/white, yin/yang, positive/negative, the ultimate law of opposition. I soon began to realize that nothing would exist without its counterpart, and this Law of opposition was much too obvious to be challenged or ignored. I began to wonder if God would be without the Devil. One month is made up of two two-week periods, one year of two six-month periods. From the New Moon (black dot on your calendar) to the Full moon (a circle on your calendar), the light is green.

Those two weeks are called "the waxing time." Then when you see her full, white and round, the light is amber. Those two weeks are called "the waning time." As she starts her positive waxing time, you should plant your seeds for life. Go out, meet new people, socialize, get engaged, get married, buy a new car, go shopping, sign important contracts, travel, visit family members and generally promote all you can during this positive trend. My Starguide has all the New and Full Moons available for entire year. Also, Starguide tells you when and in what sign the New Moon or the the Full Moon will mature. You can use this knowledge to master the outcomes of all your endeavors. Initiate ideas or projects as she climbs happily in the heavens. Then when she finally becomes full, be aware of the approaching "yellow light," as this signals a time to slow down and reflect. Use your will to fight depression, clean your house, prepare your next move, write letters but don't send them just yet.

Observe and listen to all the people around you. Many will suffer the waning Moon's power and will become negative, moody and lunatic. Watch the news and see for yourself the dramatic differences in the two periods. However, good things can happen then. This means, officially, that somehow you started "that" situation during her waxing, positive time, and you are now being paid off. Bad things can also happen to you when the Moon is supposedly positive. It might only be a tap on your hand, compared to what you could really experience for yourself in the future. Keep in mind that you have been going through your life not knowing — not using the Universal Law. You did not interact with the Moon's fluctuations (the gearbox of our system) and many gears (your experiences) have broken down. Apply your knowledge right away and take the time to invest in your understanding of Astrology (the dynamics of our Universe).

Women's menstrual periods are also commanded by the Universal Clock, and both the Moon and women share the same twenty-eight-day time period. Work non-stop around the Moon's passage thoughout every sign of the Zodiac, and then her deepest secrets will by yours. As she travels through the belt of the Zodiac, she will be residing between two and three days in one sign, she will melt your emotions with the energies (positive or negative) found in that specific astrological sign. Never forget that an ultimate higher order has been established, and the essence of our emotional life is within. Learning and adapting to the Moon's power will help you to understand what it really means to be human. This lunar consciousness will lead you towards the understanding of your own strengths, and the ability to use them to further your life, while minimizing your weakness day by day!

Some people often tell me, "But Dr. Turi, I cannot leave my life this way. New Moon or Full Moon, I have business to take care of!" Well, I understand the dilemma, but to me it sounds like, "Dr. Turi, the light is red, my car is stopped at the light, but I can't stand still any longer here because I am going to be late for my appointment." Go ahead! You see, you came and asked me for spiritual rules, I gave them to you, now you have to deal with them. You took the chance and were curious enough to "ask"; now that you receive the "discipline," it's pretty much up to you to heed them or not. The world is not necessarily ready, willing and unenlightened pertaining to this "lunar" code, you are! The idea is to plan well ahead of time and synchronize with the universal law to plan all your important endeavors. It is as simple as that.

Since the dawn of time, the Creator has shown his truth to the humble, a truth that is hidden from the vain blinded by worldly pleasures, but which is written in the skies, which nightly speaks of the glory of God.
— Nostradamus

Chapter 6

Your Personal Horoscopes for 1998
Welcome to Each Sign of the Zodiac

Important Note from Dr. Turi:

Born and raised in Provence, France, I rekindled and only exercise Nostradamus' 16th-century Divine Astrology method. This formula does not reflect the modern disciplines you may be used to. Realize that over 500 years ago the famous Prophet did not use a watch or any sophisticated computers. Thus like the great Seer, I investigate the outer space and the Universal mind with my inborn spiritual telescope. A "microscopic attitude" will not help anyone to gain the Golden key of spiritual knowledge. This limited explorative attitude is for "astronomers" who have long lost their cosmic consciousness with their rigid scientific minds. We all heard of missing the forest looking at a tree. Every one of them is aware of the twelve constellations of the Zodiac, somehow impossible for them to pass the limitation of their five rational senses. To penetrate the intuitional domain and decode the subtle meaning behind each symbol does take more than numbers. Realize that Divine Astrology is both an art and a science and it must be practiced as such. For those born on the cusp of any zodiacal sign, simply refer to the month of your birth which reflects the exact constellation of your nativity. Divine Astrology is the original way at looking at the stars, and my students and I have found it to be incredibly accurate.

Philosophical Astro-Poetry
By Brigitte Turi
Copyright 1995

Saturn Governs the Power-Oriented,
Structural Constellation of Capricorn

Builder of the greatest towers
Holding all the social powers
Striving to climb to the highest peak
For honor has no place for the weak
I am CAPRICORN, child of Saturn

1998 — Forecast For Those Born In January

The month of January is controlled by structural Saturn and, traditionally, the practical sign of Capricorn. Souls born in January are strongly motivated by their career, and all are gifted with a strong organization principle. More than any other sign, they strive for respect and position in career accomplishments. This sign is ruled by Saturn (a karmic planet), and Capricorn must avoid depressive thoughts. The part of God in ourselves is stronger than the stars we inherited, and our will must be used correctly in promoting faith and positivity. Capricorn will realize that during the course of their life, nothing will come easy. Like the symbol of the goat, slowly but surely, against all odds, the soul must climb towards the top of the mountain. Usually, the first part of Capricorn's life is a constant struggle. Only around middle life (after many ups and downs) they reach a well-deserved position and career. Saturn will reward Capricorn with a very long life, an appreciation of all in old age and solid financial security. They also tend to marry younger or older partners. The fluctuation of the Moon strongly affects their moods and success in their career. A wise Capricorn will use his fish tail, be aware of the Universal law and synchronize his life and business with it. Steadiness, organization, patience and charm belong to them. This sign has a strong architectural or mathematical ability and their keen sense of observation will help them succeed in their endeavors. In the meantime, karmic Saturn will exact payment for manipulation and will throw the soul back to the painful start. Capricorn is attracted to successful people, and many of them marry into wealth. Emotional and sensitive, this sign is responsible and protective for the security of the family circle. However, they must learn to communicate deep feelings openly. Capricorn's real gifts are psychology, electronics and careers promoted by Uncle Sam. The awareness of the natal Dragon's Head can propel Capricorn to the highest position of supreme power, but their challenge is to open up to the intangible world of the spirit and its accompanying Universal rules. The natural tendency to organize people and business at all times could hinder Capricorn's sensitivity to others. They are good home makers, love real estate and can produce great food. Trouble in 1997 came from some guilt and depression produced by important decisions involving others. Those resolutions have forced many of Saturn's children to re-structure their future. As a rule this sign is favored to be within a successful business environment where they can apply their tremendous organizational gifts.

Personal: In 1998, You will be receiving the impact of the Dragon's Head in your Virgo, 9th house of higher learning, traveling, publishing and academic accomplishments. A new way of thinking has been induced by the Dragon and many hard-working Capricorns will finally be able to publish their work. This will open exciting doors to promising business endeavors and rewarding financial contacts. The Dragon's Tail's location is still in the sign of Pisces (until October 20th, 1998) in your 3rd house of communication. This could give you mental stress and depression. Thus, you are strongly advised to use your will and "amuse" yourself with a challenging and regenerative spiritual endeavor. Do not let the nasty pull of the Dragon's Tail get the best of your mind. The positive Dragon's Head will send you interesting circumstances, and the fruits of many years of hard work will begin to pay off in 1998. Opportunities will be offered by foreigners and they will still play an important part of your life for another year. Foreign business association, partnerships, traveling and luck in general will be presented to the hard-working Capricorn this year. Providing you keep busy and avoid nurturing pessimistic thoughts of the past, an advancing time is ahead of you. As a rule, those born in January strive for public standing and career promotion. Saturn is slow in his rewards but when he does it usually lasts for-ever. Keep in mind to respect the Universal Law (the fishtail of the goat) as this is a major contribution for your success or failure in your life. The opportunity to make serious progress in 1998 is available to you. This celestial process will bring you much luck if you take on the challenge of investing in computerized education, traveling and if you associate with foreigners. Most of the stars are on your side, especially on foreign ground and in publishing.

For the entire month of January 1998, Jupiter (luck) will be still in the electronic sign of Aquarius (astrology/computers/radio/TV). On February 4th, 1998 the lucky planet will move into the creative and spiritual sign of Pisces until February 13th, 1999. Pisces will be offering you great opportunities to invest and study in the arts and many new-age endeavors. For those who take on the challenge of spiritual rebirth a new wonderful self-esteem will emerge. Be ready for romance or a great business deal with someone born in July, May or September soon. Those born in November will bring you great luck. Good luck to all of those born in January.

1998 — Forecast For Those Born In February

Uranus Governs The Ingenious,
Freedom-Oriented Constellation Of Aquarius

Holder of knowledge of the dimensions
The spark of all the inventions
Lover of all things in simplicity
Charged with the power of electricity
I am AQUARIUS, child of Uranus

The month of February is governed by the eccentric planet Uranus and the futuristic sign of Aquarius. This sun's sign belongs to the most original souls walking this earth and has produced many inventors. This revolutionary Uranian energy rules the future, the incredible UFO phenomenon, astrology and drives staid traditionalists up a wall. Blessed by the stars, those born in February are attracted to the professions of science, research, electronics, psychology, the police force and astrology, just to name a few. This sign rules aeronautics, advanced computers and many an Aquarian dreams of becoming an astronaut. They usually reach fame and fortune during the course of their lifetime and secretly wish to master the enigmatic "time machine." The motion picture *Back To The Future* is one of the best ways to represent Aquarius ingenuities in terms of creative art. Strong and fixed, they inherited from the stars an accurate intuition, tremendous common sense and a powerful will. Yet they have to learn to listen and participate in conversation with equality. Even when the ideas being presented are not of your own making, much knowledge can be gleaned. Lend your full ear, do not race ahead with only thoughts of what you want to say or you will miss much. They must also learn to positively direct Uranus' innovative mental power for the improvement and well-being of the world. Acting eccentrically without forethought is a sure downfall. Aquarius' idealistic views are legendary, their soul's purpose is to promote universal brotherhood with the use of all technological advancement.

However, before working on others they must work on their own cosmic consciousness and awareness of the Universe. This sign handles the difficulties of life with a smile and the advanced ones transcend setback by always using the knowledge to their benefit. The women of this sign are somewhat original, independent, beautiful, intellectual and tend to use their incredibly magnetic sexuality to reach their purposes. As a rule, women born in February produce extraordinarily intelligent children or twins. They are strongly advised not to eat when upset as Aquarius is sensitive in the stomach. In 1997, The Dragon's Head was in their 8th house of corporated money and regeneration; this configuration has promoted the Aquarius' spiritual awakening, bringing with it perhaps some financial hardships, but only because you were not going in the direction you really wanted. You were offered many new opportunities to diversify; those who went fearlessly ahead are beginning to reap the rewards, while others are just beginning this two-year journey.

Personal: 1998 will be another rewarding year for you. The powerful Dragon's Head is still rolling through your 8th house in the sign of Virgo. This will positively affect your corporate financial endeavors, metaphysical growth, contracts, legacy and your partner(s) resources. Many years of hard work will finally pay off and some big-time money is on the way. On a spiritual level, a fascination with the unknown, death, and ethereal matters will generate many stimulating studies. Some of those subjects will be used to further your financial security and increase your wisdom. In 1998, many of you born in February will excel in rich supernatural instruction. You have another year ahead of you where a new way of handling or making money will be offered by the stars. More opportunities to wheel and deal with new-age matters (computers, video, healing, television, radio, UFO etc.) are on the way. New doors will open to plentiful, interesting endeavors if you keep active. The possibility to get worldwide recognition and get your work(s) published will be a strong possibility this year. Keep your eyes open for any business ventures involving foreigners and their well-managed gifts and support.

Trouble may come from mental exhaustion or from your impulsive intellectual nature in dealing with others. You must realize and control the depressive impact of the Dragon's Tail in your 2nd house of finances in Pisces (until October 20th, 1998). Planning on more education will further your ability to manage your finances better, always a weak area with you. Do not let failures of the past diminish your self-esteem and be practical with your money. Invest in your education and look for people who can use your natural talent, especially if you use your communication gifts. Use the knowledge of the Universal Law based on the Moon's fluctuations and you are a guaranteed winner in 1998.

On February 4th, 1998 Jupiter (luck) will enter the sign of Pisces in your 2nd house of money. Expect much traveling, education, teaching and good financial reward even fortune in most everything you will try. This celestial process will bring you much windfall if you take the challenge of trusting yourself and trying the "devil." A romance or business deal may be coming from those born in August, December or February. Good Luck to all of those born in February.

1998 — Forecast For Those Born in March

Neptune Governs the Soft, Dreamy,
Intuitive, Artistic Constellation Of Pisces

Mystical and magical
Nebulous and changeable
I work my way up life's rivers and seas
To my place at God's own feet
I am PISCES, child of Neptune

The month of March is governed by dreamy Neptune and the artistic sign of Pisces. Pisces souls are born teachers, philosophers, perfectionists and will exercise more intuition than logic in dealing with life in general. Pisces naturally does well in holistic endeavors and many are involved in the medical profession. This sign is also noted for his creativity and artistic values. Michaelangelo and George Washington were Pisces' and used their creative attributes to the fullest. The downfall of this sign is an overpreoccupation with others and a blind acceptance of religious dogmas. Nevertheless, the "good heart" of this sign is not surpassed by any other sign of the zodiac, and the advanced ones possess spiritual healing powers. Many of the highly evolved Pisces can lead us out of the deep clouds towards the brilliance of reality. Pisces soul's purpose is to swim upstream (as represented by both fishes) towards the ethereal light of God. A young Pisces spirit is deceiving, complaining, and easily addicted to chemicals, drugs and alcohol.

Pisces MUST respect the laws based on the moon's fluctuations to avoid a negative karmic fate. This sign has within itself the potential to reach not only the light of God but also an immortality and fame through artistic or spiritual work. Pisces rules the feet. It is important for them to walk barefoot on the grass to regenerate the body using the magnetic fields of the earth itself. Pisces intuition is remarkable and should be well-heeded when confronted with serious decision making.

Personal: In 1998, The Dragon's Head will still affect your Virgo, 7th house of partnerships. The possibility to be forced to restructure your marriage or business associations will be high on your list. Inappropriate emotional (marriage) and/or abusive business relationships will be eliminated by the powerful Dragon. The same energy that has affected you in 1997 will be operational in 1998. Thus, a new attitude and a new crowd will enter your life. Those born in March must realize their attitude with others and how it affects their relationships. However, your own personal viewpoint and willingness to accept the foreseen upcoming changes will play an important role in your emotional and financial situation. The difficult Dragon's Tail, located in your first house in Pisces, (until October 20th, 1998) will directly affect your temperament. Great friends will be there to provide you with spiritual support, but don't be too heavy on them. Depressive Saturn is still in Aries, sitting on your second house of finances and self-esteem; you will have to work harder to re-establish your own personal resources. Trouble may come from a low self-esteem and the loss of partners and some of your friends' support. Financial difficulties leading to depression or abuses of chemicals are also a threat. This painful lesson has forced many Pisces souls to "stand" firm against all odds. Towards the end of 1998, the positive impact produced by the Dragon's Head in Virgo will seriously improve and secure Pisces' emotional and financial income for many years to come. After this devastative emotional storm, the deserving Pisces soul will attract to himself new and long lasting companionships. This will result in a new found self-esteem, true love, career improvement and financial progression.

On February 4th, 1998 Jupiter (luck) will enter your own sign in Pisces in your 1st house. Expect much traveling, education, teaching and a foreign person to bring further much of your dreams. This celestial process will force you to "expand" and will bring you much joy if you take on the challenge of trusting yourself and your new future. Romance may be coming from those born in September, July or November. Interesting business deals may be offered to you by those born in May or January. 1998 will be another year that you will not soon forget, loaded with stress but incredible results. Stand strong, swim upstream and respect the Universal Law; you can't lose. Good luck to all of those born in March.

1998 — Forecast For Those Born in April

Mars Governs the Aggressive — Warlike and Impatient Constellation Of Aries

All will hear my views and voice
Trial and error is my school of choice
Dashing and daring I appear
Fighting for those that I hold dear
I am ARIES, child of Mars

The month of April is controlled by aggressive Mars and impatient Aries. Aries souls are born motivational leaders and are prone to learn by mistake. The strong, impatient desire to succeed must be controlled and hasty decisions avoided. They are classified as the warrior of astrology. More than any other sign of the zodiac, Aries must learn steadiness, organization and most of all, DIPLOMACY! When confronted, grace and charm doesn't really belong to them. This sign has a strong leadership and engineering abilities, and the men of this sign are attracted to dangerous endeavors, sports or a work related to Uncle Sam. Due to their "turbocharged" personality, Aries is accident-prone to the head and should protect it. They must also learn to listen, control impatience, focus on their needs steadily and finish what they have started. At work, the strong Aries personality will be felt and may hurt those more sensitive, damaging the chances for respect and hasty promotion. Aries' explosive behavior is mainly due to an inborn inferiority complex, and this sign must learn not to take opposition personally. The Aries "child-like" attitude could attract manipulative spirits wishing to structure or use the immense creativity and energy of the Mars spirit. They do love home and take responsibility with their family. Nevertheless, they prefer to be where the action is. Providing Aries learns patience, tolerance and diplomacy, there is no limit where Mars would take his children. The main lessons for Aries to learn are the diplomatic and loving traits of the opposite, Venus-ruled sign Libra.

Personal: In 1998, the Dragon's Tail in Pisces will be passing through your 12th house (until October 20th, 1998). This house deals with your subconscious, thus you can expect serious improvement in your spiritual nature. Secret affairs will flourish for some and many secrets will come to light. You will still feel the urge to investigate the unknown, your own motivations and hidden personality. An important metaphysical study will bring you many of the answers you seek; however, avoid falling prey to deceiving groups especially if your financial support is requested. Foreigners will play an important part of this spiritual awakening but make sure the "spiritual" information received is factual and usable. On a positive note, the new and practical celestial knowledge will promote your cosmic consciousness and your life in general. Severe stars will affect you again in 1998, but the positive Dragon's Head will force great changes upon your service to the world and your general health. Do not become too concerned with your physical appearance and stay clear from oppressive diet programs. You may involve yourself in an healthy exercise program that will improve your looks in many ways. Doing so will save you a lot of trouble and accelerate the chances of a long and healthy life.

As the child of Mars (ruler of the animal kingdom), red meat or wine is a must in your diet. In 1998, you will still be compelled by the Dragon's Head in Virgo (your sixth house of work) to further your service to the world. Opportunities to bring yourself to a leadership position or starting your own business will be offered to you.

On February 4th, 1998 Jupiter (luck) will enter the sign of Pisces in your 12th house. Expect much spiritual growth and traveling on or by the water. A foreign person will promote much of your wishes. This celestial process will force you to "unravel" the secret side of yourself and will bring you much joy. Channeling, writing and publishing will be high on your list. Romance may be coming from those born in December, August and October. Interesting business deals may be offered to you by those born in February or June. 1998 will be a year of progress loaded with great accomplishments. Be patient, listen, stand strong, and respect the Universal Law, and 1998 will be a success. Good luck to all of those born in April.

1998 — Forecast For Those Born in May

Venus Governs the Beautiful and Financially
Oriented Constellation Of Taurus

Luxurious and elegant
I have the memory of an elephant
Loving all of life's finer pleasures
Gifted am I at acquiring more coffers & treasures
I am TAURUS, child of Venus

The month of May is governed by the loving planet Venus and the stable sign of Taurus. This Sun sign is seen in Divine Astrology as beautiful, stubborn and practical. They are classified as the money sign in Astrology. Taurus souls have a lot to offer to others, providing they control their strong insecurity complex and powerful emotions. Gifted Taurus people are attracted to the professions of banking, real estate, the arts, computers, radio, television, psychology, aeronautics and investigation, to name a few. Many "Bulls" will reach fortune "and a big house," if not fame in their lifetime. Strong and dominant, they have inherited a deep intuition, tremendous common sense and a powerful will. This sign must learn to control all negative thoughts about jealousy, stubbornness and insecurity. Doing so, Venus' constructive power can be channeled towards love, gracious mental exchanges, diplomacy and produce the finest of all hosts and artists. However, behaving in a stubborn and intractable manner is a serious downfall for them. Taurus' down-to-earth approach to life must not interfere with their spiritual growth. Part of the Bull's challenge is to keep an open mind to the world of the spirit and use the metaphysical information to ensure financial growth and material security. This sign's strong desire for riches is legendary, but in some way, Taurus will promote the New Age of Aquarius. They courageously handle the difficulties of life with a solid attitude and the advanced ones possess nobility of purpose. The women of this sign (like Scorpio) are somewhat classic, intellectual, magnetic, sensitive and will always combine Venus' beauty and sensual magnetism to attain their goals. As a rule, Venus women are picky about their mates, so it is important that they marry someone who is respected. In 1997 the Dragon's Head location in their 6th house of health and work has promoted Taurus in a new and different way.

Personal: In 1998 the progressive Dragon's Head will be cruising through the sign of Virgo (your 5th house of love/romance, creativity and children). This governing body will stimulate your natural talents and will bring many new opportunities to prove yourself to the world. The way you present yourself to the world will play an important part of your upcoming success. Thus your image along with a busy program involving plenty of exercise will boost up your magnetism and self-confidence. Meantime, avoid criticizing your partner or forcing him/her into your own perfectionist health schedule. The resolute Dragon's Head may also compel you to review your love relationships and may induce badly needed changes. You will feel the urge to give life, either to a great artistic project or a child. Stress may come from confused friends or from impractical wishes. Do not allow any friend to abuse your caring nature, and learn to say "NO" if they become burdensome on you. The Dragon's Tail in Pisces (until October 20th, 1998) will force many old friends to "disappear" from your daily life; they will be replaced by new ones. Make practical demands on those new friends and test their willingness to help you. Don't let guilt take over your rational mind as the Dragon will try you to your limits; just be "practical" with friends.

On February 4th, 1998 Jupiter (luck) will enter the sign of Pisces in your 11th house. Expect some of those new friends to further much of your wishes. The deserving Taurus soul will be given the opportunity to get published, and travel on or by the water will bring great joy. Older, wiser and respected people will be helping you to promote much of your wishes. This celestial process will force you to tap on your creativity and may lead some Taurus to the cinematographic or television industry. Channeling, writing, acting and publishing will be high on your list. Romance may be coming from those born in January, September or February. Interesting business deals may be offered to you by those born in March, November and July. 1998 will be a year of progress loaded with great accomplishments for many of the Venus children. Stand with faith and respect the Universal Law; 1998 will be a year of great achievement. Good luck to all of those born in May.

1998 — Forecast For Those Born in June

Mercury Governs the Nervous and
Witty Dual Constellation Of Gemini

Free-thinking and intelligent
You will not find me under rigorous management
You may think you know me well
Then my other half over you casts a spell
I am GEMINI, child of Mercury

The month of June is governed by sharp Mercury and the witty sign of Gemini. Gemini souls are born intellectual, nervous and adaptable. They are classified in Greek mythology as "the messengers of the Gods," also, the Lord of the Thieves, because of their double-personality characteristics. As the rule, this zodiacal sign does well in communications, radio, language, photography, sales, movies and any type of PR work. Their natural zest to experience life makes them impatient and unusually nervous. They are born with a gift of youth and a quicksilver mind enabling them to adapt easily.

Once Gemini learns to focus and crystallize the mind, they have the potential to produce interesting publications of all sorts. Due to their strong desire for security, many of them are attracted to the real estate and the food industry. Their financial potential is unlimited if they respect the Universal law controlling their second house of income. Children born with a strong Mercury in their chart will often be classified by the psychological field with A.D.D. (attention deficiency disorder). This is not a disorder but a gift from God, as the soul is rejecting traditional education. Thus, if the teacher is mistaken, Gemini and his sense of curiosity will help him to find the real truth, somewhere, somehow in life. Impatience, nervousness, mental curiosity, and a short attention span are the characteristics, and these have produced many a genius. Gemini souls must not and will not follow long established dogmas. Whatever is accepted by the majority as the only true answer must be intellectually challenged by Gemini's natural curiosity, thus opening new doors to mental exploration. Promoters of common sense, Gemini (like all air signs) has a low tolerance for stupidity. Nevertheless, basic education and discipline must be induced at an early age. Mercury (ruler of Gemini) is naturally in opposition to Jupiter, (ruler of Sagittarius), which rules the codification of thoughts, dogmas, traditional education and religion. Mercury controls Gemini and will always make them question all. Thus, expect notes from the teacher about class disturbances and your Mercury-ruled child to challenge the rules. Some of these children will, in the course of their lifetime, surprise many people.

Personal: In 1998 the powerful Dragon's Head will be still cruising your 4th house (home/family) in the sign of Virgo. This will force you to restructure your base of operation, move, sell or buy a house. Be prepared to further your education into a new home. The positive impact of the Dragon head under your roof will further a couple of important studies. Some Geminis will benefit from the possibility to start a home-based business. A form of rebirth of your basic security will be imposed upon you by those stars. You will feel the need to get in touch with your roots and ancestry, so that you may further yourself. Much of your close associations will also have to undergo that difficult but rewarding transformation. In 1998, the negative Dragon's Tail in Pisces (until October 20th, 1998) will spend most of the year in your 10th house of career. His passage in Pisces will induce stress, uncertainty, and finally a difficult but solid restructure. Another year where you're advised to be prudent. Avoid taking chances in your career and think twice before investing your resources imprudently. Your investments could be wasted in wrong endeavors or deceiving partnerships. Avoid the worst of the Dragon's Tail impact in your career by respecting the Universal Law, which is based on the moon's monthly fluctuations.

On February 4th, 1998 Jupiter (luck) will finally enter the sign of Pisces in your 10th house. The great benefic Jupiter will tone down the negative Dragon's Tail, thus, soon after this date, expect a slow but solid progress in your career area. Great opportunities to travel or study will be offered to you by foreigners. The hard-working and deserving Gemini souls will be given the opportunity to get much of their artistic work published. Many will find opportunity to work and travel on or by the water. Free from the negative Dragon's Tail pull, many of you will feel a relief as many people will be helping you to promote much of your wishes. Jupiter's helping hand will force you to use your creativity, knock down some doors and may even lead some Gemini to the cinematographic or television industry. Advertising, writing, acting and photography will be high on your list. This celestial process will bring you much luck if you take on the challenge of education or if you associate with foreigners. Love may be coming from those born in February, October and December. Friends born in August will further some of your wishes. Good luck to all of those born in June.

1998 — Forecast For Those Born in July

*The Moon Governs the Nurturing and
Caring Constellation Of Cancer*

I am mother, I nurture and provide
In my soul the physical and spiritual collide
I say "ask and you shall receive"
But also as you sow so shall you reap
I am CANCER, child of the Moon

The month of July is controlled by the "lunatic" Moon and the emotional sign of Cancer. Cancer people are strongly affected by the Moon fluctuations, and family matters will always play an important part of their lives. They are classified as the "caretakers" of astrology. This sign is particularly touched by the Universal law, and their success depends on the awareness and practical use of it. This sign is distinctively gifted with food (cooking or eating it!), real estate and strongly motivated by security. During the course of their lives, Cancers will attract to themselves a position of power or management, thus, financial security, if they learn to recognize and synchronize with the flux of the Moon. They will be allowed to shine through their ability to amass riches and possession, so spoil yourself with luxury.

They must avoid depressive thoughts of the past and control their powerful imaginations. Steadiness, organization, warmth, love and charm belong to them. Cancer's powerful emotion can be channeled positively with music, singing and the arts in general. (Country music is a Cancer vibration.) Cancers are attracted to successful people (older or younger mates) and usually marry rich. The natural tendency to smother family members and friends at all times makes these souls admired and deeply loved. Nevertheless, they must learn to control sensitivity and participate with life outside of the home a little more. As a rule, Cancer is a great home maker unless the soul selected a non-domestic Moon position such as Aries, Leo or Aquarius.

Personal: You went through a lot of trouble the last few years, but in 1998 the stars are still on your side. The great Dragon's Head is still traveling (until October 20th, 1998) through your Virgo, 3rd house of communication. Thus mental exploration, study, writing and traveling is on your agenda. Many opportunities in 1998 will be given to you by the stars to accomplish serious mental progress, especially if you decide to do something practical about it. Use the great Dragon's location to further your education, and a long-lasting reward will be offered to you. As a rule, Cancers tend to be too critical with everyone around, including themselves. Do not allow yourself to be trapped into a wrong or disturbing thought process. Naturally concerned with health, you are strongly advised to let go of fears and negative thoughts, thus your body (temple of God) will stay healthy. Rest assured that your positive thinking alone can take care of your spiritual and physical bodies. Give a good look to yourself and realize your potential for success this year. Trouble may come from the location of the Dragon's Tail still crossing the sign of Pisces, your 9th house of higher learning and traveling. Avoid exhausting yourself mentally in order to accomplish great academic feats and take some time off from the heavy burden of your traveling. Sad news may also come from foreigners or visiting foreign places. Take plenty of fresh water with you and think twice before eating unfamiliar food. To avoid trouble, learn to keep your eyes wide open on the Moon's fluctuations and initiate your endeavors only after the New Moon. Respecting the Universal Law will save you much trouble or unwanted legal action.

On February 4th, 1998 Jupiter (luck) will enter the sign of Pisces in your 9th house. The great benefic Jupiter will tone down the negative Dragon's Tail, thus, soon after this date, expect a less hazardous, even a better time abroad. Great opportunities to travel or study will be offered to you by foreigners. The laborious Cancer soul will be given the opportunity to get much of his education to pay off and flourish in artistic endeavors. You could also find a great opportunity to travel and use your managerial abilities abroad. Liberated from much of the negative Dragon's Tail pull, many of you will finally be able to relax. Then, many people will be helping you to promote much of your wishes close to beautiful exotic places. Jupiter will make you feel very spiritual and closer to God and may even lead some of you to a deep research into your spiritual identity and purpose in life. Channeling, psychic work, writing, spiritual studies and traveling will be high on your list. This celestial configuration will bring you much luck if you take on the challenge to expand your cosmic consciousness and learn to understand the tools and recognize the face of the creator in the stars. Great spiritual progress will be offered by foreigners. Watch for love or a potential business proposition with souls born in January, March, and November. Love may be coming from those born in February, October and December. Friends born in May will further some of your wishes. Good luck to all of those born in July.

1998 — Forecast For Those Born in August

The Sun Governs the Flamboyant and
Majestic Constellation Of Leo

Powerful and Charming
All things living find me disarming
I step to the center of God's stage
In the books of history I have always a page
I am LEO, child of the Sun

The month of August is governed by the all-powerful Sun and the magnanimous sign of Leo. This sun sign is seen as the most dignified energy in astrology. It is classified as lifegiver and shines over all signs of the Zodiac. These souls have a lot to offer, providing they exercise serious control over the strong egos and authoritative nature of the untamed King of the jungle. Naturally gifted Leo souls are attracted to the professions involving the arts, public life, medicine, research, management and fame in general. Just as the Sun's rays penetrate the depths of the rain forest, Leo was born with the potential to bring and promote life to all that they touch. This Sun sign is fixed and strongly motivated by the will to succeed, and usually in the course of their lifetimes, they will reach fame, power and fortune. Strong and dominant Leo was born with the deep desire to organize and rule others. If Leo becomes too overbearing, he will be forced to learn and accept the lesson of humility. Destructive outburst of emotions and unfettered pride are the enemy of the king. He must positively direct and control the Sun's creative rays without burning himself or others.

The challenge of Leo is to recognize the powerful Sun's energy and diligently work toward a better understanding of other life creative forces at work. Acting eccentrically and pridefully without forethought is a serious weakness of Leos. This Sun's sign courageously handles the difficulties of life. The wise ones possess nobility of purpose. The women of this sign are stunning, intellectual, magnetic and attract others with their natural auric power. As a rule, Leo produces the most protective of mothers, but they should avoid being overbearing with their children. Health-wise, all Leos were born with a subconscious fear of death, but nature gave them a strong mind and robust body. Leos are weak and accident-prone in the knee and joint area (President Clinton is a Leo!), so use precaution and moderation when running or jogging.

Personal: In 1998, the great Dragon's Head will drift through the sign of Virgo, (until October 20th, 1998) your 2nd house of self-esteem and general finances. The Dragon's impact has forced you to a full restructure and will soon be offering you several business and financial opportunities. Many new ideas to enhance your personal income will come to your mind or be presented by new business associates. As a rule Leos must work for themselves and use the Sun's creative power constructively in building a pyramid of success. For another year, the general re-structure of your finances will also involve spending for the office, reorganization and for health improvement. You could also use this positive trend to enroll in an advanced financial or tax class. This will allow you to get a broader view and more control over your financial endeavors. The Dragon's Tail in Pisces is still in your 8th house of corporate money for much of the year. This may bring you some stress, either with a lawsuit, unsuitable partners or Uncle Sam claiming the lion's share for his tax purposes. Thus, you are strongly advised to keep a close eye on your financial duties and joint finances in 1998 to avoid any form of future trouble in this area. With the Dragon's Tail crossing your 8th house of death, in the deceiving sign of Pisces (imagination/deception), avoid worrying too much about your health. On a sad note, many Lions who are done with their "schooling" will pass away through the golden doors of heaven. But for the rest it will be a shining year of rewards and riches, if they use all the knowledge of the ancients.

Expect the signing of important legal matters; some of it will be related to a legacy or a loan. The Dragon's Tail could also produce some emotional stress but, as usual, the King will win the battle. 1998 will force you to restructure both your finances and your self-esteem. The understanding of handling your income in an organized or different way will bring you many great opportunities to further your financial security.

On February 4th, 1998 Jupiter (luck) will at last enter the sign of Pisces in your 8th house. The great benefic Jupiter will seriously alter the negative Dragon's Tail energy thus, soon after this date, expect a slow but solid progress in all your financial endeavors. Great opportunities to join groups and enjoy their financial support will be given to you. The hard-working and deserving Leo soul will be finally given the opportunity to get some rest and organize his brilliant future. Many will find financial support and opportunities to prove to the world they are real artistic talents. Free from much of the negative Dragon's Tail pull, many of you will feel a relief as many people will be offering you great contracts promoting much of your wishes. Jupiter's helping hand will induce contracts, commitment, luck and expansion in all you do. This celestial process will bring you much advantage if you take on all the challenges early in the year with faith in your ability to succeed. Love may be coming from those born in February, December and April. Friends born in June will further some of your wishes. Good luck to all of those born in August.

1998 — Forecast For Those Born in September

Mercury Governs the Precise and
Critical Constellation Of Virgo

Cleansing impurities large and small
Don't think yourself immune, for I see all
Attending to every chore and task
Perfection being all that I ask
I am VIRGO, child of Mercury

The month of September is governed by witty Mercury and the critical sign of Virgo. Virgo souls are born intellectual, picky and workaholics. They can become great writers and will combine logic and intuition in dealing with life in general. They are classified as the "perfectionists" in Astrology. As a rule, Virgo souls do well in the fields of medicine, teaching, writing, designing and office work. Many of them are refined artists. The downfall of this sign is sarcasm and an overly concerned attitude with trivial matters. Some Virgos are overwhelmed with health matters, while some ignore it completely. Letting the rational mind scrutinize everything could hinder Virgo's spiritual gifts and slow down their cosmic consciousness. This sign has a natural investigative mind, and many of them are involved in science, research, radio, television, newspaper reporters, computer programming and the law. The advanced ones are great leaders and masters in communication.

As a rule this sign is prone to headaches or head injury, eye and sinus problems. They are strongly advised to keep away from alcohol and narcotics. On the medical side, Virgo controls the elimination principle (bowels) and they could be their worst enemy by being overly concerned with health matters. An advanced Virgo soul will soon realize that diets that are too restrictive cause just as much problems as over-indulgence.

God designed our bodies as Omnivorous, thus our metabolism is well equipped to deal with all types of food, including red meat. If your natural desire for perfection prevails and you eliminate this "red" source of food, you must then substitute it with different red foods such as red wine, hot peppers or any other thermogenic food. The balanced diet imposed by God must be respected to avoid digestive tract problems and a loss of "power" due to a lack of energy and body heat. A word of caution — if Virgo happens to suffer headaches or migraines, he may find comfort by walking in grass barefoot to regenerate from the earth's magnetic field.

Personal: The powerful Dragon's Head is still located in your 1st house of personality, so again there won't be much that you will not be able to accomplish in 1998. A strong feeling of independence and competitiveness will prevail while you are restructuring yourself and your future. Much work will be directed to a general improvement and the image you want to project to the world. As mentioned earlier, do not be overly concerned with health matters or you may end up stressing every moving part of your body, especially your digestive tract. A good diet will pay off for you; however, try not to exclude meat or fish from your daily food intake. Trouble may come from the Dragon's Tail in Pisces (until October 20th, 1998) in your 7th house of marriage and partnerships. A full restructure of this department did or will take place within the next few months, and letting go of the past must become your sole priority.

On February 4th, 1998 Jupiter (luck) will at last enter the sign of Pisces in your 7th house of marriage and business associates. The great benefic Jupiter will seriously alter the negative Dragon's Tail energy thus, soon after this date, expect a slow but solid progress in both your emotional and business relationships. Great opportunities to join specific groups and enjoy many new people will be given to you. The hard-working and deserving Virgo soul will be finally given the opportunity to find someone who fits their nature. Many will find financial support in partnerships and opportunities to work harder with new partners to improve their artistic talents. Free from much of the negative Dragon's Tail pull, many of you born in September will feel a relief if you keep active on the social front. Many people will be offering you great contracts promoting much of your wishes. Jupiter's children (foreigners) will induce new contracts, traveling, education, luck and expansion in all you do. This celestial process will bring you much advantage if you take on all the challenges to let go of the past and trust your capability to succeed.

Watch for love or a potential business proposition with souls born in July. 1998 promises to be another rewarding year for you. The opportunity to be born again and "clean up" incompatible associations will be forced upon you by the Dragon's Tail, but he has your best interest at heart. Love may be coming from those born in May, January and March. Good luck to all of those born in September.

1998 — Forecast For Those Born in October

Venus Governs the Diplomatic and
Peaceful Constellation Of Libra

Lover of grace and harmony
Seeking the balance of matrimony
Though there are those that hold to opinions tight
I will see it in all the different lights
I am LIBRA, child of Venus

The month of October is controlled by diplomatic Venus and the charming sign of Libra. Libra souls are strongly motivated by a strong desire for justice and must create harmony in all areas of their lives. Libra is classified as "the peacemaker" in Astrology. They succeed in career matters due to their gentle personalities, sense of diplomacy and natural "savoir faire." They rarely learn by mistakes but, as a rule, must avoid prolonged indecision. Libra's soul's purpose is to achieve "balance" during the course of their lifetime. Nevertheless, they must learn decision making, by following not only the rational mind but also their accurate intuitions. This sign possesses a strong psychological aptitude, doing well in the real estate, the food industry, stock market, interior design, marriage counseling and the arts in general. Libra must focus on what they need first, using inner stamina and their practical and intuitive mind. Libra will be attracted to competitive people, and can expect much respect and trust from them. These sensitive souls could be easily offended by the abrupt or assertive manner of business partners and should avoid taking remarks too personally. Libra loves a good home and likes to be in company of business-oriented partners where they can apply their tremendous diplomatic skills.

Personal: In 1998, the Dragon's Head will be still going through the sign of Virgo and your 12th house of subconscious. The Dragon's Head in this subtle area will impose a full restructure of your inner self. Thus, many Libras will feel like taking a course in astrology, psychology, even metaphysics. This study will bring you subconscious knowledge and help develop your psychic ability. Your imagination, psychological and artistic gifts will be enhanced and this realization should be used to create something solid. Thus, your ability to perform or write will be sharpened and should also be put to use in the form of artistic endeavors. The occasion to recognize your feebleness and do something about it will heal much of the emotional wounds you had to suffer since 1990. Trouble may come from your working environment or your health due to the Dragon's Tail in Pisces (until October 20th, 1998) cruising this section of your life. In any case do not let yourself down, let go of the past and keep a positive attitude no matter what. If you behave this way, the negative Dragon will not be able to harm you. Still, be ready for a full restructure of your working life, and again, avoid stressing yourself as the changes are taking place. These transformations are needed and very positive in the long run. The positive Dragon will lead you toward great accomplishments if you decide to be practical about a study ahead of you. The opportunity to realize your creative potential and start a new business could also be offered to you. The restructure must take place and you will have a lot to gain if you make and accept the upcoming changes.

On February 4th, 1998 Jupiter (luck) will finally enter the sign of Pisces in your 6th house of health and work. The great benefic Jupiter will tone down the opposing Dragon's Tail. Soon after this date, expect a less strenuous working environment and more opportunities to improve yourself. The laborious Libra soul will be given the break he hopes for, but much depends on the education accumulated in electronics. If so you will be given a chance to flourish in some artistic endeavor. You could also find great fortune in traveling and use your managerial abilities abroad. Jupiter's power will liberate you from much of the negative pull of the Dragon's Tail and you will finally be able to relax. Many new people will enter the new scenery and promote much of your wishes in beautiful exotic places. Jupiter may also lead you into a research of your relationship with God and the universe. You will feel the urge to do a deep research into your spiritual identity and real purpose in life. Channeling, metaphysical work, creative writing, ethereal studies and travel will be high on your list. This celestial configuration will bring you much luck if you take on the challenge to expand your cosmic consciousness and learn to understand the tools and recognize the face of the creator in the stars. Watch for love or a potential business proposition with souls born in August. Friends born in August will also further some of your wishes. Love may be coming from those born in February, June and December. Good luck to all of those born in October.

1998 — Forecast For Those Born in November

Pluto Governs the Mighty Constellation
of Scorpio — "The Eagle or Lizard"

Holder of all the secrets deep
Never speaking for they are mine to keep
For those who plunder without care
Tread carefully for I see you there
I am SCORPIO, child of Pluto

The month of November is governed by dramatic Pluto and the intense sign of Scorpio. Gifted with a powerful will, Scorpio souls are attracted to the medical profession, the police force, government and investigation, just to name a few. They are classified as "the Eagle" (positive) or "the lizard" (negative) in Astrology. This Sun sign is seen as the most mystical sign of Astrology and, like all water signs, they are attracted to the study of metaphysics. Unless you are aware of their innate "negative" qualities, you are well advised to play right or keep away from them. Those souls carry with them an element of life and death, and their magnetic thoughts can reach anyone, anywhere, for good or for bad.

Many "young Scorpio spirits" will experience despair and imprisonment during the course of their lifetimes. However, the destructive energies of Pluto can be channeled positively to accomplish tremendous results. This sign rules the Mafia, the police force and the absolute power of creation or destruction, including sex. The message is quite clear when representing Pluto. No one should take chances under his command. If Scorpios realize their own birthright of creation or destruction, they should have no fear and will "fly" well over destructive emotions and legendary jealousy, using mystical gifts to succeed were many would fail. Strong, private and dominant, they have inherited a practical mind and an acutely accurate intuition.

Scorpios must learn to control their deep emotions and, at the same time, positively direct Pluto's power for the well-being of society. They do regenerate themselves with investigation, spiritual growth and must uncover the fantastic mission of leading others towards the undiluted truth. The women of the sign are seen in Divine Astrology as "la femme fatale." They are sensual, classic, intellectual, reserved, magnetic and tend to use sexual power and beauty to reach their purpose. However, the powerful Scorpio is weak with affairs of the heart and tends to be in love with love.

Personal: In 1998, the great Dragon's Head will be slowly passing through your 11th house of wishes and friends. By birth you are naturally endowed with super spiritual tools and in 1998 the Dragon will grant many of your personal wishes. Additional friends will enter the panorama of your life and will bring with them ability to reach a higher purpose. They will introduce you to worthwhile group organization, new business ventures and lots of traveling. In 1998 your social life will undergo gradual changes and opportunities to find love. Much will be accomplished this year if you decide to participate with life with a positive attitude. As with all the water signs, your swift accomplishments will also depend on your ability to respect the moon's fluctuations in all you do.

Trouble may come from the Dragon's Tail in Pisces (until October 20th, 1998), disturbing your 5th house of creativity, love, romance and children. The fatalistic Dragon's Tail may force you to re-evaluate your love life and put some stress in your relationships with children. You are strongly advised to stay clear of narcotics, limit alcohol and use common sense, patience and diplomacy in all your dealings. Dramatic happenings are a part of a Scorpio life if you let the "Lizard" take over your common sense.

On February 4th, 1998 the great planet Jupiter (luck) will finally enter this difficult area in Pisces. Dignified Jupiter will then tone down the hostile Dragon's Tail for your benefit. Soon after this date, expect a less strenuous atmosphere and a more courteous attitude with others. The likelihood to travel will also be high in your mind and love with an Asiatic or artistic person on the horizon. The tireless Scorpio soul will also be given a chance to perform on a much higher level. Many artistic Scorpios will finally be given a chance to flourish in creative endeavors. Great fortune may come your way close to the water or on an island; however, use your legendary intuition to make up your mind about any situations you may encounter. Jupiter's power will liberate you from much of the negative pull of the Dragon's Tail and you will finally be able to enjoy life and relax more. A new lover will enter the scenery and promote much of your wishes in beautiful exotic places. Jupiter's philosophical side may lead you into research of your relationship with the universe. The urge to do some deep research into your spiritual identity will be challenging but rewarding. Watch for love or a potential business proposition with souls born in September. Friends born in March will also further some of your wishes. Love may be coming from those born in July and May. Good luck to all of those born in November.

1998 — Forecast For Those Born in December

Jupiter Governs the Philosophical and
Educated Constellation of Sagittarius

I have traveled the world wide
With naught but the law on my side
Yearning for the higher knowledge
All of God's creation as my college
I am SAGITTARIUS, child of Jupiter

The month of December is governed by majestic Jupiter and the lucky sign of Sagittarius. These souls are born philosophers, teachers and intellectuals and classified as "the truth seekers." As a rule, Sagittarius does well in professions related to the codification of thought, the law, religion, communication, radio and language. Many of them are attracted to holistic healing and the world of sports. Their subconscious desire to travel foreign lands will take them far away, bringing back home the results of their learning to teach the rest of us. They are born with the gift of teaching and will always promote a form of purity in life. Sagittarius also does quite well in office work and can be extremely organized. They inherited from the stars a quick mind and can keep up with anyone willing to listen to them philosophize. Once Sagittarius realizes the importance of education and learns to focus on chosen goals, their ruler, Jupiter (the lord of luck) will throw blessings to them. This sign has also the potential to produce interesting books, even novels. Sagittarius are by birth too concerned with finances and must learn to give, so that they may receive help from accumulated good karma. They must adapt to the saying, "to be a millionaire, you must act like one." Word of caution: Children born with an overbearing Sagittarius energy must guard against overzealousness; their lesson is to realize that God cannot be confined to any man-made building or any man-made doctrine. The advanced ones (truth seekers) will lead the rest of us towards the reality of God's manifestation through all creation. Realizing, learning and teaching the face and the tools of the Creator is their challenge and their real contribution to the world.

Personal: In 1998 the Dragon's Head will be still cruising your Virgo, 10th house of public standing; this will load you with incredible opportunities to promote your career. If you worked hard, last year was a year of slow but solid progress. This year, once more, be ready for another progressive re-structure of your position in your corporation as well as a deserved promotion in the face of the world. In 1997, you were given the opportunity to start your own business; if you did not do it yet, do not despair. You may do so within the next few months ahead of you. You are strongly advised to make the most of the protective Dragon as luck may strike you anytime, anywhere. Get active on the social scenery, especially after each and every New Moon. Word of caution: with karmic Saturn in Aries, as with all the other signs of the Zodiac, remember that karma is also very real and if your progress is selfishly oriented, you may be brought down to a painful crash.

Trouble may come from the Dragon's Tail located in Pisces (until October 20th, 1998) your real estate and home area. Be gentle with those you care about and if you did not move yet, be ready for a relocation before then. Find time for those you care about, as your challenging new career may take up your thoughts and plans.

On February 4th, 1998 Jupiter (luck) will at last enter the sign of Pisces in your 4th house of domestic affairs and will affect some real estate endeavors. Majestic Jupiter will seriously modify the negative Dragon's Tail energy thus, soon after this date, be prepared for substantial progress in both your emotional and business relationships. Great opportunities to expand the base of operation or relocate to a warmer climate and enjoy the water and many new neighbors will be given to you. The hard-working and deserving Sagittarius soul will be finally given the opportunity to find a more secure home life. Many will find financial aid and new opportunities to work right from the security of their home. Free from much of the negative Dragon's Tail pull, many of you born in December will find relief in a cutting-edge endeavor. Many groups outside of your home will need your talents and will be offering great contracts. In 1998, foreigners will also touch you, begetting financial and educational agreements promising expansion in all you do. The possibility for writing, appearance on radio and television programs are also part of this trend. This celestial process will bring you much if you let go of the past and trust your capability to succeed. Watch for a potential business proposition with souls born in October. 1998 promises to be another challenging but excellent year for you. Love may be coming from those born in April, August or June. Good luck to all of those born in December.

Starguide 1998 Daily Guidance

New Moon — December 29th, in Capricorn:

Expect the beginning or ending of important phases of your life. Watch for friends and family members too as the stars will force them into a new section of their life experiences. Everything around you must change and those changes will be positive. Count on the government to make important political decisions during this trend. The waxing moon (positive) is a sure sign of progress within the next two weeks. Push now, be confident and swim with the tide.

Chapter 7

Your 1998 Starguide Day-to-Day Guidance

Welcome to Your Day-to-Day Guidance For January 1998

THU., FRI., SAT., SUN. — JANUARY 1st, 2nd, 3rd, 4th:
RULERS — Uranus (astonishment) & Neptune (dreams come true)

Work, Career and Business: Even during a waxing Moon time, Neptune may make you feel a bit depressed or overemotional with people at work on Sunday. Whatever you do, stay clear of alcohol or you're in for serious trouble. On Friday, keep your eyes and ears open; with Neptune's "dreamy" nature, you are prone to make serious errors or forget to do something important. Go ahead with contracts, but read between the lines; in the long run, you will be happy if you do. Count on the new Moon to further all progress.

Partnerships: Crazy things may happen now; behave appropriately in public. Things done or words said to some people, especially without forethought, might have disturbing consequences. Expect interesting, even surprising news by mail or telephone. With Neptune in the air avoid fears as insecurity could take over your common sense. All will be fine; there is a Divine plan for your future. This timing is ideal for meditation and renewing your faith in each other and the universe.

Family and Friends: Expect the affairs of the heart to progress or even get better. Teenagers may get themselves in trouble as Uranus will make them irrational. Friends may call you asking for spiritual support or direction. Confusion is in the air with Neptune and if you socialize during the night hours, keep mindful of who is going to drive home as alcohol will be flowing. Don't misplace your keys. Find humor in life's little problems, use the new Moon for happiness.

Love Affairs: The Moon is still waxing (positive); this means a time to look for love. If you're single, now is the right time to socialize, looking for that special person. The happy moon can only further your chances and will promote your endeavors. With spiritual Neptune around, you will find relief close to God in your local church. If you are single and born in January, Cancer, Pisces or Virgo will be strongly attracted to you.

Travel and Communication: Expect the telephone to be busy and loaded with surprises these days. However avoid gossiping or supporting a negative discussion. Go ahead and plan for trips in faraway places close to the water.

Environment: Again, Neptune rules the oceans and combined with Uranus anything out there can happen. It is a great time to go for a cruise or any other enjoyable water sport. Always use your head around water as it is mighty and unpredictable.

Famous Personalities: Great movies will be available to the public and some well-known actors will sign important contracts. Some of them would do anything to gain attention; watch for weird news.

Events: As usual with Uranus in charge, expect anything to happen. This planet rules the sudden release of energy (earthquakes, volcanoes, explosions, etc.) Let's hope the waxing Moon will stop him from disturbing the earth. As usual for those interested in the incredible UFO phenomenon, keep your eyes open now, especially if you happen to be in the desert or open spaces. Many incredible experiences happened under Uranus' power. We may hear of some wonderful news pertaining to possible cures for old diseases.

Shopping: Surely a great time to purchase a new car or any electronic equipment; the salesman will compromise for you; challenge him, take a chance. Use Neptune's philosophical energy to promote your knowledge; you may gain a lot by investing in a spiritual class. A good movie will help you to enjoy life.

MON., TUE., WED., THU. — JANUARY 5th, 6th, 7th, 8th: RULERS — Mars (devastation) Venus (sweetheart)

Work, Career and Business: With Mars around, your emotions will run high in the office; a single spark and you could start an emotional fire. The beginning of the week begins with some frustrations and will get tense as we are approaching the Full Moon. Use Venus' diplomatic power to save trouble and propose a meeting.

Partnerships: Pretend you don't hear anything negative from anybody. Don't take anything personally and laugh "inside" at all the victims of Mars. You know better; use your knowledge and the soft tendency of the planet of love to make a good day.

Family and Friends: Use your will, control your speech and your temper, especially with your loved ones at home. Mars' aggressive manners will be felt with the behavior of your friends and family members. Use "savoir faire" with them and be patient. Insure your home and be aware of fire. You will also hear that someone got a promotion for extra diligence in their work.

Love Affairs: During a New Moon period (positive), Venus, the planet of sweetheart and charm, should stop real tragedies. Secrets may be shared with you; however, do not make the situation worse; keep the secrets of your friends secret. For the singles, Venus passion will rule the nights. Physical attraction could lead to sex; think of the future and do not take any chances on your health. If you are single, wear light blue and those born in December will attract Leo, Gemini and Aries.

Travel and Communication: If you have to drive to work, keep in mind to be polite and courteous with the unaware mass out there. The majority of people will fall victims of Mars and will fight for the road. They don't know about the hostile celestial energies upon them and are nothing less than robots of the stars. You will notice that people will want to drive very quickly, but be sure to watch your own speeds.

Environment: Mars won't care much about the positive moon and could manage to stir trouble. This up-coming weekend should be spent away from the roads, bridges, piers, tall buildings and anything that could fall on your head. Mars will have fun doing his own destructive things, and you should be aware of it.

Famous Personalities: News of accidents may be coming from some rich and famous man. You may hear of a celebrity wedding during this trend as well.

Events: Mars likes explosions and fires. Expect nature to rumble a bit; hopefully, earthquakes or dangerous explosions will happen far from you.

Shopping: Money will play an important part of your life these days and you could invest in anything that will promote your business. Expensive, sharp and dangerous tools bought now will attract work and will pay off later. For those of you into a little luxury, money spent to surprise and woo another will pay off. If you are alone, then indulge yourself a little.

January 10th, 1998 — Venus enters Capricorn: Souls born now will have an opportunity to master classical arts and many will marry well. They will attract much older partners when young, then much younger as they grow older. The opportunity to mix business, love and pleasure together is offered to the soul. They may also experience depressions due to loneliness and spend long periods of time without love. Thus if you were born with Venus (love) in Capricorn (class), you must get active after each and every new moon period. Often, love and success are experienced later in life. Avoid criticism and participate in many activities.

January 12th, 1998 — Full Moon matures in the emotional, family-oriented sign of Cancer. Expect some serious career or personal developments to take place. Some will be starting a new job, and others will drop one; this may also include a business relationship. Promotion or deception, whichever happens to you (or others) will mark an important part of your life. Just be ready to accept the upcoming changes with faith in your new future. Be ready to provide a supportive shoulder to the victims. Nature may also decide to do some nasty things in some states, promoting bad weather or earthquakes. The government will have to take serious steps to promote peace in the world. This sign is ruled by the Moon. Expect the beginning or ending of important phases of your life. This lunation could represent a very important part your destiny. You may be forced to let go of your past, accept your new future with confidence. Many will be affected and forced to move on around you.

January 13th, 1998 — Mercury enters Capricorn: Souls born now are blessed with a scientific mind. They will excel in mathematics work, astronomy, geology, mechanics, computing and any science requiring an extreme attention to details. A top position involving the rational thought process will lead the soul towards political activity and an ability with architectural endeavors. By birth, many of them will miss the natural ingredient to assimilate the essence of any spiritual matter or enter the intuitional domain of metaphysicians (or astrology). Fortunately for them, later on in life they will be able to see the "forest not only the trees."

FRI., SAT., SUN., MON. — JANUARY 9th, 10th, 11th, 12th:
RULERS — Mercury (intellectual power) & the Moon (new starts)

Work, Career and Business: The Moon is now waning (difficult) and the universe won't further any new opportunity now. This may force you into a change in your business endeavors. Use Mercury's mental power to promote yourself or clarify a difficult situation with others. For those involved in sales, this lunation will not bring worthwhile arrangements and some of us will have to deal with important legal documents. During a waning moon, you can sign any important paper work if you have to finish or get rid of a situation (or a person!).

Partnerships: Nothing is made to last forever not even relationships. This process will impose many changes, prodding you towards new experiences and valuable knowledge. Do not hold tightly to your past; you only make yourself miserable until you can't take it any more. Only when the changes are accepted will the stars will shine upon you and your new destiny. Keep a positive attitude no matter what.

Family and Friends: Many will enjoy good food and the family circle this weekend. If you decide to dine out on Saturday, it would be wise to make reservations as the local restaurants will be busy. Surely a good time to enjoy the wild, wide open spaces with children and pets. Expect news from mom, brothers or sisters.

Love Affairs: Do some listening; avoid talking too much about you or your past. Nurture positive thoughts about life in general. A trip close to nature or the water would do great for both of you. Candlelight, good wine, great food, and soft music are there for you to enjoy with your partner. If single, go out with friends you know and do not be too trusting of a stranger's words. Participate with life wisely. Those born in January will be attracted to older or younger people born in September, July or May.

Travel and Communication: Do not expect much good news to arrive via mail or telephone. A person you know who is going in a direction that you disapprove of could benefit from your advice. This individual might need more emotionally upheaving experiences; don't let this affect your relationship. Soon new friends may come into your life, but they are from the waning moon; don't expect much from them. Avoid being critical with old friends as your remarks could be misinterpreted and could haunt you for a while. Be aware if you're invited to a party; don't believe in all you hear. Be nice and happy, impress everyone. Much of your wishes can be granted, after the new Moon, if you participate a bit more with others. A trip to your past could bring you joy. Keep in mind to service the car before leaving and drive safely.

Environment: Thousands of people will be forced to relocate during this type of celestial configuration. Nature may decide to throw a nasty message to man; quakes, volcanoes, floods are very high on the list. Let's hope for the sake of many that this lunation won't be too devastative.

Famous Personalities: Many prominent people will come in or out of a situation, business or a bad marriage. The beginning or ending of important phases of life is active for all of us. Famous or not, they are under the same stars and will suffer the reality of life.

Events: Be ready for the government (foreign or the U.S.) to make important decisions. Some elected officials might be forced to a departure from office. The United States, France and Japan could be touched directly.

Shopping: Avoid spending too much money on anything. If you need a new answering machine or a new telephone, wait for the next new Moon. Great time to purchase any book(s) that could teach you something spiritual.

TUE., WED., THU., FRI., SAT. — JANUARY 13th, 14th, 15th, 16th, 17th:
RULERS — The Sun (entertainment)& Mercury (printed word)

Work, Career and Business: With the waning Moon upon you, do not expect much luck these days. A new job or a better position may be what you need and could be attained in the near future. Renew your confidence and support to your worldly ambitions and don't let the waning moon affect you negatively. Keep a low profile for now.

Partnerships: Come clean with what you mean with a partner; miscommunication does happen and usually leads to trouble. Go easy in expressing your feelings; don't let the sad Moon blur your vision or your words. Re-schedule an important meeting.

Family and Friends: Don't expect much with family members or friends either. Expect disturbing news from them and help them to get on with their lives. Avoid stressing for them and let them know when they abuse your telephone. Children will also be a bit unmanageable and nervous. Use lots of patience with them and remember their sensitivity if they are teenagers. They could be hurt with your attitude and this could damage your close relationship later on in life. Discipline them carefully, assist their young will and help build up their self-esteem.

Love Affairs: With the waning moon above your head, a reliable love relationship won't be available for a while. An unexpected invitation to a gathering could bring an interesting person into your life. Use your head, not your heart, and you'll be fine. The Sun's revitalizing power should be used to rekindle your feelings for some of the friends or lovers you really trust. A good love story movie will help you to release some feelings you have for someone you care about. If you are single, and born in February, spend valuable time with those born under the sign of Leo, Gemini or Libra.

Travel and Communication: As always with Mercury in charge, take good care of your car and drive cautiously. You may be surprisingly asked to drive somewhere soon; whereever you go slow down. Be aware of the waning moon and don't take any chances with the cops. Avoid gossiping about someone close to you. Words travel fast; be aware as you, may lose that person's friendship.

Environment: With the waning Moon in progress, mother nature might respond to our closest satellite's disturbing magnetic field. Some lives may be swept away with flooding. Some surprising development will make the news on CNN. Explosions and volcanic eruptions are on the way. Some naturalist groups will be concerned and active in making the rest of us aware of her wonderful blessings.

Famous Personalities: A celebrity may engage in a disturbing matter in public or a distressing happening will affect some of them. Sad news involving legal battles, marriage and children will reach the media.

Events: Under the same type of energy on February 19, 1997 in Beijing. China formally declared six days of mourning for Deng Xiaoping as the nation began to come to terms with the death of its leader of two decades.

Shopping: If you are an investor, hold on to your gold assets or you may be stuck in a bad transaction and lose. Presents will be offered to those deserving loving souls. Do not invest in a specific interest or creativity. A garage sale is where great bargains are available now.

> **Note**: Attention Pluto is back with us — Expect dramatic happenings all over; control is a must. The Lord of Hades doesn't forget and doesn't forgive; don't be a victim. Be aware of Pluto's destructive power.

SUN., MON., TUE., WED., THU. — JANUARY 18th, 19th, 20th, 21st, 22nd:

RULERS — Venus (commitment) Pluto (drama)

Work, Career and Business: If you are tempted by any form of unlawful shortcut, consider Pluto and the real potential for disaster, even death before jumping right ahead. You may be forced into a wake-up call of sorts. Do not expect anything to go your way these days. Be easy with letters, meetings, phone calls, etc. Don't let Pluto sting everyone and everything to death. Use your intuition in all you do and be ready for concealed business to surface.

Partnerships: Spend time re-organizing the home and the office. Throw old things away and be busy at all times. Your unaware principal and coworkers are also affected by those negative stars and could make your life misery. Be diplomatic as your weakness or errors won't go unnoticed. You may want to listen carefully to what is said for or against you; those comments deserve your attention. Pluto will damage your partnership if you do not consider, re-think or be cautious. You may have to use your rational judgment caps concerning key partnerships. Some changes are imminent.

Family and Friends: A family member or a friend will undergo dramatic endings to a portion of their life. You'll be asked to offer your judgment and a supportive shoulder. At home or at work expect arguments, and this may get those days off on the wrong track. Aggravations that could continue into the evening hours could have serious repercussions and may bring the police in the neighborhood. Keep your head cool; stay calm and patient.

Love Affairs: Be ready for secrets to surface; however, bits and pieces of information may be wrong or missing. Do not make important decisions about a situation or a person just now. Concealed love trysts will take place all over and will keep a bunch of insidious investigators active. Don't trust strangers; Pluto always induces drugs, alcohol and rapes. Protect yourself at all cost if you're sexually active now; the signature of Pluto is AIDS! If you are single and born under the sign of Pisces, those born in September, November or July will be strongly attracted to you. Use your head, not your heart!

Travel and Communication: Avoid long trips by air, plane or ship as the stars do not care — they just do the work they were intended to do by God's higher order.

Environment: Islamabad, Pakistan — Be ready for nasty surprises, especially the ones with nature's forces at work. A powerful earthquake shook southwest Pakistan. The death toll climbed and scores more people were injured when the 7.3 magnitude earthquake shook Pakistan's province of Baluchistan.

Famous Personalities: Pluto likes to take away famous personalities when in charge. Expect a well-know figure to pass away soon. A lot of secret activity will take place and the unaware wealthy and famous souls will have to pay a heavy price for involving themselves with the wrong elements. The Las Vegas assassination of a prominent rap music artist is a clear signal of their future.

Events: Awful news involving tragic accidents, mass murderers, suicide and drama will plague the media. Everything you say or do now will have serious repercussions later on.

Shopping: Anything bought now that could kill and destroy any form of life will be efficiently used. If you need to purchase a firearm, you are strongly advised to wait until after the New Moon. Insecticides and other things to get rid of insects and household nuisances should be high on your list now. And for the single and sexually active: Condoms.

January 25th, 1998 — Mars enters Pisces: With both Mars (explosions) and the Dragon's Tail (negative) in Pisces, expect dramatic news involving the Middle East, religious activity, abortion or oil. Many diplomats will be active on the political front to avoid war in different parts of the world. With Mars fueling acts of terrorism, explosions are now high on the list of every terrorist. Prominent politicians run the risk of assassination and some unlucky souls will not survive this dangerous trend. Souls born now will further love and faith in their respective religious belief systems. Many of them will be gifted in the arts and medical fields and will live in exotic places. Their sensitive nature combined with a strong religious purpose could lead many of them toward the pulpit. Thus a breed of advanced souls (teachers) or inferior spirits (terrorists) will be reincarnated with this Martian spirit. This planetary position will lead the soul towards danger, competition and great success if the energy of Mars is applied positively.

FRI., SAT., SUN., MON., TUE. — JANUARY 23rd, 24th, 25th, 26th, 27th:
RULERS — Jupiter (optimism) and Saturn (alteration)

Work, Career and Business: With the guardianship of Jupiter, the finances, resources and expertise of others could spell a profitable opportunity, especially after the upcoming new Moon on January 28. Real estate deals, trade, credit approval will be among workable developments. However, with the waning Moon still with us, better keep a low profile and avoid asking too many favors. Be ready for the beginning or ending of an important portion of your business life. Surprising news is ahead of you; be ready to welcome the changes. Again, realize that life is a constant process of changes and your existence has specific reasons. Be wise, be patient and promote your business life only after the next New Moon.

Partnerships: Just keep in mind that Saturn may make you feel depressed, especially during the very last days of the waning moon. Do not put any strain on your relationships, and faith in your significant other is advised. Be ready to aid those close to you, but sometimes saying "NO" is the best assistance you can offer. Work toward your heart's desire and don't let Saturn drag you down. If you operate with a partner, don't be too concerned with too many details or feel that you must do everything perfectly. Errors are parts of your business life; don't hate yourself if you make some. Use computers or learn a different program to make your business life easier.

Family and Friends: Assign your spiritual help but save your feelings about a difficult situation with a family member or a trusted friend. Further hopes give solid directions and don't be pessimistic about the end. With freedom-oriented Jupiter above our heads, an out-of-doors trip for the family will be rewarding. A trip to your local church on Sunday could also give you a sense of faith in the creator and in your future.

Love Affairs: With the waning moon, prudence in your union would be wise. Expect surprising news soon, related to the legal activities of marriage or divorce. If you happen to be the victim, be patient; sooner or later you will find peace of mind and true love with the right partner. If you are single and born in April, Leo and Libra will be strongly attracted to you. An Aquarius friend could bring a wish true.

Travel and Communication: Be careful on the road as the waning-moon influence may bring bad temper to some drivers. Keep in mind that nobody ever attracts bees with vinegar; use honey instead! Avoid arguments at all costs and use diplomacy to save a situation that could turn dangerous. Be careful driving; don't trust anyone and keep your eyes on your speed.

Environment: Gloomy news may come from Mexico, Japan and some faraway continents. Nature may decide to stretch herself and do harm to many people in different places. She may decide to produce a bad quake or a volcano eruption within the next few days.

Famous Personalities: Some government or entertainment figures may make dramatic news.

Events: Under the same celestial energy, flight 800 was blown out of the sky, killing all people on board and 04/19/95 — in Oklahoma City, an explosion felt for miles around rocked a downtown federal office building, blowing away an entire 9-story wall and killing scores of people. Let's hope nothing of this sort will ever happen again.

Shopping: Use this trend to find great Indian or foreign bargains in a garage sale or enjoy shopping your local antique shop with a Capricorn or Cancer friend. Do not buy any plants now; the ones that you will pick won't stay alive for long.

New Moon — January 28th, in Aquarius: The New Moon will mature in the futuristic sign of Aquarius. Expect surprising developments all over. The waxing "positive" moon means a progressive time to launch any new project. The next two weeks are going to be full of surprises, and a chance to move forward will be offered to those asking for progress. Try anything now, aim as high as you are capable of; coincidence be will magical. Don't waste this great lunation: be original, ask and you will receive!

WED., THU., FRI., SAT. — JANUARY 28th, 29th, 30th, 31st:
RULERS — Saturn (maneuver a course) and Uranus (upheaval)

Work, Career and Business: With the New Moon upon us you will encounter interesting people and incredible situations, especially if you decide to take a trip for business. Many of us will be forced into new circumstances involving a career move or a job. All the CEOs, Bosses, Managers and so forth could be standing next to you and further your wishes; don't be afraid to start a conversation with an older person. Don't take anything personally if some of their comments seem harsh; they might know better than you do. A perfect trend to invest some productive time in the office furthering your business opportunities. A change in schedules or rules could affect you. Keep busy and the right profile with the authorities and be pleasant with everyone. Try not to be too critical of yourself or anyone else in the office; nobody is perfect.

Partnerships: Be ready for a wave of surprising news coming your way. Karmic souls will not benefit from that surprising news, and some will be forced to accept the reality of life. An older or significant person will play an important part in your emotional life and may give you good advice. The Lord of surprises could also bring about boating misadventures; be aware of it if you happen to get close to the river or the ocean on the weekend.

Family and Friends: Family matters may be undergoing some changes; be confident in the new situation as it may affect your security and your finances. Keep an eye on the children; they will be overactive and you do not want anything wrong to happen to them. An adolescent or a younger friend may need some of your support and may ask for direction. Do not turn down invitations, and you may invite a long-standing friend to spend valuable time in your company. Some of those friends will bring your wishes home; be active on the social front.

Love Affairs: A person close to you is experiencing some stress and may get in touch with a request for a favor that you feel obligated to grant. Be considerate or you may lose more in the future if you do nothing. Expect some people to surprise you in a public place. Love is in the air for many while others will start or enjoy a secret love affair. Be aware of weird souls hanging around, but you can still enjoy their original company. Avoid drinking during the late hours as your emotions will run unusually high and could alter your driving or behavior. If you are single and born in July, Capricorn, Pisces and Scorpio will be strongly attracted to you.

Travel and Communication: With Uranus' eccentricity with us, be aware of crazy drivers on your way to or from work during this trend. Take plenty of time to reach your destinations and be ready for some driver's unexpected behavior on the road.

Famous Personalities: Expect startling developments with some well-known people trying to get more publicity. This energy doesn't stop with famous people; regular souls may act out weird too. News of love, marriage, children will make many famous people happy and ready to throw an expensive social gathering.

Events: New moon or not, Uranus will surprise many of us with nature's destructive forces. Be ready for earthquakes, tornadoes, volcano eruptions or an incredible weather development soon. Uranus might also disturb sophisticated electronic equipment and produce aeronautical disasters. Under his power, a U.S. military cargo plane crashed and caught fire on a street in Tegucigalpa April, 1997 while trying to land at the airport, narrowly missing two gas stations. Three soldiers were killed in this U.S. military plane crash in Honduras.

Shopping: Good time to visit or call your favorite psychic or astrologer for divine guidance. Spend on anything electronic now; this will prove to be beneficial for your business life in the long run.

January 29th, 1998: — Neptune enters Aquarius: The dream planet will move from the down-to-earth sign of Capricorn to the genius-like sign of Aquarius, the planet ruling the new age. In the incredible sign of Aquarius (UFOs/microchips), Neptune's creative energy will be used to the maximum. A wave of new electronic devices will be used within the cinematographic industry, creating more movies involving UFOs and Apocalypse to "feed" the God-earing mass. On a more positive note, Neptune (imagination) in Aquarius (ingenuities) will promote a serious increase in creativity and a solid restructure within the cinematographic industry. Neptune will re-enter Capricorn on August 23rd, 1998 and will return to Aquarius again in November 28th, 1998. Neptune will remain in the futuristic sign of Aquarius well after the year 2000. The dogmatic, religious Neptunian energies will melt into the futuristic sign of Aquarius. Then the general spiritual essence of mankind belief system will undergo a full rebirth where the dogmatic views of the past will be replaced by a total cosmic consciousness. The true face of God and his celestial manifestation will be divulged to mankind.

February 4th, 1998 — Mercury enters Aquarius: If you inherited this Mercury position you are a free thinker. You also regenerate in investigations, health, metaphysics, and anything related to the new age. Work on your inventiveness and don't be afraid to use computers. You will gain fame because of your originality and your ability to communicate. Perfect time to purchase a new computer, invest in some software or start an astrological class. The future promises to divulge surprising news pertaining to Japan, France, electronics, aeronautics, NASA, inventions and UFOs.

February 4th, 1998 — Jupiter enters Pisces: With benevolent Jupiter in the religious sign of Pisces many devout organizations will land on financial opportunities that will bring relief and followers to their specific denomination. The Vatican, the Pope or a well-known religious figure could make international news. Young souls born under this configuration will travel far and fast all over the world to pass on their "specific" belief system. In the long gone past, this celestial influence produced and led many pious souls to holy crusades all over the world. This astrological condition also produced the Spanish Conquistadors' desire to convert South America to Christianity.

Welcome to Your Day-to-Day Guidance For February 1998

SUN., MON., TUE., WED. — FEBRUARY 1st, 2nd, 3rd, 4th:
RULERS — Mars (conflict) and Venus (beloved)

Work, Career and Business: The new moon will exert a revitalizing pull that will be felt in your business affairs, perhaps setting up a difficult situation to resolve conflict. Be aware of Mars' contradiction tendencies, don't let him affect your words, your attitude or your emotions. Practice patience during this Martian trend and use diplomacy; if you do so you'll make serious progress. You may also use the tough energy of Mars to do some restructure around the office such as removing furniture; in any case, don't get hurt.

Partnerships: Keep Mars in control and use Venus' diplomatic gifts to save any situation. Everyone is so intent on having his/her own way now and there will could be little cooperation around you. Time to practice tact with the same dedication as a diplomat.

Family and Friends: With lovable Venus you should trust your intuition as your psychic abilities are enhanced. Realize your limit with a friend and don't allow him/her to rely on you too much. As always, give spiritual support but avoid getting emotionally involved with his/her personal problem. You and a mate/family member can gain through a financial endeavor, but discuss all possibilities before making any commitment. You might have an idea yourself that could be used; talk about it.

Love Affairs: Your relationship may be floundering because you sense that the person in question may be deceiving in some way. Do not fall for false information or your imagination. Avoid guilt in any of your decisions and if you feel a change is needed or coming, trust your future. Expect much from a night out on Sunday if you take a chance on love or a person. Enjoy social life but don't drink and drive as Mars (action) and Neptune (deception) are not great cohabitants. When alcohol and speed are mixed, it can produce serious accidents. Keep an eye on your possessions; crooks love action and will be active. If you are single and born in June, Aquarius, Sagittarius and Libra will be strongly attracted to you.

Travel and Communication: Be watchful if you must drive a long way and don't take any chances on the road as Mars energy could make you careless. Don't let his aggressive nature make you complain about a person, and use your words cautiously. Venus has much more to offer you, and it's pretty much your choice; use your will and your knowledge.

Environment: Many of the considerate people will use Mars' power to further environmental knowledge against fire in nature. However, the red planet doesn't seem to care much for the waxing moon; he may decide to do something nasty with nature's devastating forces where all the elements could be invited for a destructive dance.

Famous Personalities: Unaware rich and famous people may become Mars victims or make sad news involving accidents, drugs or alcohol. On a positive note, Venus will shine and induce love to those often independent or unhappy famous souls.

Events: The Martian energy is tough and has in the past produced explosions and accidents of all sorts; be prudent. Venus will put a serious fight against her destructive brother's attitude and may save many souls. Violent and dangerous sports will attract many people challenging their respective side.

Shopping: Invest in anything involving love, creativity or the arts. Show someone you care the depth of your love. Tools and machinery bought now will bring financial opportunities.

THUR., FRI., SAT., SUN., MON. — FEBRUARY 5th, 6th, 7th, 8th, 9th:
RULERS — Mercury (glib of tongue)& the Moon (changes, home)

Work, Career and Business: The waxing moon is still with you for a few more days; you should make the most of her; be confident as great changes are ahead of you. You may also consider using Mercury's mental agility to pass on new ideas for improving your business. Time to invest and take care of all the advertisements and publicity. The telephone will be particularly busy; don't leave the office without your answering machine on; you could miss a great opportunity.

Partnerships: Some of you have learnt hard lessons and the scars are now healed; don't re-open them again. Keep a positive attitude in all your conversations and promote only the great time of your past. Some karmic souls will have to experience a rebirth of their relationship. Whatever unfolds, accept the changes with confidence; the stars have great news for you.

Family and Friends: Mercury rules communication, so expect family members to get in touch with you, and some will enjoy great cooking at home. "The messenger of the Gods" loves to talk, even exaggerate sometimes; do not fall for all the things you may hear now. Keep in mind that your friends have the potential to fulfill all your wishes; get active in the social arena and make good use of this New Moon. As always, you might have a karmic debt with a long-standing friend; if so, you may have to experience; annoyance for a while.

Love Affairs: You can expect the beginning or ending of important love phases of your life. Keep your eyes and ears open on the people you know as the Moon does affect everybody. If you are single and born in July, someone much older or younger than you born in March or January will be attracted to you.

Travel and Communication: Time to write those letters as Mercury does improve your mental faculties. He will reward you favorably if you decide to invest in your education or start a book. Control his strong desire to "chatterbox" and save money on your telephone bill. Mercury rules transportation and general motion; he also makes people impatient; under his command be a defensive driver. Time to plan all your future travels or visit parts of the world via a great book.

Environment: We are just a few days away from the Full Moon of February 11th and some people may experience severe weather systems in some states. If you are into videotaping lightning, storms, volcanic eruptions, earthquakes, etc., be ready for those soon. Some will see the beginning or ending of a dramatic time. This may force thousands of people to relocate.

Famous Personalities: Some famous artist or important political figure will experience shame, and children could be involved.

Events: A prominent political person either from the US, France or Japan will make an important announcement. The government may come up with important news or decisions that could affect many families in the future.

Shopping: Invest faithfully in anything that moves fast. Any office equipment purchased now will bring tons of action to its owner. This is also a perfect time to take care of your car. Mercury also rules literature, and great books will be purchased under its influence.

Full Moon — February 11th, 1998 in Leo: This lunation promises to be of a very surprising nature. Be ready for nature's devastative forces to surprise many unprepared people. Earthquakes, volcanic eruptions and blackouts will be coming from the Sun's negative spots. If you can, avoid flying on this day as the energy could be precarious for computers and will affect aeronautical systems. Be ready for a bumpy time and keep your eyes set on the children. On a more positive note, this lunation will affect positively those who deserve pure love, freedom and notoriety. The US, France and Japan could make the news soon, and be ready for nasty explosions or events to shock and shake the entire world.

TUE., WED., THU., FRI., SAT. — FEBRUARY 10th, 11th, 12th, 13th, 14th:
RULERS — The Sun (love/surprises) & Mercury (mental power)

Work, Career and Business: Some surprising developments are on the way, but with the Full Moon don't expect them to make you happy. Progress will still be made in the few weeks ahead of you, but be ready for a bumpy time. A certain study or information on a computer might help the situation.

Partnerships: Don't try anything special these days; use Mercury's creative power to clean up a business situation. Important legal papers might come your way; sign them only if it is to get rid of an unhealthy situation. Whomever you come in contact with, don't misbehave in public.

Family and Friends: Keep busy with close friends and family; watch the children as they will be accident-prone. A great time to enjoy the people you know well, but avoid overcrowded public places. Don't expect new people met under this solar affliction to bring much of your wishes. Some friends have surprising news for you and could affect you emotionally. Again, watch the children; they are accident-prone, especially with fire, weapons and explosives.

Love Affairs: Expect disturbing surprises coming your way and learn to let go of crooked people. Do not invite strangers in your home and socialize only with the friends you know well. Make a good use of the waning moon, learn to relax, enjoy nature and the sea, and look for your inner peace. If you're single, a chance to find the "right one" will be given to you at a later date. What you may perceive as love may enter your life without much notice; however, use your head, not your heart on the weekend. If you are single and born in August, an Aries or a foreigner could be a source of trouble and will be strongly attracted to you.

Travel and Communication: Not a time to take a chance at 30,000 feet above the earth; many karmic souls will pay the ultimate price. Expect all sorts of little problems that could turn lethal for some. Disturbing surprise telephone calls from friends in trouble; as usual, provide spiritual help but learn your limits.

Environment: Be ready for many activists to do all they can to protect life; some may fall victims in an ill-advised conflict. Expect unusual oceanic and earth activity that could prove disastrous for the environment. Not a good time to play with fire as explosions are very high on my list of trouble for this specific trend.

Famous Personalities: Some famous people will participate or join Green peace groups. Some will try anything to get the attention they need. Eccentricity is in the air and could lead to the use of force.

Events: Expect massive power outages without readily known causes. NASA could make some news due to poor weather conditions or an electronic malfunction. On the positive side, some great medical breakthroughs as well as high-tech scientific news are on the way.

Shopping: Do not take a chance on anything related to electronics; you will not get a great deal. Do not invest in toys for your children now; they could prove to be fatal at a later date. Some will plan to spend money traveling to Europe.

Note: Attention — Pluto will enjoy this waning Moon period; he is back with us — Expect dramatic happenings all over; control is a must. He produces much of the sensational news including the California mass-suicide. Mass murderers are again a possibility as Pluto always stimulates the criminal element, the insane and the police force, all for ill purposes. Don't be a victim; be aware of Pluto's destructive power.

SUN., MON., TUE., WED., THU. — FEBRUARY 15th, 16th, 17th, 18th, 19th:
RULERS — Venus (sensuality) and Pluto (sexuality/drama)

Work, Career and Business: Your boss may not be aware of the power of Pluto and could make your life miserable. Do not take anything too personally and forgive his temper. A wake-up call for some karmic souls where reality must be accepted is around the corner.

Partnerships: Never take a Pluto trend lightly as his impact is usually dramatic and could produce serious stress in your partnership and its future. Use all the diplomacy you know as anything you say or do will have serious repercussions. Not a time to play with anyone's emotion; stay cool in all you do.

Family and Friends: You will discover a secret from a close friend; be sure to keep it that way if you intend to keep this relationship. Don't expect everyone around you to be sensitive to your needs; instead, be ready for bitterness and harsh comments. Don't let Pluto's sarcastic nature destroy the serenity of your home life. Many ignorant souls will pay a heavy price of ignorance and lose much in the process.

Love Affairs: A dramatic time is ahead for some with Pluto's desire to destroy. Venus will make you magnetic and a prime target for Pluto's thirst for sex. If you become active on the dating scenery, don't take chances on strangers; protect yourself and avoid heavy drinking. Pluto knows how vulnerable you become to his power when under the influence, and he will make you pay. Relationships started now could be of a destructive nature, filled with jealousy and drama, and could lead you to harm or even death. This relationship could also be of a karmic nature and short but dramatically lived. Be very aware out there and avoid negative group situations. Your intuition will be very accurate and should be followed with full trust. For those born in September, people born in March, January or May will be strongly attracted to you.

Travel and Communication: Be smart and patient on the road; avoid the sarcastic remarks and be aware of Pluto's desire for drama. Some people may call you for advice or share their secrets. Better keep it a secret for now as Pluto does not like to talk. Pluto may decide to take many human lives in a dramatic accident.

Famous Personalities: You will most likely hear more about the infamous than the famous under Pluto's command. Venus will try everything she can to subdue her violent brother and smooth things out for many. The great loss of an old and eminent political, religious or entertainment figure will plague the media.

Events: Expect more headlines like this one that you saw in 1997. Bizarre and dangerous people will plague the media. Botched L.A. bank heist turns into bloody shoot-out — February, 1997 — Manhunt on for suspects. "It was like the OK Corral." Gunmen suspected in two other robberies — A blaze of automatic gunfire ripped through a crowded neighborhood after several heavily armed gunmen dressed like commandos botched a bank robbery.

Shopping: Anything related to spying or the metaphysical, especially smudges and healing products. Do not purchase guns, knives or anything made to kill under Pluto's power. They may used against you or your loved ones.

FRI., SAT., SUN., MON. — FEBRUARY 20th, 21st, 22nd, 23rd:
RULERS — Jupiter (philosophy on life) & Saturn (career demands)

Work, Career and Business: With Pluto's dramatic experiences gone by, many will keep a low profile and begin the acceptance of the tense transformation that just happened. With benevolent Jupiter, the future has much better to offer and you should be confident in all your transactions. With Saturn's touch expect a new beginning careerwise or an opportunity, perhaps even a promotion of some sort coming your way. Great Jupiter, "the Lord of Luck," will make this transition easy and may even decide to throw some luck your way; listen to your intuition and keep a positive attitude. A new beginning is on the horizon and your intuition is right.

Partnerships: Be on the outlook for a new partner and learn from a previous mistake. Money will also be on your mind and serious decisions will have to be made soon. Nothing comes easy in this life and one must strive and plan if he is to succeed. You might have to let go of someone or a portion of your business or emotional life soon.

Family and Friends: Surely a good time to spend outside if the weather permits, as Jupiter will replenish you with fresh air and a new approach to life. Spend some time with family member or dear friend and be ready to listen. Enjoy the week and the good food offered to you and if you decide to fight depression, invite a friend over. If friends are not available, a night out will not bring you much pleasure; better stay home, relax and read. A foreigner friend may stimulate your life; this will make you happy and further an important wish later on.

Love Affairs: Someone much older or much younger has interesting things to say to you; you could even be surprised. Don't look for love these days; there is plenty to gain in your own creativity, and the stars want you to be alone. You may also unearth a great idea to further an artistical or spiritual endeavor. If you are single and born in October, someone born in April, February or June may be interested in you.

Travel and Communication: Expect your telephone to be busy but do not hope for super-positive mail to reach you. If you have to drive, take extra time to get there; don't rush as the police could spoil your day. Expect an end to a portion of your life soon. Don't be depressed about anything that may come your way; the stars have better for you on a later date.

Environment: During the last breath of the waning moon, mother nature may decide to stretch herself and surprise some very soon. Environmental groups will get active and will get good support from the media to save the earth from uncaring corporations. Sad news may come from foreign ground.

Famous Personalities: A well-known foreign personality will gain international attention where sorrow, tears and memory will make many followers cry.

Events: Some terrorist groups from a faraway continent will get really ugly. Surprising destructive explosions are on the way. Also expect more news such as this from April 1997 — Shot in the back. Ashamed and revolted — An amateur photographer captured on videotape a group of police officers violently beating a suspect. But this time the setting was a poor neighborhood in Sao Paulo, Brazil — not Los Angeles.

Shopping: Not a good time for the gamblers; however, if you happen to be in Las Vegas, keep the spending in control. The Moon is still waning (negative); be patient and make major moves only after the fast approaching new moon.

New Moon — February 26th, in Pisces: Expect surprising news involving science, research, religion and the difficult abortion dilemma. The government will make important political decisions and the US Supreme Court decides on important religious/chemical/medical affairs during this trend. Nature and the weather could also turn out particularly difficult and may sink ships, produce devastating oil spills and flooding on land. However, with the waxing moon (positive) we can only hope for less damage than anticipated. A sure sign of progress for many within the next two weeks. Push now, be confident and like the fish swim with the tide.

February 26th, 1998: Today is your astrologer's birthday — Thank you for all your good wishes and wonderful birthday cards. It is an honor to receive so many blessings from all around the world. Please forgive me if I do not personally answer you, but it is from the depth of my heart that I sincerely thank you.

TUE., WED., THU., FRI., SAT. — FEBRUARY 24th, 25th, 26th, 27, 28th:
RULERS — Uranus (surprises) Jupiter (the truth seeker) and Saturn (re-structure)

Work, Career and Business: The last few days of February promise to be interesting. Expect anything to happen now and take chances; you're protected by the new moon. Uranus loves change and will reward the daring ones with incredible happenings. Jupiter's positive energy will also help to restore faith, and new opportunities will be brought about by foreigners. Be ready for interesting business developments and watch the stock market.

Partnerships: A business partner or a coworker may want to involve you in an opportunity. If it sounds practical and worth your time, it probably is! However, don't rush; listen to your intuition and do some research before coming to a conclusion. If this partner is a foreigner, the meeting could positively affect your future. Tensions may surface before the weekend about a specific project or trip. Be willing to do what it takes to knock obstacles down.

Family and Friends: With the new moon, friends will be active and may request your presence. No one should refuse invitations now as many wishes will be granted. You may plan a surprise party and share a great time with close friends this weekend. Keep your eyes open for an older person with wonderful intentions. Kids sense that they should be on a more independent path, particularly if you have a teenager living with you; be patient with their demands. A local show may prove to be an amusing place to visit. Mom or close friends may call you; don't dwell on the past and avoid gossiping. Be happy.

Love Affairs: Socialize with some coworkers Saturday night; the outcome could be surprising. You will feel positive away from the regular responsibilities and the people around you will enjoy your company. Avoid impatience where romance is concerned and drive carefully during the late hours. If you're single, do not fall victim to Saturn's gloomy power; do something about it, go out, meet people and "ask and you shall receive." The future has so much to offer if you participate with life, so put a big smile on your face and be confident in yourself. Progressive changes are ahead; take chances now. If you are single and born in November, a Pisces, Cancer or Taurus will find you irresistible.

Travel and Communication: Time to get close to God in your local church or get close to nature and enjoy the wilderness. Keep your thoughts clean and avoid poisoning your future with a negative attitude; slowly but surely the healing process is taking place. Some will fly and travel to faraway places this weekend, some just around the corner to meet their future.

Events: On a more negative note, Uranus rules the sudden release of energies and could decide to throw an earthquake or blow up a volcano; let's hope he will keep quiet and leave nature alone. He may also decide to entertain us with some surprising explosions.

Famous Personalities: Be ready for weird and surprising news from the rich and famous. Great movies are being made and some will be released soon.

Events: As usual, UFO researchers should use this timing to go to any secluded places in the desert. Anything weird can happen! Anyone interested in lightning or nature's mighty destructive powers, go for it now.

Shopping: Great time to invest in your cosmic consciousness and further your spiritual enlightenment. Use Jupiter's philosophical values to improve your teachings and learning powers or start a study. Uranus rules the future and Astrology; this is a great time indeed to visit your favorite psychic or astrologer.

Welcome to Your Day-to-Day Guidance For March 1998

SUN., MON., TUE., WED. — MARCH 1st, 2nd, 3rd, 4th:
RULERS — Neptune (creativity/faith) & Mars (action/accident)

Work, Career and Business: Do not bring any work with you this weekend; learn to relax and enjoy life. With nebulous Neptune in the air, you may find it difficult to focus at work on Monday. Be on guard for certain opportunities coming your way to upgrade your business soon. With the New Moon upon us, many miracles could happen if you take a chance on yourself. As always when Neptune rules, stay clear from alcohol this weekend; you need your driver's license for your business!

Partnerships: With Neptune's psychic power, pay attention to your dreams; one of them may come true and may be vision-like during your sleep. If you experience stress in partnerships, use the New Moon energy to discuss your desires or go out and look for them. Placing aside Neptune's self-pity feelings, your healing and psychic powers to improve your relationships will be increased. A trip by the water would do you great. Do not spoil your day and if Neptune gets you close to the water, watch the children carefully.

Family and Friends: Do not let yourself fall for depression or complaining about life in general. Life is a hard school where the only way to learn is through suffering for some. Don't fall for Neptune's deceiving thoughts or Mars' anger these days, and use your will. Make a good use to "Moon Power" and don't let the worse of those stars regulate your psyche. You might have to provide spiritual guidance to someone close to you, but realize your own counseling limit. You should heed your intuition these days, and you could enjoy visiting your future with a good psychic friend.

Many mothers may fall for Neptune's guilt feelings of the past; do not allow this to happen; stay clear from those thoughts.

Love Affairs: Neptune will lead you to enjoy the latest movie or participate in an art gathering with your lover. Neptune is somehow deceiving in nature and may lead some souls to experience undercover love affairs. This relationship may be karmic in nature and could last a long time. Do not blindly believe anyone, especially if drugs and alcohol are consumed. Don't be vague about your personal feelings or what you feel to be right. Many could fall for Mars' appetite to further Neptune's wish to reach a higher plane with the use of drugs. Be aware not only of karma but the consequences involving drug dealings. Don't be suggestive to others; come out strongly with what you really mean. If you are single and born in December, a Gemini, a Leo or a Libra will be strongly attracted to you.

Travel and Communication: Once more, with the planet of daydream in charge, don't drink heavily, and realize the importance to take plenty of rest before driving long distances. Be watchful to the road signs and realize that Neptune (drugs) and Mars (impatience) are a dangerous combination on the road. We are still on the waxing positive moon and crooks won't be caught! Be alert, especially during the late hours and keep your eyes on your belongings; thieves will be active. Be firm in all you do, ask questions, sample and if you worry about a situation, go straight to the point. Neptune can sharpen your intuition and save you trouble, you'd better listen to the little voice inside.

Environment: On a negative note, Neptune regulates the sea, thus many accidents, oil or chemical spills were often produced because a lack of judgment and a mixture of alcohol. The new moon and your rational mind will protect you if you decide to take a cruise or play around the water, even the frozen kind.

Famous Personalities: Neptune rules the Middle East and oil, thus news from this area is to expected. You may also hear news about Elizabeth Taylor or gossiping about secret love affairs involving your favorite actors and actresses.

Events: Sadly enough, Mars' aggressive nature is also with us and the "Lord of War" may decide to stir nature's destructive forces and manmade explosions. Don't fall for his aggressiveness nor impatience and all will be fine for you.

Shopping: Mars will lead you to invest in sharp dangerous tools; purchase now and the white power of the moon will protect you from accident. Neptune will also favor any shopping related to water or anything related to the art. Great time to do a candle ritual to clean up negative energy around the house; this magical endeavor will attract a secret wish into your life.

March 5th, 1998 — Mars enters Aries: Perfect time to launch a business or start any program involving leadership and structure. If you are a Virgo or a Scorpio or born with an Aries Dragon's Tail (see year's Dragon's tables), you will be accident-prone on the head for a while; don't take chances; slow down and wear your seat belt. Use Mars correctly, invest in yourself and give birth to your own business. Souls born now will inherit a natural gift in enterprise and will establish themselves as powerful CEOs or leaders. These souls are born aggressive and impatient, and do learn by mistake. A top position in sports, the Army, the Navy where fire, danger, speed and courage are needed.

March 5th, 1998 — Venus enters Aquarius: One of the best windows of opportunity is offered to all the single souls out there. Venus will reward those willing to try anything to find pure love. Sweethearts can be found in places where people group together and where the new-age topics such as astrology, UFOs, alternative medicines, etc., are prevalent. Souls born now will be extremely magnetic, original and many will travel the world in their lifetimes. They will be attracted to beautiful, intellectually stimulating partners and some will be inclined to marry foreigners.

THU., FRI., SAT., SUN. — MARCH 5th, 6th, 7th, 8th:
RULERS — Mercury (power to use the mind) and the Moon (new starts)

Work, Career and Business: The Moon is waxing (positive) and the universe will further your opportunities, take chances — you still have a few more day to reach for your dreams. This could also mean a full change in the way you handle your business affairs. Promote yourself or clarify a difficult situation with a different attitude. If you are involved in sales, these days will bring worthwhile deals and important legal documents. Sign the paperwork before the upcoming Full Moon of March 13th if it's to keep; if you decide to get rid of an old business, sign after the full moon.

Partnerships: We all know that life as it is, is a constant process of changes forcing all of us toward numerous experiences and solid knowledge. With this lunation, holding to your past or a situation can only make your life distressed to the point where you can't take it any longer. Thus, accept the changes with a positive attitude, and the stars will shine again upon you and your new destiny. Learn to let go of the wrong people and the wrong things in your life.

Family and Friends: Many will enjoy good food and the family circle this weekend. Mercury will promote verbal exchanges and friends and family members will be calling you. If you decide to dine out on Saturday and you don't like to wait, it would be wise to make early reservations as the local restaurants will be busy. If the weather is appropriate, it is a good time to enjoy the wild, wide-open spaces with the children and your pets. Expect news from brothers or sisters or some people of your past from faraway places.

Love Affairs: Don't let Mercury's desire to talk over everyone take over. Do some listening and avoid any form of gossiping. A trip away from stress and close to nature would do great for both of you. A perfect time to enjoy great discussions with candlelight, good wine, great food, soft music, all is there to enjoy your partner. Get active and participate with life; use the waxing Moon while you can. If you are single and born in January, a Virgo, a Taurus or a Cancer will want to know more about you.

Travel and Communication: Expect some good news to arrive via mail or telephone. A wise person who sees better than you do may disapprove of a situation you are in; you could benefit from some inside information. This person has been where you are now and need to help you in your decision making. Whatever is said, don't let this affect your friendship. New friends will come into the picture soon; they will bring more joy and greater opportunities to reach your wishes. Control Mercury's gossiping nature; avoid being critical with some friends; your comments will fly back to them and you could be sorry later. Throw a party in your home; your natural skills as a hostess will impress everyone. Some of your wishes can only be granted if you engage a bit more with life and others. Perfect time to plan a trip. Keep in mind to service the car and to drive safely; especially if you're about to take a long drive.

Environment: As always nature is always active and under this celestial configuration, thousands of people have been forced to relocate, starting a new life. Nature may decide to throw a fit: quakes, volcanoes and floods are high on the list. Keep in mind that we are approaching a Supernova "window" and you should be aware of it. South Africa's Cape of Good Hope was hit by a fierce winter storm under a Supernova Window in July 1994. Hundreds of people were left homeless and forced to relocate. This energy also brought to shore an oil slick that destroyed vegetation and much of the local wildlife. Let's hope the new moon will see for it and stop the predicted upcoming damage.

Famous Personalities: Many prominent people will come in or out of a situation, business or a bad marriage. Some will enter fierce legal battles disturbing the family circle. The beginning or ending of important phases of life is active for all — not only the rich and famous.

Events: Be ready for the government (foreign or the U.S.) to make important decisions that will affect millions of lives. Some elected officials will step down and others will take over during this lunar timing.

Shopping: Time to invest in anything that will further communication or a car. A new answering machine or a new telephone will bring good news and might be a necessity soon. Great time to purchase any books that could further your cosmic consciousness. With Mercury, called in Greek mythology "The messenger of the Gods," let people know about *Starguide*, help me to pass on the message. Share the light, keep in mind that *Starguide Moon Power* is a perfect present for anyone's birthday.

MON., TUE., WED., THU., FRI. — MARCH 9th, 10th, 11th, 12th, 13th:
RULERS — The Sun (enlightenment) & Mercury (intellectual powers)

Work, Career and Business: We are getting closer to the full moon; make the most of the opportunities offered to you. Some will land on a new job or a better situation by surprise in the near future. Renew your faith and your dedication to your worldly ambitions and use what's left of this positive timing if you want to succeed. Your ability to communicate is enhanced by Mercury; take a chance on a project that means a lot to you.

Partnerships: Use both Mercury and the Sun to come real clear of what you expect with your partners. Miscommunication does happen and usually leads to unwanted trouble. Go easy in expressing your feelings; don't let your ego or your emotions blur your vision of the future or your words.

Family and Friends: On the family level you might have to revise a course of action or the timing involving your plan. Expect family members to ask you for details, or go and see them to discuss a situation with children or a house. You can bet on surprises and interesting news from them over the telephone or your mail these days. Due to the vitality of the Sun, the children could also be a bit unmanageable and nervous. Take them out and let them vent out their youth. Use tons of patience with them and remember not to suffocate their sensitive will. Do not be a promoter of future subconscious stress; instead, discipline them carefully, and reinforce their self-esteem.

Love Affairs: Love is in the air and can be found for those who mean business looking. A surprising invitation to a party could bring that special person into your life; don't turn it down. Use the Sun's revitalizing power to rekindle your feelings for those close to you. An artistic gathering or simply a good movie will help you to release some hard feelings with life. If you are single and born in February, those born in October, June and August will want to know the real you.

Travel and Communication: Don't let speedy and impatient Mercury take over your driving. Slow down, be patient and prudent wherever you go. Other souls out there are not aware of Mercury's pull and will drive dangerously. Talk about love, talk about your sincere desire to reach happiness and avoid putting stress on others.

Environment: With the swelling Moon with us a little longer, mother nature should be quiet these days. Some groups will be concerned and active in making the rest of us aware of nature's wonderful blessings. Planting or saving many trees will be on their mind.

Famous Personalities: Many celebrities will engage in important gatherings and many will be rewarded for their creativity and artistic gifts. Much of the profits will go to honorable causes and the children. Some will offer great news involving marriage or children to the media.

Events: We are getting closer to the full moon; some surprising development with children, explosions or volcanic eruptions is on the way.

Shopping: If you are in investor, gold will be a great buy. Presents will be offered to those deserving loving souls. A perfect time to invest in anything related to your specific interest and creativity. Invest in clothing for children; great bargains are available now.

Full Moon — March 13th, 1998 in Virgo: Be ready for the ending of a portion of your working life. Disturbing news is ahead of you, be ready to accept these changes as you might have to serve this world in a different manner. Life is never stagnant, so learning to embrace change is part of the whole lesson. Don't let critical, health-oriented Virgo affect your mental process and over-worry about your health. This is indeed a perfect time to join a club and rebuild your physical figure. On a negative note, expect oil spills and aeronautical accidents; avoid flying if you can. Not a time to take chances; avoid signing important contracts. To travel or start new projects, wait until the next New Moon of April 28th, 1998.

> **Note**: Attention — Pluto is back with us — Expect dramatic happenings all over; control is a must. Nothing you say or do now will be taken lightly! Be aware of Pluto's deadly nature; don't become his victim. Major drama is about to unfold.

SAT., SUN., MON., TUE., WED. — MARCH 14th, 15th, 16th, 17th, 18th:

RULERS — Venus (commitment) Pluto (tragedy)

Work, Career and Business: Wake-up call time for many unaware souls. You will be forced to realize your limits and face your real self. Plans must be suddenly abandoned and this could mean business and career momentum losses. If you are tempted to make money fast or astray, consider Pluto's ugly claws and the real hazards before jumping straight to jail. Expect to be harassed these days with letters, meetings, phone calls, etc. Something must be done.

Partnerships: Spend time reorganizing the office; throw old things away and look busy at all times. Your unaware boss is now under the malignant destructive power of Pluto. Coworkers are also affected by the "Lord of Hades" and could make your life misery. Show them Starguide when it's all over and help them to deal with the stars. Doing so, you will gain a great karma for your future reincarnations. Someone may try to show you the error of your ways, perhaps an older person or a critical friend on your bad habits. You may want to listen carefully as Pluto is speaking through them and what is said may deserve your attention. The stars want you to consider, re-think and be cautious in all you do and say these days. You may have to use diplomacy now and put on your thinking and rational judgment caps concerning key partnerships. Anything else and you're in for serious trouble.

Family and Friends: Some of your friends or close family members will have dramatic experiences and your supportive shoulder will be requested. At home or at work expect nasty conflicts and this may get those days off on the wrong track. Don't bring it back home as Pluto will follow you home and the aggravations could continue into the evening hours. Keep your head cool; stay calm and patient. Secrets will pop out of the closets and Pluto's sexual urge will raise its ugly head. Don't invite strangers into your home; many children were abused under his sexual powers.

Love Affairs: On the emotional side of your life, bits and pieces of information may be wrong or missing, so do not make important decisions about a situation or a person. Investigate all the information with a cool head and see if jealousy is the reason behind it all. Use common sense; love with your head first, then give your heart if he/she deserves it; you might have to let go of an abusive partner. Love associations started under Pluto's dramatic powers could lead you to your own death. You know better; stay home and keep the worse of society from entering your life. If you are single, wait for better stars to go "hunting." If you are in a healthy relationship, use Pluto's passionate nature to re-kindle your sexual nature. If you're born in March, November or July, stay clear from alcohol during this trend. Souls born in September, November or July will be strongly attracted to those born in March.

Travel and Communication: Avoid long trips by air, plane or ship as the stars do not care — they just do the work they were intended to do by God's higher order.

Environment: Be ready for nasty surprises and drama, especially the ones with man and nature's forces at work. In my conferences and in many radio and televised programs in Seattle, WA, San Diego, CA and Tucson (Ted Loman AZUFO) I gave the date of April 26th, 1997 (mass suicide). Be ready for nasty quakes and drama. In February 1997, Teheran, Iran experienced an earthquake that killed at least 100 people and injured 250 in northwestern Iran. This is Pluto at work. Be ready!

Famous Personalities: Pluto likes to take away famous personalities when in he is in charge. In May 1996 in Los Angeles, counterculture guru Timothy Leary died at 75. For many, Timothy Leary is a name forever frozen in the 1960s.

Events: Expect the government to make important announcements and drastic actions for many of the "karmically" affected. Under Pluto's power in June, 1996, a Russian province named Murmansk experienced heavy rains and thawing snow that swelled rivers in northern Russia, causing the worst floods in the region in more than 50 years. We will be hearing more of this kind of news during Pluto's control over the earth.

Shopping: Invest in any products that can destroy any form of pests. You'll carry Pluto's deadly signature in a can. Be aware how you use it and place it away from your children. Get rid of it as soon as possible to keep his poison from affecting your own life later on. If you decide to abide by a budget or to lose weight, the stars will help you. Some will make plans to go to Las Vegas; enjoy yourself but now is not the time to bet the farm.

THU., FRI., SAT., SUN., MON. — MARCH 19th, 20th, 21st, 22nd, 23rd:
RULERS — Jupiter (sense of right and wrong) and Saturn (dedication unmatched)

Work, Career and Business: With Jupiter's protection, the finances, resources and expertise of others could provide support this week. All sorts of financial deals will be attainable, especially where foreigners are involved. With the waxing Moon upon us opportunities to rebuild the damage inflicted by Pluto will be offered to the valiant. Be ready for a restructure of a portion of your business, these changes could also affect your emotional life. Take chances, sign contracts, travel and promote your career while the moon is still waxing.

Partnerships: Saturn's gloomy attitude may make you feel insecure about life in general. Don't taint those close to you; put a smile on your face; caution in relationships is advised. You may find yourself forced to help someone; if you feel like saying no, don't feel guilty about it. This publication's purpose is to help and guide those who need help on a daily basis. If your partner becomes too heavy, mention my work and release yourself from guilt. Work towards your heart's desire with a practical mind. Saturn wants you to go out and find out all the answers for yourself. Don't be too concerned about doing everything perfectly; you can only do your best. Use or learn computers to make life and your business easier and don't be afraid of technology.

Family and Friends: Share your feelings about a difficult situation with a family member or a trusted friend, but don't be pessimistic about the end. With benevolent Jupiter a trip close to nature in an Indian reservation with the children will be regenerating your soul. A trip to your local church on Sunday could give you a sense of faith in the creator and in yourself. Some juveniles may ask for tuition help; educate yourself and the child with valuable history books.

Love Affairs: Be particularly attentive to a fascinating foreigner. Being cautious in relationships is always a good thing; be sure to take your time before committing your heart. Expect a significant development with marriage or divorce unfolding with some karmic relationships close to you. If you happen to suffer one at the present time, don't stress yourself; be patient. Sooner or later it will all be gone and you will find a well-deserved peace of mind and true love with a suitable partner. If you are single and born under the sign of Aries, a Libra or a Sagittarius will be tenacious about you.

Travel and Communication: Perfect time to make travel arrangements if you have to be away from home after the full moon. Be easy on a person who may be quite troublesome; use diplomacy, or the situation could turn nasty, even against you. Keep a firm control over the outcome; you won't attract bees with vinegar; use honey instead! Don't let another's radical judgment ignite a harsh argument at work; again, use diplomacy to save a situation that could turn nasty later on. Your presence may be requested for a gathering, and a wise person may play an important part in a critical decision. Enjoy the road and keep your eyes on the signs.

Environment: Sad news may come from foreign countries experiencing problems with emigrations or education. With benevolent Jupiter with us these days, some "saviors" may become active in respect for nature.

Famous Personalities: Your management or some important government figures will impose some new rules. An old person will make his voice heard to the young generation. The message will bring a new beginning for the children's education.

Events: 04/19/95 — Under the same celestial energy, in Oklahoma City, an explosion felt for miles around rocked a downtown federal office building, blowing away an entire 9-story wall and killing scores of people. Let's hope nothing of this sort will ever happen again. On a negative side, this lunation may activate destructive news pertaining to fanatical foreign groups.

Shopping: Use this trend to find great bargains in a garage sale or enjoy shopping your local antique shop with an exuberant friend. If you have an Indian guide, invest in their work of art to channel spiritual information. Pets bought now will live a long and happy life and give you tons of love. Green and brown colors should bring luck today; you may wear black at night.

SUPERNOVA WINDOW

Concentration of Negative Celestial Energy Approaching.

First SUPERNOVA Window: MARCH 1998 / APRIL 1998.
— From Tuesday March 24th through Sunday, April 26th, 1998.

Specific dates of extreme caution:
March 24th, April 3rd, April 13th, April 21st and April 26th.

March 24th, 1998 — Violent weather in parts of the US and many other parts of the world with the potential to produce volcano eruption, earthquakes, floods, tornadoes, hurricanes and aeronautical disasters. High seismic activity. Earthquake well above normal in Japan and California.

April 13th & 21st, 1998 — Violent weather in parts of the US and many other parts of the world producing earthquakes/floods/tornadoes/ hurricanes and aeronautical disasters. Quake activity well above normal in Japan and California.

Be extremely prudent in driving and expect chain-reaction accidents. Be prepared for delays, strikes, nature producing awful weather, including hurricanes and tornadoes. The same energy that produced both the Northridge, Los Angeles, and Kobe, Japan, earthquakes is approaching us again. Double-check all your appointments, and if you can, postpone traveling and flying during this Supernova "window." Communication and electricity will be cut off, and general loss of power is to be expected. Appliances, computers, telephones, planes, trains, cars — all of these "tools" will be adversely affected by this energy.

They will be stopped in one way or another. The people of the past will make the news, as people from your past will reenter your life. Expect trouble with the post office, education, students, prisoners, newspaper, broadcasting industry and computer viruses may bother us again. As usual NASA, which is not aware of the science of astrology, will waste our tax money with a failed mission due to bad weather and/or electronic malfunctions.

All these malevolent predictions do not have to hurt or touch you as they unfold. Instead, they are printed to prepare you for setbacks and frustrations, thus advising you to be patient and prudent during this trend. Smile, it's just a short time really.

In the stormy game of life, to be victorious is to reject defeat.

— Bradley

TUE., WED., THU., FRI. — MARCH 24th, 25th, 26th, 27th:
RULERS: Uranus (sudden happenings) Neptune (trickery)

Work, Career and Business: The new moon is getting near and may bring a higher level of emotions in your business affairs. Keep a cool head to set up a difficult situation to avoid a conflict. Don't let Neptune's deceiving powers affect your attitude with life in general; be positive and practice patience during this trying trend. Beware of get-rich-quick schemes, clean up your act and be ready to get rid of some pieces of equipment that may let you down soon. Use the ingenuousness of Uranus to do some investigation around the office and let him provide you with great ideas to promote your career.

Partnerships: Keep Neptune's complaining attitude in check and control your thought processes. Don't expect much from coworkers and supervise them closely; they might forget something important, errands or returning vital telephone calls. Everyone will feel the "dreamy" side of Neptune; be patient with those you deal with. Time to build up others' confidence and practice diplomacy with the same dedication as a diplomat.

Family and Friends: With Neptune in charge, you may trust your intuition but control your imagination. With Uranus sitting next to him, your psychic abilities are enhanced; just tune in and you will receive the wisdom of the stars. A friend may become difficult; do not let this person rely on you too much and avoid getting emotionally involved with the problem. Both Uranus and Neptune strive in new-age endeavors; you may decide to share your own psychic knowledge with a friend. You could gain through new-age financial endeavors if you educate yourself in metaphysics. Do not allow Neptune's deceiving tendency to make your life misery. Clean your thoughts, you have a choice, be happy.

Love Affairs: A romantic relationship may fall short of your expectations, mainly because your intuition tells you differently. Neptune will make you sense that the person in question may be deceiving in some way. Someone may try to lead you into a secret love affair and you may fall for it. Don't be deceived, especially if the person in question happens to be married. Avoid any form of guilt in your decision and stay miles away from alcohol during the night hours. With the upcoming new moon of March 28th, expect much from weekend dating and social plans. If you are single and born in May, Pisces and Virgo will be strongly attracted to you.

Travel and Communication: With Neptune and Uranus in charge, wherever you go, keep an eye on your possessions; crooks will be active. Enjoy life in many ways this weekend; go after your wishes but don't drink and drive. Mars/Neptune are not great cohabitants and when alcohol and speed are mixed, it produces serious accidents. Be cautious if you must drive a long way; take plenty of rest as Neptune's energy could make you sleepy. Don't let Neptune grasp you and complain; use positive words and keep busy to avoid depression just before the new moon.

Environment: Mars (explosions) will be strong and this trio could bring about serious surprises with nature's devastating forces. Crazy people and all the elements will be invited for a mad dance. Just before the new moon, this energy will be quite strong and will disturb electronics and could produce aeronautical disasters.

— E-Mail —

Memo: to Dr.Turi@worldnet.att.net
Subject: Swarms at Mammoth
"RED ALERT" JULY 30th, 1996
Date: Tue., 30 Jul. 96 14:49:37
Organization: America On-line, Inc. (1-800-827-6364)
sender/@newsbf02.news.aol.com/
Mammoth Mountain had over 150 Shallow focus low magnitude quakes on July 30, as predicted by Dr. Turi and it looks like today is going to be a repeat. These swarms have been happening for some time but usually no more than 15 or 20 a day. This is quite a change in EQ activity — quite similar to the activity before the eruption of Mt. St. Helens. Keep an eye on this area for some time. The USGS has issued a level D status which it says it will lift on Tuesday if EQs subside.

Famous Personalities: Some rich and famous people may make sad news involving drugs or alcohol. Both 911 emergency calls placed by Nicole Simpson were made under the same negative energy. O.J. was probably under the influence when he had beaten his wife.

Events: The Lord of accident (Mars) could also bring about explosions and misadventures, especially if you happen to get close to the river or the ocean this weekend. October 1996 — BLUE ISLAND, Illinois — An explosion rocked an oil refinery south of Chicago, jolting neighborhood homes for miles around and sending clouds of black smoke into the air.

Shopping: Avoid making any financial commitments and do not sign any important documents now; wait for the upcoming new moon. Invest in anything related to the arts, fishing or metaphysics. Put a big smile on your face; use your will and your knowledge; the dying Moon won't bother you for too long! Visit a good friend or your local church for comfort and direction.

New Moon — March 28th, in Aries: The New Moon will mature in the sign of Aries. Explosive and destructive news involving fire, wars, explosions is to be expected soon. Mother earth is alive and may stretch herself vigorously, producing powerful volcanoes or earthquake activity. Souls born with this celestial identity will be competitive, aggressive and will use their inner leadership ability to gain a position of power during their lifetime. Discipline and patience must be induced at an early age to avoid serious head injury. Many endeavors will be launched successfully within the next two waxing weeks and you should be confident of the outcome.

SAT., SUN., MON., TUE. — MARCH 28th, 29th, 30th, 31st: RULERS — Mars (leadership) Mercury (traveling) and Venus (devotion)

Work, Career and Business: With the new moon don't miss an opportunity that may come your way and should be used to improve your business endeavors. This fortuitous method will strengthen your chance of success in the near future. Trust your ability to communicate with Mercury and follow your intuition. The next few days will be vital to launch yourself and Venus' lucky touch will bring additional developments. With the waxing Moon at work the next two weeks should be used to the maximum in promoting your business life.

Partnerships: This timing is perfect for many of us and participating with all the activities around can only further your wishes. Remember, Mars is also around and you should use his strength and concentrate on your efforts to get things done. The future promises to bring about good results from interviews, employment applications, promotions and other job opportunities. A pivotal turning point is to be expected this week in a key relationship. As always consider the long-term implications and respectability of the offer before making up your mind.

Family and Friends: With the "Lord" of communication, Mercury in charge these days, expect your telephone to be busy; everybody will have something to share with you. Use Venus' loving touch in your verbal exchanges and avoid Mars' invective remarks about an unlucky friend. Don't be shy: pass on your message, be confident and be direct in your approach, your impact on others will surprise you. Do all this with "savoir faire." Enjoy the wilderness with the children as Mars will make them restless.

Love Affairs: With the New Moon upon all of us and the kind-hearted touch of Venus, you may decide to treat someone you truly love with your best intentions. You're apt to make significant progress with love this weekend and you should really make the most out of this trend. Social life and romance is up; a trip is on the way for some. If you are single and born a Gemini, a Sagittarius, a Libra or an Aquarius may fall for you.

Travel and Communication: Anything related to selling or general communication will go particularly well, and progress is imminent. This week promises to be worthwhile for the more creative souls and your writing skills will improve dramatically. Under Mercury's and Venus' auspices, especially in time of a new moon, a new book could be started or finished. A trip to Vegas will pay off for some. Don't let Mars make you impatient or accident-prone on the road; be patient.

Environment: Let's hope that Mars' destructive temper will not produce any tornadoes, explosions, high wind or flooding.

Famous Personalities: Be ready for some good news from famous people's creativity or great projects to come to the light.

Events: Remember, Mars is around; don't take any chance with confrontation or the police. A positive attitude and diplomacy will take you out of trouble. Impending breakthroughs with medicine or science are expected soon.

Shopping: Great time to buy interesting books and telephone appliances for your business. As Mercury rules transportation, it would be a good idea for you to take care of your wheels or shop for a new car.

Welcome to Your Day-to-Day Guidance For April 1998

WED., THU., FRI., SAT., SUN. — APRIL 1st, 2nd, 3rd, 4th, 5th:
RULERS — The Moon (commencement) and the Sun (faith in oneself)

Work, Career and Business: Some people will see the end and the beginning of a business situation. New people will move in to replace others. The Moon is still waxing (positive); make the most out of these two weeks ahead of you and have faith in your ability to deal with any changes.

Partnerships: For the deserving soul, this lunation means a great new start, a relocation, a promotion, even the start of a new life. Those changing stars do not care about your sadness, guilt or anything else; don't turn back, move on to your future. Your situation or feelings do not match your wishes; changes must take place. You'll be glad you did it.

Family and Friends: The family will be on your mind and Mom may get in touch with you. The moon will make the children quite emotional; they will need your attention and will be demanding. With the Sun's vitality invest some time with them and do something special they will cherish these days in their heart forever. A friend surprises you with an invitation; restaurants will be busy, so you'd better make a reservation if you do not want to stand in line for a long time.

Love Affairs: Some relationship might end with sorrow, but the stars are on your side. Control your feelings about the past and let them lead you towards your future. Promote your next section of life without delay. Expect some surprises too and go full speed after your desires; anything incredible can happen especially during the weekend. These surprises should be positive and unexpected and there is much to gain if you interact with others. Not a time to stay home at all: visit friends, socialize or throw a party to celebrate this great solar and lunar energy. This lunation has the potential to bring about one of your greatest wishes. Again, don't waste it, go out there now, push and have faith. If you are single and born in July, a younger or older person born in January, November or March won't be able to resist your magnetism.

Travel and Communication: Expect news from brothers and sisters; be part of the action and communicate with those you love. Use plenty words of love and care for others; somehow you'll be rewarded. Traveling is fine; bring your camera; great things and great surprises are ahead; however, concentrate on the road.

Environment: Many people are forced to relocate during this celestial energy, sometimes due to nature's destructive forces. Typhoons and other water disasters are to be expected. Let's hope the new moon will alleviate the drama and make the transition safe for many souls.

Famous Personalities: Famous and powerful personalities will be ending or starting a very important part of their lives. Some will have finished their work on earth and will work as guides for those they cared for on earth.

Events: Under the same star pattern, foreign governments will make important decisions such as the Seoul, South Korea dilemma. In June 1995, worried about its capital's growing population, North Korea reportedly began moving hundreds of thousands of people out of the city of Pyongyang. Thus, thousands will be compelled into a new section of their lives due to a forced relocation.

Shopping: Perfect time to invest in silver or gold. All real estate endeavors are protected; a new house bought now will bring much reward and protection to the owners. Some will be forced to move to a different location. If you do so, make sure to do a candle ritual. Burn white, green and blue candles, and mix them with an incense to clean up some psychic residues left behind disturbed souls. Some stores may also be affected and may rebuild or close down completely.

March 6th, 1998 — Venus enters Pisces: Ideal celestial position to invest in an artistic or spiritual study. Empower yourself with spirituality and display your creativity to the world. Souls born now will inherit a natural gift in music and the arts. A top position to lead in the artistic fields. A weak or badly asserted Venus in this sign will induce deception in love, leading to secret love affairs. If you're born with Venus in Pisces, you are strongly advised to love with your head, not your heart to avoid awful guilt later. When well assisted by other celestial bodies, this is a perfect position for total commitment and endless love.

Full Moon — April 11th, in Libra: Be ready for the beginning or ending of a portion of your business or emotional life. Disturbing, surprising news is ahead of you; be ready to accept those changes as you might have to find a better partner or a new way of serving the world. Keep in mind that life is a constant process of changes and the future usually has better to offer. Take chances, sign contracts, travel and promote your life only after the next New Moon of April 26th, 1998. Be ready for a bumpy couple of weeks ahead of you. You'll need to be strong but when all is said and done you'll be in a much better position.

MON., TUE., WED., THU, FRI., SAT. — APRIL 6th, 7th, 8th, 9th, 10th, 11th:
RULERS — Sun (amazement) Mercury (information) & Venus (love)

Work, Career and Business: The Moon is waxing (positive), and opportunities to further your position in life will depend on your interaction with others. Social contacts will pay off if you use Venus' gentle touch in all you do. Remember the power of your own thoughts; don't be crippled by our own fears and anxieties so that you may attract setbacks to your life. Go after what you really want and don't be afraid to communicate your feelings. Expect some surprising development soon. Fruitful contracts will be signed and will bring great financial rewards.

Partnerships: Do not assume the worst without finding out all facts, nor break your spirit by suppressing all faith. Mercury could make you talkative; listen to your partner. Keep an open mind and be receptive when direction is being offered, especially if the person in question is older than you. Being patient and working harder to attain your goals are the key. If you are inquisitive enough, secrets of a financial nature may be revealed to you. Important legal paper work may be on the way for you to sign; be confident in doing so, the moon is waxing.

Family and Friends: Use your exceptional insight into the secret motives of a friend close to you and avoid all unnecessary gossip. Be patient and practice "savoir faire" with loved ones as Mercury may promote intellectual challenges, even a confrontation. Use plenty of words of love for those you care about and keep your eyes on the children. Friends may ask for financial favors; provide help, but don't overstress your own security for them. People from the past will reappear soon.

Love Affairs: Those stars above your head are tough, but your will is much stronger; use your will in all occasions. The kindhearted touch of Venus can only promote your wishes if you decide to be part of the activity around you. Avoid being too critical about someone you value; no one is perfect. Learn to love yourself and concentrate on the qualities you and others possess. If you are single and born in August, a Scorpio could be giving you trouble; however, a foreigner born in December or June may fall for you.

Travel and Communication: Venus' diplomatic powers will be felt in your words and will further many of your requests. Just remember, you will not attract bees with vinegar. Plan a trip now: invest in your thought power and expect the money to be there. Many souls will be forced to deal with their past, and some will take a long journey.

Environment: With the waxing Moon and the gentle touch of Venus, nature should be quiet. Many environmentalist groups will be active; some may get out of hand trying to get their words out.

Famous Personalities: A prominent person will promote a new diet or a specific product. It will use only natural goods and be very Eastern in conception. Some will announce and enjoy a new baby arrival.

Events: Some disturbing, even shocking news will arrive soon pertaining to unhappy people willing to start a strike. A new line of clothing may attract investors from Europe or the US.

Shopping: A perfect time to invest in health, clothing or beauty products. You may also find a great deal involving children's products; look for it while the Moon is waxing.

SUN., MON., TUE., WED, THU., FRI. — APRIL 12th, 13th, 14th, 15th, 16th, 17th
RULERS — Pluto (rebirth from death) & Jupiter (foreign impact)

> **Note**: Attention — Pluto is back with us — Expect dramatic happenings all over; control is a must. Don't be a victim, be aware of Pluto's destructive power. Anything you say or do under his power will follow you for the rest of your life. Time to use extreme caution in all you do.

He who reigns himself and rules his passion,
desire and fears is more than a king.

— Goethe

Work, Career and Business: Pull in a safe place and be quiet; that is the best advice I can give you now. You are at this time of the month where you must wait for the green light; take no chance on anything, keep a low profile and all will be fine. Watch the type of dramatic news during this trend and realize the importance of having your Moon Power close by. As always, if Starguide works for you, it also works for others, so don't be afraid to tell others to "cool" down. We are all under the incredible will of the cosmos, and Pluto will reach some unlucky souls.

Partnerships: Be courteous with everyone as your over zealousness is sure to be heard and felt. Time to use your will and apply your knowledge of the stars. Avoid outbursts of emotion, even if your partner gets completely out of hand with jealousy or bad temper. With Jupiter's presence these days, some of the upcoming dramatic news might involve religion, foreigners or the justice principle.

Family and Friends: In time of a full Moon, Pluto might go completely berserk; use Starguide's wisdom or you may be very sorry you didn't. Many of us will undergo some form of metamorphosis as Pluto gives serious wake-up calls. If friends and family members need help or guidance, share your knowledge for the common good. Not a time to plan a visit or get away from home; wait for better stars. Many disturbances are reported during this trend, especially the one with domestic violence, and the police will have their hands full.

Love Affairs: Be ready for some secrets to surface. Some people you care about may become very uncooperative and could lead you straight to depression or decide to fight with you. These days could bring an element of drama with them, and you are advised to stay away from other people's problems. Better enjoy your own home and cooking on Monday and Tuesday night; social life can only bring unwanted situations, even serious trouble. Don't take chances with sex and stay clear from strangers. In the game of love, protect yourself. If you are single and born in September, a Taurus or a Capricorn could be difficult to deal with. If you know a Pisces who has a problem with alcohol, move on; look for a better soul.

Travel and Communication: Do not travel unless you absolutely have to. Your car may decide to let you down, so take care of the wheels before taking a risky journey. Doublecheck all plans and arrangements to avoid further hazards. Now is the time to speak clearly and concisely as you're prone to miscommunication. Do not broach subjects that are controversial and emotions are running high and logic is out the window. For those who find themselves in a difficult communication situation it may be better to save the subject for later and excuse yourself before it's too late. You will usually find that the argument occurred as a result of what might happen rather than what will. Lots of secrets will come to light and money will be a disturbing topic for some.

Environment: Under this planet immense destructive power, chemical plants explode, airliners crash, nature goes crazy, prod-

Moon Power — Starguide 1998

ucts are tampered with, and potentially dangerous technology is sold to hostile powers. Time to get close to God in your local church and pray for the unaware victims of deadly Pluto. On April 16th, I posted a "window" for April 23rd and 30th, 1997 saying "Be ready with nature's devastating forces producing quakes well above 6.5."

> **Note**: A window is always operational a few hours before and after the given date!
> Results:
> Santa Cruz Islands. (8.0Mb)
> Tonga islands (6.5 Mb)
> 97/04/22 09:31:26 10.97N 61.17W 33.0 6.5Ms A
> Trinidad
> 97/04/23 03:47:18 13.54S 166.02E 33.0 6.1Ms B
> Vanuatu Islands
> 97/04/23 19:44:28 14.22N 144.58E 100.2 6.3Mb A
> Mariana Islands
> 97/05/01 11:37:34 18.87N 107.26W 33.0 6.7Ms A
> Off Coast of Jalisco, Mexico

Famous Personalities: The world will lose a famous personality under Pluto's command. He may also decide to do it dramatically (assassination). Pluto will not stop at famous people, so watch yourself and choose your environment carefully.

Events: All the dramatic news involving the police, sex, drama and death was promoted by this disreputable planet. Be ready for a bumpy one. Pluto is also a factor that stimulates and dramatizes ethics issues and makes them even more complex. On the posted window for April 23rd, 1997 I also mentioned on the Internet to watch for surprises with the police and explosions.

Results: April 23rd, 1997 — Peru, Japan relieved by hostage rescue: 14 rebels, 3 others die. The assault by Peruvian police and soldiers started at around 5:23 a.m. Japan time on Wednesday April 23rd and was covered live by Japanese television stations. Fujimori said 25 other captives were injured in the gunfire and explosions that rocked the compound. Japan had been urging a peaceful end to the crisis, which began on Dec. 17. Explosions — April 23, 1997 — MOSCOW — A bomb ripped through a railway station in southern Russia on the night of Wednesday April 23rd, killing two people and wounding some 20 others, news reports said.

Shopping: Anything related with the unknown, magic, candles, incense. Some old souls will be busy writing their wills. A great time to visit your favorite psychic or astrologer or deal with the unknown.

March 13th, 1998 — Mars enters Taurus: With Mercury (communication) going retrograde, this is not a time to launch any financial business venture or start any program involving corporate money. If you are a Taurus or an Aries or born with a Taurus Dragon's Tail (see year's Dragon's tables) you will be accident-prone on the neck for a while; don't take chances, slow down and wear your seat belt. Use Mars correctly: do not allow the planet of hunger to disturb your business life. Souls born now will inherit an interest in music, geology, massage, chiropractic, plants and jewelry. Forging into one of those enterprises will establish security and a solid position. These souls are born aggressive and impatient where money is concerned, so a more tolerant partner is a good suggestion to deal with sensitive financial endeavors. A top position involving finance or the arts is usually achieved during the subject's life.

SAT., SUN., MON., TUE., WED. — APRIL 18th, 19th, 20th, 21st, 22nd:
RULERS — Saturn (karma) Uranus (sudden events) Neptune (water/drugs):

Work, Career and Business: With Mercury still in retrograde motion, you can only experience stress and conflicts all over. Moreover, we are on the waning time (negative) and faith could be quite low for many. Hold on a little longer for the upcoming New Moon (April 26th) and life will get much better for all of us. Use patience with everyone around you and wait before launching important business or signing documents. Don't trust any business proposition now and don't take any chance with your finances.

Partnerships: Be aware of Saturn's gloomy nature and try smiling if you can. *Moon Power* mentions a concentration of negative influences in this long trend and telling you otherwise or to expect good things to happen won't work. Take care not to fall prey to depression or self-destruction. Use all your abilities to deal with life and help the one you care about. Enjoy a good movie and a good bottle of wine at home.

Family and Friends: A friend or family member's surprise visit has you scrambling to make your home presentable in advance of the arrival. This person may bring a lot of excitement but also some unwanted turmoil. If you decide to socialize, keep an eye on your possessions and lock your car. Under Neptune's grip, people drink too much and crooks become active. Get rid of unwanted things: have a garage sale or give it away to the Salvation Army for the unfortunate. A good time to clean around, take care of your gardens or even your house-plants. Don't fall for guilt; avoid depressive thoughts of your past. Look for happy people and try to enjoy what life has to offer for now. Keep an eye on the kids, especially if there is water around you, Neptune may play tricks on them.

Love Affairs: Do not trust strangers! Not a good time get involved sexually; take precautions. A badly aspected Neptune promotes sexually transmitted diseases and narcotics abuse. Secret love affairs may start now, but if you are in one, make sure you are not taken for a ride, as all those promises may be too good to be true! Be practical and review any promises with common sense. If you are single and born in October, an Aries or an Aquarius will find you quite attractive and may ask you out.

Travel and Communication: Travel ideas may be too risky for comfort; be sure you're prepared for any road emergency or difficult weather. If you must take a long journey, be very careful on the road and if possible avoid flying. With the waning Moon your energy level won't be that high and if you must drive, take plenty of rest before taking the road. Keep to the speed limit as the police will be out there ready to penalize you. Avoid drinking at all costs during the evening hours and keep a positive attitude in all you say.

Environment: Uranus (surprising disruptions) and Saturn (karma) are good friends and they all like to upset the poor unaware human on earth below. Sadly enough many oil spills happened under this energy when either the weather or miscalculation is the real reason. *POSTED* April 20th, 1997 on the Internet — Expect SRE "Sudden Release of Energy" for April 30th, 1997. On this window expect explosions/volcano eruptions/blackouts/drama/police/ death etc. April 29, 1997 MEXICO CITY — The Popocatepetl volcano erupts near Mexico City. Scientists were keeping a close eye on the Popocatepetl volcano in central Mexico Tuesday after red-hot rocks from small overnight eruptions ignited huge fires on grazing lands and frightened farmers on the mountainside. — April 30, 1997 — Explosion at Albanian weapons depot kills 20 — TIRANA, Albania — At least 20 people were killed Wednesday when a weapons depot exploded in a central Albanian town. Police said the cause of the explosion at Burell, about 20 miles (35 km) northeast of Tirana, was unknown.

Famous Personalities: Sad news coming from famous people and their involvement with deceiving activities. Some will be incarcerated or receive emergency care.

Events: On a large scale disturbing news is to be expected and may disturb the population. The government may be forced to make very important decisions that could affect some of us. Be ready to hear about disasters such as the following. Moon Power Supernova windows for 1997 gave the date of April 29th. "Flood seeps through Winnipeg dike; thousands flee — The date of April 30, 1997 was also posted as a window on the Internet — Red River still rising. Dike, large ditch may offer protection — The flood could be the worst seen in Manitoba since 1852. More than 28,000 Canadians and 50,000 Americans have been forced from their homes by the rise of the Red River.

Shopping: Difficult energy coming from the Universe will manifest itself, thus not a time to deal with metaphysics or trust psychics. Neptune may blur their vision of the future. Avoid investing in Uranus' tools (computers/electronics).

THU., FRI., SAT., SUN. — APRIL 23rd, 24th, 25th, 26th:
RULERS — Neptune (losing hold on reality)& Mars (God of war):

Work, Career and Business: Be nice with others at work; use your knowledge and don't expect your boss to be aware of Mars' impatience and irritability. The waning Moon won't provide you with many opportunities just yet; keep a low profile and wait for better days. Neptune may make it difficult for you to concentrate these days. Postpone everything important until the new moon of April 26th. Important matters related to finances will be on your mind, and all will be fine soon.

Partnerships: Make a good use of Starguide and don't be afraid to offer its guidance to others. You may also suggest it to your partner as two souls aware of the stars are better than one. Using Neptune's intuitive power may save a situation, but avoid complaining and do something about it. Control Mars' impatience and understand the need of your partner too.

Family and Friends: Use tons of diplomacy with your friends and loved ones as patience is not Mars' quality. A great time is to be expected soon when the New Moon will shine once more on all of us. Enjoy the love and good food provided by those who really care for you. Spend some time with the children; teach them love and harmony as Mars may make them play rough. As always with Neptune around, be aware around water.

Love Affairs: Avoid any intense situation with your partner; support, love and respect will take you miles. Use Neptune's responsive nature to apologize to someone you deeply care for and control your imagination. Offer a present or some flowers; this always works. If you are single and born in November, a Pisces or a Cancer will want to know you.

Travel and Communication: Be aware of Mars' speedy nature and drive carefully; be courteous with others; psychotics share the road with you and one of those dangerous drivers may get you in trouble. As always, stay clear of alcohol if you take a long trip, and rest if you feel tired. Anticipate the upcoming new Moon and put a big smile on your face; life will get much better soon for all of us.

Environment: Combined with Mars' explosive temper and the waning Moon, expect sad news from water, oil or the Middle East. Once more, Mars' destructive instinct is unpredictable, so avoid dangerous situations, especially if you spend time close to the water this weekend.

Famous Personalities: Life is a constant process of change, and famous figures must also accept the sad reality of demise. Light will be brought up to some famous people's hidden problems with alcohol or unlawful endeavor. Soon, the end of a notable person's life will reach the media.

Events: Difficult weather including tornadoes or flooding may affect some parts of the states and surprise some people. Much of the difficult news may be coming from foreign places. With Mars, fires, destruction, violence, war and nature's devastative forces at work are on the agenda.

Shopping: Perfect time to purchase a camera or get a good deal on paint. Dangerous tools or a car should not be bought now. You may be asking for trouble later on if you do so.

New Moon — May 26th, 1998 in Taurus. This sign is ruled by the peaceful planet Venus; however, combined with the magnetic pull of Mars still present these days, we may experience explosions, accidents and damaging earthquakes. Hopefully, gracious Venus will stop her turbulent brother Mars from disturbing the earth's entrails. Use this lunation to further your finance and utilize Venus' diplomatic power to deal with others. If you play your cards right, she may also reward you with love.

MON., TUE., WED., THU. — APRIL 27th, 28th, 29th, 30th:
RULERS — Mercury (speech) Moon (changing cycles):

Work, Career and Business: This lunation will force you into many changes; those changes, no matter how painful they may seem to be, are for the best in the long run. Thus be ready for a variety of new starts concerning some areas of your life. Some deserving souls will land on a great opportunity for a new career. Make the most of the new moon and have faith in all you do.

Partnerships: Expect the beginning or ending of important phases of your life. Keep your eyes and ears open on the people you know as this new moon will affect them too. Many will be forced into new partnerships; accept the changes with an open mind. Surely a great energy to be spent in the outdoors close to the water or in the high mountains. The wilderness will do great healing on your spirit and recharge you for future challenges. Be aware of offensive·Mars and use plenty "savoir faire" with your partner.

Family and Friends: Friends will be active, calling or going to parties. Don't turn down any invitation from friends; many of your wishes may come true through them. Some, not without tears, will be going away for a while or forever to a different location, to a different fate, to a different life, even to a different world. Expect the family circle to be emotional, busy with Mom and the kids to be the center of attraction. Surely a good time for you to enjoy the warm family circle and appreciate all the children around you. They would love you forever if you decided to take them to the zoo, food will be everywhere and happiness will rule these days.

Love Affairs: Many interesting people will be out there enjoying what life has to offer. This energy will affect the "executives," so meeting one of them can seriously promote your career. Do not be afraid to take chances on anything or anybody; these stars are extremely lucky and your competitiveness will pay off. Do not stay home this weekend; you may have to wait a long time to get this type of positive energy around again. Go out, ask and you may even find true love. If you are single and born in December, an Aries or a Leo will drive you crazy. A Gemini will be strongly attracted to you.

Travel and Communication: Mercury will make you curious and will help you to communicate adequately with others. Your telephone will be busy as this rare beautiful energy will boost everybody around you. Surely a great time to enjoy your holidays, but if you have to be at work, be ready for an interesting meeting with some after work.

Environment: Expect the weather to especially beautiful as she shows off her finest garments. However, we may get some freak accidents, so stay prepared.

Famous Personalities: Expect to hear some surprising news about some behind-the-scenes personalities.

Events: Look for larger than usual earthquakes and maybe some other spectacular sight of nature showing off around the new moon. Unfortunately this energy does sometimes see aeronautical disasters or force thousands of people to flee either nature or man's madness. Let's hope the new moon will stop any dramatic happening.

Shopping: Anything and everything for your children. Tools used for the home or the arts will also bring luck to future projects. Purchase your plane ticket now if you need to fly far away this summer.

Welcome to Your Day-to-Day Guidance For May 1998

FRI., SAT., SUN., MON. — MAY 1st, 2nd, 3rd, 4th:
RULERS — The Moon (readjustment) & Sun (love & surprise)

Work, Career and Business: The month will start on a note of faith with many new financial breaks ahead of you. You can expect the serious beginning and ending of important parts of your (and others') life. Be ready for those upcoming progressive variations and be ready to accept them. Life is a constant process of change and the stars are, even if you don't agree or realize it, working for your benefit in the long run.

Partnerships: Let go of disapproving people and depressing situations; take a chance on your new future with faith. Many will experience the sad end of their relationship and their lucky souls may see the new beginning; however, under this lunation there are no excuses; just get on with it. Many of your wishes may see the light soon.

Family and Friends: The Sun rules love, romance and children and with the waxing moon expect surprising news. If something wrong happens to a child under a good moon, maybe you should check out when you invested in the toy that was used. The Sun gives life to anything that he touches but for some mystical reasons, fatalistic experiences do happen. As usual, watch over them, especially close to the water. On a more positive note he will put his undiscriminating light on the incredible UFO manifestation. You may hear about someone's heart problem or surgery.

Love Affairs: Be ready for new starts in love matters and provide spiritual help for the victims suffering a painful broken heart.

The right partner might not be the one you want to be with. You should use the new-found freedom to look for someone who deserves your love. With the waxing moon, keep looking for the special person and by miracle it will happen. Some teenagers may suffer or find their first love. If you are born in January, a much older or younger person born in September or July may want to let you know how much you mean to them.

Travel and Communication: If you decide to take the children with you, be aware on the road; you are responsible for their young lives. Order them to put their seat belt on and be ready for anything. Enjoy all that nature has to offer and be prepared for surprises; enjoy — a great time is ahead of you.

Environment: What was once built by man (cities/homes) or nature (forests somehow with time will have to be destroyed. What was once born must sooner or later die and this is what life is all about. There is nothing else to do than to accept the ultimate changes imposed by God, and usually the future offers better. The Sun regulates fires, so be aware and be prudent if you happen to go in the wilderness.

Famous Personalities: Expect interesting, even weird surprises with the rich and famous. Be ready for the unexpected in their words and actions. You may take some calculated chances with the Sun in charge but understand your limits.

Events: Terrible tragedies such as the Kobe, Japan earthquake and many volcanic eruptions are around the corner as Pluto soon will reign upon the earth. If he is early, he will force thousands of people out of their homes because of nature's destructive forces. Let's hope the powerful life-giving Sun to be able to stop him and his tragedy.

Shopping: Anything for children as long as it is new. Great time to invest in gold or expensive items. You may also invest in computers and anything involving creativity or the arts.

May 4th, 1998 — Venus enters Aries: Perfect time to concentrate on improving your looks and start an exercise program. Invest in your desire for action; this will lead you to stronger health. Souls born now will be competitive in matters related to the arts and love. Many of them will have to learn to love with their head first, to avoid heartaches later on. A natural gift in acting and considerable magnetism will lead them to a successful career. These souls are born to love and be loved. A top position leading to any endeavor demanding a mixture of arts and danger. The soul will use Mars metal (steel/skates) to represent beauty in action.

TUE., WED., THU., FRI., SAT. — MAY 5th, 6th, 7th, 8th, 9th:
RULERS — Mercury (letters) and Venus (Goddess of love).

Work, Career and Business: Just a few days away from the full moon, make the most of Venus' new fresh breath of life. With Mercury's vital intellectual genius, push your business now. Advertisements, important calls, traveling, and meetings will pay off and social interaction will bring good luck. Respect the Universal Law, use Moon Power and your knowledge and have faith in your abilities.

Partnerships: Mercury rules the mail, telephone and communication in general; expect anything from anybody. Venus may decide to offer you with a get-together after work and Mercury will have everyone "gossiping." Promote only faith and love, and pass on your message to the world around you.

Family and Friends: Use the New Moon to provide a generous shoulder to those who suffered karmic experiences the last few months. However, let no one exhaust your spirit, and avoid showing frustration with loved ones. Some of those friends really need spiritual regeneration, even a helping hand; do so, but realize your limits, especially where money is a concern.

Love Affairs: Your sense of perfection will expand with Venus in charge these days. Don't be too picky or demanding with those you care about; no one is perfect. You may feel like starting a diet; but don't get too concerned with your appearance or your health. Work first on yourself, and the results will stimulate those close to you. Venus hates cigarette smoke, so with her help, apply your will and try to give up smoking. Doing so, the opportunity to find real and healthy love will be given to you. If you are single and born in February, someone born in August or June may fall in love with you.

Travel and Communication: Get your wheels in action; traveling and shopping is under the protection of the New Moon. Use Venus' touch of love to show your affection to those you care about, and offer them flowers. Mercury will get your telephone busy and much of your important mail should be done and sent now. Further happiness and love and you will benefit from your own positive attitude.

Environment: You need to recharge your batteries; a trip in the wilderness is strongly recommended if you have been under stress lately. Venus' energy will make you appreciate the beauty of mother nature and the people around you. Many animal rights activists and environmentalists will make serious progress and get the attention they deserve in passing out their important message.

Famous Personalities: A new diet, a new product or a health-oriented presentation will be promoted by a famous person. A new line of cars or electronics will also be promoted by famous personalities.

Events: With the New Moon upon us, mother nature may decide to relax a bit and keep approaching Pluto in control. Some large financial corporations may decide to fuse together to secure themselves against competition.

Shopping: Great bargains will be offered if you want to invest in products to improve your life and your body. Some may decide to join the local gym or enroll on a weight loss program.

> **Note**: Attention — Pluto is back with us — Expect dramatic happenings all over; control is a must. Don't be a victim; be aware of Pluto's destructive power. Anything you say or do under his power will follow you for the rest of your life. Time to use extreme caution in all you do. Killers, rapists, psychotics, and the worst of society will get active. While Pluto reigns, you'd better stay home and let the ignorant get killed. Time to make a good use of my work.

Full Moon — May 11th, 1998 in Scorpio. Be ready for a bumpy one. As always with the Lord of hell in charge of this trend, better think twice before saying or acting on impulse. Expect secrets to be divulged, affairs of sex, and nature's devastative forces at work. The police and blackguards will make the news. More than ever, use diplomacy as whatever you do now will have very serious repercussions in your future.

SUN., MON., TUE., WED., THU. — MAY 10th, 11th, 12th, 13th, 14th:
RULERS — Pluto (death/drama) and Jupiter (new faith):

Work, Career and Business: You are now walking on a razor blade! You'd better use all the "savoir faire" you know if you are to go through this lunation without trouble. A serious wake-up call will come to many abusers as the heavy hand of karma will fall on the victims. The possibility to lose it all (and rebuild it all) will be a serious consideration for some karmic souls. Not a time to deal with money matters; keep a low profile.

Partnerships: The ugly secret life of a person may surface; you may learn something valuable about a partner. Whatever you find out, do not divulge the secret. Stinky money-making schemes will play an important part of this trend; listen to your intuition in all you do. Stay clear of dark alleys; your life hangs upon your awareness.

Family and Friends: Do not expect anyone you care about to be diplomatic with you during this trend. Do not fall for Pluto's destructive or sarcastic remarks; words of love and support will pay off in the long run. Be ready for some dramatic news from someone close to you. Whatever happens, be strong; life must go on as Pluto has important work to do and he is part of a celestial design imposed by God.

Love Affairs: Secret affairs of sex and passionate love may be divulged to the public, forcing people to take a stand in destroying and rebuilding relationships. This might happen to you too. In any case use tons of diplomacy to save unwanted trouble in your love life. If you are a Scorpio, a Pisces, or a Cancer or have any planet in Scorpio, be ready for a wake-up call of some form.

Travel and Communication: Expect news pertaining to secrets, sex, the police force, and medical discovery. Be careful of what you do or say during this trend. Drive carefully, stay clear of strangers and strange places. Be ready for dramatic news to plague the media.

Environment: Pluto belongs to the divine family and has a specific work to do, and his impact on earth (and the people) is needed. As Pluto demolishes he also gives the opportunity to rebuild stronger and better bridges and buildings. Be ready for dramatic news with the police and nature's forces soon.

— E-Mail —

From: mary41@ix.netcom.com
Date: Thu, 1 May 1997 23:43:29-0500 (CDT)
To: drturi@pacbell.net
Subject: Earthquakes
Dear Dr. Turi, I posted a note on alt.astrology that cited the 6.7 quake off the coast of Mexico in the Pacific Ocean. I included it under the rather "nasty" piece of mail that someone sent indicating that they believed your window of probability for April 30 to be invalid. Not that I think you need defending, as I have found your work very compelling. I just thought I'd let you know — in case you didn't — that you were "right again." On the late night of April 30, the 6.7 quake took place. Mary

---

Famous Personalities: Some famous people will be called back to God. Many famous spoiled children get involved with the wrong crowd and some are found shot to death alongside a road. Pluto could not care less about the famous. Saving the name of the famous parent is usually a priority, so the media get confused signals of what really happened. I'll let you be the judge and make your own association to this comment.

Events: Hopefully knowledgeable Jupiter will slow down Pluto's rampage and thirst for blood.

> — Posted on the Internet —
> Date: Tue, 30 Apr. 96 02:07:28 GMT —
> Organization: C-Group-Link,SanDiego,CA,
> News.CGL.COM!DrTuriFromdrturi@cgl.
> Newsgroups: ca.earthquakes —
> Subject: Big and bad quakes "window" of May 3rd!
> Result: (1) May 3, 1996 — BEIJING, China — Chinese officials said that at least 15 people have died and over 200 were injured in a magnitude 6.4 earthquake that rocked Northern China. (2) May 3rd, SEATTLE, Washington — the Seattle Mariners and the Cleveland Indians will finish what they started Thursday night — playing the last innings of a baseball game halted when an earthquake struck the Pacific.

Shopping: Taurus will see an important part of their business or financial life taking a specific direction within this lunation. With Jupiter with us too, the worst might be avoided by some miraculous development. A visit to your local church to pray for Pluto's victims will do you good. Do not invest in weapons; if you do so you might have to use them later. Anything bought now that can be used for metaphysics will bring unusual power to you.

May 15th, 1998 — Mercury enters Taurus: Perfect time to review a new financial endeavor or to investigate the possibility for future investment. Empower yourself to structure your financial security and sign the legal forms after the new moon only. Souls born now will inherit a natural gift in handling corporate money and will slowly but surely secure themselves financially. These souls are born financial planners and much of their patience will pay off in the long run. A top position to lead in any way they choose where organization of resources, the arts and beauty will prevail.

FRI., SAT., SUN., MON., TUE. — MAY 15th, 16th, 17th, 18th, 19th:
RULERS — Saturn (congress) and Uranus (consternation).

Work, Career and Business: Expect a forced ending passed upon your service to the world or your career. Something must be done, something must change; be ready. The undertaking that you are doing leaves you unsatisfied and is a source of stress; you might be forced to modify your direction. Resolve to find a new way of handling your career soon and for the lucky ones expect a well-deserved promotion.

Partnerships: Don't let anyone pressure you into using their ideas instead of your own. You came across this plan to stimulate you and your entrepreneur spirit to become more independent. Meditate to understand where this partnership is going in your life. Did you make the right choices and can you live with them? If not, there won't be a better time to deal with those questions; these days will help you to change it all. Some surprising news is ahead of you.

Family and Friends: Your friends will be requesting your presence and may invite you to a gathering. Enjoy this opportunity, but you will be amazed with what you are about to hear. Uranus also makes the children very active and accident-prone; watch them closely. They will be heavy on you; be patient with their young demanding spirits. Let them enjoy Uranus' world of miracles, maybe by going to a place you went before like Dixieland or the Zoo. Keep your eyes on everything they do and everywhere they go and you will have a smashing time.

Love Affairs: Expect piquant surprises during these days as many people will surprise you with the people of their past. With Uranus' disturbing touch these days, avoid going places or doing things you never did before. Stay with what you do or know best. Karmic love is around the corner for some, especially if you were born in March. Someone from your previous life born in July or November will be attracted to you. A Cancer may bring someone much younger or older in your life.

Travel and Communication: Here are some ideas for a small trip not far from town. Uranus rules electronics, the future, astrology, psychic phenomena, and UFOs. If you want to see something unusual, talk about it and do it now! Who knows, Uranus may decide to grant one of your wishes. Stay clear from storms; a sudden blackout and danger coming from lightning is very real.

Environment: On a sad note, keep in mind that Uranus rules earthquakes and volcanoes. He may also decide to throw a tornado or produce violent explosions. Let's hope he won't.

Famous Personalities: Be ready as usual for an unusual type of news from some extroverted celebs. Much will be done for children during this trend as the negative trend will touch some of them. Let's hope I am wrong, I hate to say anything drastic about the children. Sadly enough, Uranus or Pluto couldn't care a bit about my personal feelings and will do what ever pleases them. A famous person will provide and help to make important decisions pertaining to the young generation, computers and education.

> **In article**
> <4khsfi$v02@bugs.cgl.com>, drturi@cgl.com (Dr. Turi) wrote: Next negative "window" is for Wednesday 17th — 12 hours 04/16/96 thru 04/18/96.
> : > Surprises and nasty earthquakes are to be expected.
> — HalBlonde@aol.comPath: news.goodnet. .com!usenet — 8.0 QUAKE JOLTS INDONESIA: 21-Foot Tidal Waves Recorded.
>
> Dear Dr. Turi. Please forward me your predictions for 1996. I was very impressed by the accuracy of the past few of your "windows," especially this most recent one earthquake/explosion. For the last few months I have followed your predictions with increasing interest. You have some astonishing insight in the way the world acts.

Events: Under Uranus' surprising power, Newsgroups: ca.earthquakes —
From: lpease@n.com (Lisa Pease) —
Subject: Re: FORECAST (Dr. Turi) —
<lpeaseDq2L8x.6su@netcom.com>Organization: NETCOM On-line Communication Date: Thu, 18 Apr 1996 18:12:33 GMT — Lines: 1-Sender: lpease@.com I don't know yet who Dr. Turi is — but we just had an earthquake here in Los Angeles. Time: 11:10 a.m. Date: 4/18/96. Exact date was posted on the Net!

Shopping: Do not turn down an invitation as a professional contact could bring people who will positively influence your career. For this occasion, you may feel like spending time and money on your appearance; great time to shop for new wardrobe items, or consult a beautician. Not a good time to pay a visit to your local psychic; stay practical and use your own intuition.

WED., THU., FRI., SAT. — MAY 20th, 21st, 22nd, 23rd:
RULERS — Neptune (losing hold on reality) and Mars (flare-ups and hot-headedness).

Work, Career and Business: Make good use of the information printed in Starguide; this work translates the energies ahead of us. With the waning moon upon us, time to slow down and do a clean-up around the office. Avoid signing important contracts and postpone every important meeting until the approaching new moon of May 25th. Slow down, be patient; there won't be much that you can do apart from finishing up and preparing your next move. Anything else could be wasting your time and your money.

Partnerships: Do not let anything bad happen to your psyche; avoid Neptune's deceiving nature. With Mars around, you'd better use a diplomatic attitude in all your endeavors and avoid any confrontation with coworkers or your supervisor. Time to rescue some depressed spirits without letting yourself be affected by their personal problems. A good movie or a great video will do for tonight.

Family and Friends: Friends and family in trouble will call you. They might be experiencing anxiety in their relationships; provide them with your support. Talk about the moon's impact upon their lives and psyche and mention my book. In all, a difficult time where you should be prudent and patient with others. The depressive power of Neptune also affects your friends; sadly enough some of them will abuse alcohol and may pay a heavy price. DO NOT DRINK and drive and if you do drink designate a safe driver or have a cab take you back home. Neptune could seriously blind your vision and with Mars' impatience you could visit the emergency room (or the cemetery!). Don't take a chance on your life; stay clear of chemicals and use tons of patience with your family members.

Love Affairs: Secret love affairs may be a temptation to some and will bring deception to the unaware initiator. Time to give strong support to your mate, especially if they are water signs as the waning moon will make them "moody." If you are a Pisces, Cancer or Scorpio do not expect much with love, romance or with your children. Just be patient, control your imagination and do not nurture guilt from past endeavors. A long walk to the mall or the sea will keep your mind away from Neptune's depressive liturgies.

Travel and Communication: The majority of people are not yet aware of the power of Mars and Neptune upon their psyche and will behave like foolish robots. Drive slowly, be alert and most of all stay calm in any situation. Be very forthright and patient in your speech as miscommunications now could have disastrous results. Further love and understanding and all will be fine.

Environment: This celestial duo has in the past produced oil spills, chemical plant explosions and extremely high tides. Avoid the sea if you can or be safe, as many vessels will go down to Poseidon's world. Stressing news about floods is to be expected soon.

Famous Personalities: Elizabeth Taylor, Mohammed Ali, Michael Jackson and many other Pisces celebrities could make the news. Many Virgoans will see the end of their famous associations. The Pope and the church could give us sad news as abortion and religious groups will insist on their personal war.

Events: Neptune rules religion; under his power on May 3, 1997 the Pope made an important announcement. VATICAN CITY — When Pope John Paul II makes a choice for sainthood, it's often to make a point. On Sunday, he draws attention to a long neglected and often despised group in Europe, beatifying a Gypsy for the first time in the history of the Roman Catholic Church. Beatification is the last step before possible canonization or sainthood.

Shopping: Good deals will be offered on a garage sale or your local flea market. Anything related to chemicals to clean up the house of pests or the garden of unwanted weeds. Avoid buying any medicines and stay clear of prescriptions.

> **Note**: Losing much of its financial support the church must change its approach to gain more followers. Mars (the warrior) rules Germany and parts of Europe; disturbing news may come from there. The weather could turn real nasty again and water and slides could be a serious threat to some regions of the US.

May 24th, 1998 — Mars enters Gemini: This sign is ruled by the faster orbiting planet around the Sun, Mercury. With dangerous Mars there, you are strongly advised to slow down for a while if you want to keep your car (and your life). Much of your desire for communication will be enhanced, but don't let yourself fall for verbal challenges. During this trend people have a bit of problem listening and will display quite a lot of impatience. Some others will take things personally, so use "savoir faire" in all your dealings. Souls born with this celestial signature could pursue a racing career or educate themselves to become fine attorneys. When well supported by other planets, a gift in communication and writing is usually present.

New Moon — May 25th, 1998 in Gemini. A perfect time to start any intellectual pursuit, start a book, find a publisher and communicate your feelings to all. You may invest in a new car or anything related to communication. Traveling and foreigners will play an important part of this lunation. Plans made to travel under this new moon will bring excitement and many wishes. On a large scale, witty Mercury will help in promoting better relations with other countries around the world.

SUN., MON., TUE., WED. — MAY 24th, 25th, 26th, 27:
RULERS — Mars (danger) Venus (caring)& Mercury (roaming).

Work, Career and Business: Mars is still active, so emotional reactions in the office should be avoided. Use patience and diplomacy with whoever is around you and good progress will be made. Make plans for the future and act upon them while the moon is new. Money and communication will play an important part of this trend.

Partnerships: Some interesting news may come your way. You have a free will, and Mars won't let anyone force his opinion on you. With Mercury's sense of exaggeration, do not fall for all you hear now and don't be afraid to challenge people's information. You need to use your intuition, and sensitive Venus can help you in doing so. Use words of love and be patient with everyone; the new moon will induce a new energy in them.

Family and Friends: Venus will bring an element of love and joy in the anticipation of the upcoming weekend. Mercury will make us very communicative and Mars will further a desire for action. This trend will be an interesting one where friends and family members will try to get in touch with you all at the same time. Make the most of those beautiful stars and enjoy life.

Love Affairs: If you use Venus' "savoir faire" power in any situation, you will win over Mars' argumentative temperament. A great time to show love and affection to those you care about. Avoid depressive conversation of your past, stay in the future, look to the bright side of life. If you were born under the fiery sign of Aries, keep a cool head with someone born in August or December. A Libra may fall in love with you. If you are single, get going and reach your wishes.

Travel and Communication: Don't let this trio drive you crazy as you will have a million things to do at the same time. The strength of Mars combined with the speed of Mercury may bring trouble in your driving, so slow down. Use precautions and take your time if you have to travel far away to visit people; don't let accident-prone Mars stop you. Be alert and slow down and nothing wrong will happen to you.

Environment: Keep in mind that Mars is with us and he doesn't care for any of your plans; he may decide to throw an earthquake or produce disturbing weather all around. News of war and the Middle East (terrorism) could be upon us again. If he wins over Venus and Mercury, his destructive power will be felt with an explosion.

Famous Personalities: This powerful trio configuration may take the life of an important political person. Some famous person may also meet a sad fate in the water or on the road.

Events: Pluto (ultimate power/life and death) is still in retrograde motion in the sign of Sagittarius (religion). He will keep enforcing a slow but sure decay of dogmas. Religions as they are known at present will be completely transformed. The rebirth will result in one religion based on man's direct cosmic consciousness with God. This celestial configuration will bring real spiritual leaders to the fore passing on their inborn gift of teaching the fundamental laws governing all life in the universe.

Shopping: Invest in anything brand new or tools, as great deals await you. Be confident in spending large amounts of money on clothes or jewelry now, but they will not bring you any luck or the magnetism you're looking for.

May 30th, 1998 — Venus enters Taurus: Perfect time to concentrate on improving your wardrobe and shaping the body for the new you. Invest in your desire for beauty and perfection. Souls born now will be possessive in matters related to love and lucky with money. Many of them will have to learn to let go of wrong relationships and trust again. This position makes for one of the most beautiful women of the Zodiac. A sincere gift in loving, creating and a distinguished magnetism will lead them to a successful career. These souls are born to reach emotional, financial and spiritual security, teach genuine love and be loved back. A top position involving financial security, communication and success in any artistic field.

THU., FRI., SAT., SUN. — MAY 28th, 29th, 30th, 31st:
RULERS — The Moon (changes ahead) & the Sun (life and love).

Work, Career and Business: Do not try to hold on to your past; accept the upcoming changes with faith. The stars' pattern and changes are imposed by God to continually promote experiences and a better life. Surely an interesting Universal trend full of changes and surprises. With the waxing Moon, try anything new and take chances on new opportunities. Someone's advice regarding an investment may be worthwhile. Examine all business propositions carefully and sign the paperwork now. With the Sun around, expect some surprising progress in the near future.

Partnerships: Be ready for the beginning or ending of an important part of your life. To involve or find a new business partner is a strong possibility. You may feel comfortable with the person involved and sense that you can succeed with his inborn talent. Make a full commitment to succeed and work harder to get there.

Family and Friends: The Sun will give tons of radiant energy to the children. If you don't take them out to the park, your hands will be full for a couple of days with them. Let them get rid of the superfluous solar energy and keep your eyes on them. Many kids get hurt under this energy. You may be requested to enjoy Mom's great food at home in the security and safety of your own family. The family circle will be active these days and mother would be happy to hear about your progress. Expect an element of surprise coming your way with some friends' surprising arrival. You may want to plan a special gathering for a person to whom you are close. Great food, love and joy are on the agenda. Make the most of those rare and beautiful stars.

Love Affairs: Romance is on your mind more than ever, and a meeting with some friends could lead to an exciting love affair with an interesting stranger. Visit or call your friends; they need to share interesting news pertaining to love, romance and children. Enjoy the artistic intonation of the Sun during the night hours in a great show. If you are a Taurus, Capricorn or a Virgo will need to know you better and a Pisces might fall in love with you soon.

Travel and Communication: Again a time where anything you really want could happen if you ask hard enough. The Moon is still waxing and much of your trips are protected if you take precautions on the road. Flying is also under good auspices and planning for trips now will add more protection.

Environment: This will be an important time for the government to make decisions about a situation which needs to be dealt with. Many will be forced to relocate and start a new life due to previous natural catastrophes. Food and clothing could also be needed and sent to some parts of the world.

Famous Personalities: Many famous people will take part in some charity duty and many will donate money to alter the suffering of the world. Great news pertaining to new arrivals will make the family happy.

Events: The Sun's expansive power may affect some organizations. Expect some conservative groups to make the news about the earth, abortion or religion.

Shopping: Invest in gold; the stock market will take some by surprise. Anything charming and beautiful bought now will further fame or love.

Welcome to Your Day-to-Day Guidance For June 1998

June 1st, 1998 — Mercury enters Gemini: Witty Mercury enters his own sign in Gemini and with impatient Mars there too you will feel like being in orbit. Caution: be prudent on the road as Mercury rules speed and Mars danger. Many people driving with you are not aware of this duo and could pay the price of their cosmic ignorance. Make a good use of "Moon power" and keep reminding yourself of those two expeditious planets. Your telephone will be red hot and action will be everywhere. Mercury rules all the motion parts, your arms, fingers, shoulders, etc. Don't let Mars crack some of your bones. Be prudent and be patient in all you do and you will be protected.

MON., TUE., WED., THU., FRI. — JUNE 1st, 2nd, 3rd, 4th, 5th:
RULERS — Sun (power) Mercury (moving) & Venus (caring)

Work, Career and Business: This trio will make this week an interesting one in terms of actions and news. You will be occupied trying to cope with all the demands made on you. Local errands will keep you busy and bring you in contact with interesting people. Don't rush if you feel you don't make progress or if things don't go your way; all will change soon. Use the waxing moon to your advantage.

Partnerships: Expect new partners to show you their talents and be patient with them if they cannot follow your pace. The deserving hard-working souls will benefit soon with well-deserved promotions or a new opportunity for growth.

Family and Friends: A family member or a friend in trouble may need your advice. Be willing to consider the issue from their point of view; avoid emotional outbursts or forcing your opinion on them. You may receive an invitation to be part of a gathering; use this opportunity to get some of your wishes. Some of the people you know well will have to move away from you or you may decide to relocate soon.

Love Affairs: Don't be shy; go after the person you are attracted to. Propose to dine out or offer flowers. With the great Sun in charge your romanticism will be accepted. Use positive words and further your life now. With Mercury in the air you might also use a convincing approach to stimulate someone you care about. Your words can make a difference with a person who has lost some of the feelings they had for you. If you were born in June, a curious foreigner born in December or an original Aquarius may be looking for your love. Keep busy on the social scenery.

Travel and Communication: Some will decide to take a trip to Las Vegas and enjoy the night life. The waxing Moon (positive) may bring you luck. If you plan to travel far away, always make all your plans within the New Moon to protect yourself and further your wishes. Enjoy the wilderness and enjoy the best of what life has to offer. Use the growing new moon's energy to your advantage.

Environment: Wind could be a problem and speedy Mercury could produce sudden tornadoes some parts of the US. Expect activity from environmentalists fighting for the survival of wildlife and the earth.

Famous Personalities: Much talk and gossip will be available from celebrity magazines. A brother, a sister or a pair of twins may make the news.

Events: Hopefully Venus will stop any damage from explosions. News from France or Japan or the Middle East could be troublesome. Interesting new developments in biology, science and research are to be expected soon.

Shopping: Gifts offered to those you care about will bring much luck to their happy owners. You can find a good deal on a big-ticket item by comparison shopping. A perfect time to offer Starguide to a birthday person and bring the light of the Sun into someone's life.

June 9th, 1998 — Saturn enters Taurus: The great planet of structure will force many of us to plan for future financial security. Many deserving souls will benefit from Saturn's passage in the money sign of Taurus. Many important contracts will be signed and secured, and many progressive investments will be added to the security principle involving both earthy elements. Saturn is a karmic planet, so those who have used and abused society will be forced down from their high position of fame to shame and to the painful start. For the deserving souls, wherever Saturn is in your Taurus house you can expect a full and positive restructure of your self-esteem and finances. Children born with this position will gain a position of power where money, the arts or the earth (geology) is concerned. In time of stress they will experience problems with their neck. Thus massage is recommended and will be a part of their celestial gifts.

Full Moon — June 10th, 1998 in Sagittarius. Disturbing news from foreign lands is to be expected. Jupiter, the Lord of law and religion, will impose his righteous, dogmatic views on some lost souls. Dramatic transformations in the world of faith and the church are ahead. The previous wake-up call provided by Pluto's impact will induce a form of death and rebirth for some people. Pluto will bring to light the shameful manipulation, sexual and financial secrets of organized religions and some of their religious leaders. Pluto is still interacting with Uranus to further the truth and the new Age of Aquarius against the dying Pisces age. There is still a war in heaven.

Moon Power — Starguide 1998

> **Note**: Attention — Pluto is back with us — Expect dramatic happenings all over; control is a must. Don't be a victim; be aware of Pluto's destructive power. Anything you say or do under his power will follow you for the rest of your life. Time to use extreme caution in all you do. Killers, rapists, psychotics, and the worst of society will get active. While Pluto reigns, you'd better stay home and let the ignorant get killed. Time to make good use of my work.

SAT., SUN., MON., TUE., WED., THU. — JUNE 6th, 7th, 8th, 9th, 10th, 11th:

RULERS — Pluto (death principle) Venus (love principle) and Jupiter (faith principle)

Work, Career and Business: So close to a full moon, don't let Pluto make you too direct or radical until you really know what you're talking about. Be cautious in all you say or do. Pluto likes to further the animal side of man and will make us behave like such. Be aware that whatever you say or do now will have serious repercussions in your life. Stay on the side of the law and make a good use of Venus' diplomacy or you could end up sorry. Money will play an important part of this trend; use your intuition and turn down a hazardous business proposition.

Partnerships: Pluto is very choleric and nothing will stop him from inducing trouble in your life. Death, secrets, power, manipulation, sex and extra-marital affairs are his favorite. Venus is no match for her powerful brother Pluto and this duo will change you into a walking sexual magnet to others. Be aware and stay close to the one you trust.

Family and Friends: Be aware of everything and everybody around you. Keep an eye on the children; Pluto takes their young lives swiftly. Be patient with family and friends, avoid gossiping habits, help by cooling things down. Perfect time to mention my work just before this celestial trend; the skeptics will receive a full wake-up call pertaining to the stars' impact in their life.

Love Affairs: With Jupiter around, a foreigner you know will play an important part in the next dilemma of your life. Pluto will also make you highly sensual and magnetic; you should take all the precautions needed to avoid sexually transmitted diseases. Any love affairs started now will have a profound, even dramatic impact in your life. All water signs, especially Scorpios, will be affected by this plutonic impact; be aware, be prudent. Better stay home and watch TV.

Travel and Communication: Not a time at all to plan a long-distance trip or even to travel to faraway places. Use diplomacy in all your conversation and listen carefully; you will hear about secrets. Understand your investigation limits and do not let sarcasm or the Scorpio stinger affect your self-esteem. Stay clear of psychotic leaders and crowded places loaded with maniacs suggesting castration, suicide or drugs.

Environment: With the fast-approaching full moon of June 10th, nothing will stop Pluto from doing something tragic to the earth. Be ready for some serious mess with the worst of our society to shock the media.

Famous Personalities: Many financial or sexual secrets about a famous person will reach the media. Some unlucky souls will get a wake-up call from the dramatic planet. A public figure will make dramatic news or may be called to God. Under Pluto's power in May, 1997 sad news reached the media from New York when talk show divas Oprah and Rosie fought to a draw in the 24th annual Daytime Emmy Awards ceremony. And Susan Lucci lost again.

Events: As usual, be aware of the power of Pluto as dramatic news will plague the media. Expect news related to the police force, sex, scandals, earthquakes, secrets, abortion and AIDS. The police will be busy trying to catch the villains and hopefully none of the brave public servants will die doing so. The police force will make the news as they always do when their Plutonic ruler is in charge. Certified letters were sent to many prominent governmental figures and police chiefs all over, before and after the dramatic happening unfolded. A copy of both pages 87 and 36 of Starguide 1996/1997 where I predicted (over a year ago) the "Mass suicide" of March 26th, 1997 and "Bill Cosby's loss" were sent without any reply. None of those "educated" high board of directors had the decency or the courage to answer my mail. Events with the plain facts in their face, none of those public executives ever acknowledged my work in predictive astrology. Fear of ridicule kills your children and our police officers and I would think and hope that they would do something valuable for our valiant and courageous cops, such as training them and advising them of the incredible danger they face when Pluto is in charge. My research is unarguable and too many police officers have died in the name of their superiors' ignorance and fear of ridicule. Too many wasted lives, and this must change.

Shopping: Avoid investing in dangerous tools, weapons or ammunition. Pluto's awful signature of death should not be stored in your home. Doing so could kill your own. Beware of what cannot be seen or understood yet in terms of metaphysics could greatly cost you or those you care about. You may invest in anything that can be used to kill nuisances. If you buy dangerous substances, keep them well away from children.

June 15th, 1998 — Venus enters Cancer: Perfect time to plan on launching any real estate endeavor after the upcoming new moon of June 24th. Home improvement, buying or selling a beautiful house is on the agenda for some. You may also plan to invest in anything beautiful for the home, but be patient before spending money. Souls born now will be soft and emotional in matters related to love and family. They will make money with business endeavors involving hotels and restaurants. Many of them will strive to find a partner willing to exchange deep emotions and spiritual research. Some will have to learn to let go of wrong relationships. This position makes for one of the most sensitive signs of the Zodiac. Usually a gift in cooking is present with this position. Those souls are born to feed the world with food and love. A top position involving financial security, communication and success in any real estate, sales and the artistic field.

FRI., SAT., SUN., MON. — JUNE 12th, 13th, 14th, 15th:
RULERS — Saturn (mastering self) & Uranus (shocking surprises)

Work, Career and Business: With a waning Moon (positive) many of your wishes won't be granted just yet. Don't invest in your future; you may regret it. Do not turn down an invitation offered by friends that you know well; they may require your presence at a gathering. People you meet now should be heard with a grain of salt. Those of a certain age will offer valuable intellectual guidance.

Partnerships: Expect the beginning or ending of important parts of your life and be ready for surprising developments. Your life at work may be unstable now and those changes will give you the opportunity to focus on plans for a better future. Support your partner with words of courage.

Family and Friends: The weekend could be spent with family members, good friends and Mom's good food. Some will prefer to dine out with lovers or business partners, but the experience could be troublesome. Time to experience patience with everyone around you and avoid doing anything original.

Love Affairs: Absolutely anything great can happen if you are lucky enough to be involved with the right partner who really loves you. Don't gamble on anything or try to reach for your dreams just yet. Throw a party, but avoid new faces; old friends have the best to offer. Participate with life to avoid depression and if you are a Pisces, a Cancer or a Scorpio may fall for you. If the person is new in your life, don't dream, use your head.

Travel and Communication: Make the best of Saturn and "Moon power" in your life by planning future trips and by being prudent on the road. Curiosity is the pathway to fulfillment and happiness and Saturn will reward you for your celestial planning. Take care of the children and let them participate in all the great activities in your city. Be aware of eccentric Uranus affecting them; have a good time and enjoy it all. Some may have to relocate to a different residence; make sure you do your Astro-Carto-Graphy before then, as these "new" stars may affect you positively or negatively. Read the section Astro-Carto-Graphy if you need more information and don't be afraid to call the office at 1-619-275-4416. Being at the right place at the right time has a lot to do with your progress in terms of opportunities. This work would be a major contribution to your success (or your failure) in one of these new locations. Keep this opportunity in mind and give it a try — it works!

Environment: Stay clear of thunder and lightning; Uranus takes many lives by surprise. Expect him to throw a quake, a tornado or blow up a volcano soon. Let's just hope you won't be in his way!

Famous Personalities: Crazy behavior in public by some famous people is high on the list. Some will get engaged, married in a very large gathering and some others will expose their strong desires for freedom.

Events: Under Uranus' power in CONROE, Texas — A fire ignited a small oil tank causing several explosions outside an Exxon oil refinery and forcing the evacuation of 40 refinery workers and nearby residents. Disco death Philippines — 150 people died in a discotheque fire. Alaska fire burns 'out of control' June, 1996. HOUSTON, Alaska — Fueled by gusty winds, a wildfire has swept "out of control" in south-central Alaska, where it has engulfed 7,000 acres and destroyed as many as 100 homes.

Shopping: Invest in Uranus now: visit your astrologer or favorite psychic only if you know him well. Don't bring new spiritualists into your life now, especially if you have never dealt with one before. Unless you feel strongly about one of them, don't do it. Any of those light workers are karmically attracted to you and the reading could be one of your best or your worst psychic experience. Uranus rules astrology and if you are attracted to the stars there won't be a better time for you to realize what the old science has to offer you.

TUE., WED., THU., FRI. — JUNE 16th, 17th, 18th, 19th:
RULERS — Neptune (deception) and Mars (aggression).

Work, Career and Business: As usual with Mars' aggressive personality, expect all sorts of trouble with business partnerships. You are strongly advised to use diplomacy to avoid serious complications, especially during a waning Moon. If you are experiencing some trouble in your career, a serious change may be ahead of you. Neptune will make you absent-minded; try to concentrate. A little walk by the water would do your spirit good.

Partnerships: The Lord of dreams may make your spiritual life busy and some of your dreams may come true in the near future. Learn to translate your subconscious impressions and write your dreams first thing in the morning. You or your partner may be responding to Neptune's power, so you may want to reach your inner self asking for God's help in your prayers. Some may feel tuned into the universe and miraculously guided out of a bad situation.

Family and Friends: As usual with Neptune's sad touch combined with the waning moon, sensitive friends may get depressed. Be there to help, but don't let their problems get to you. The lonely old ones will feel the impact of Neptune upon their life and its accompanying deception. Give a thought and pay them a visit or send them a little card. This gesture will make them feel less lonely and will make their own world more exciting. Be ready to offer a strong shoulder and realize the impact of Neptune upon your world. If you are an Aries, an Aquarius friend needs you.

Love Affairs: Keep your eyes on your possessions as things may "disappear" now. Don't let yourself into a deceiving business deal or worthless situation; learn to love with your head first and give your heart later. Your intuition will be sharp; use it to your advantage.

Travel and Communication: Remember, Neptune is also part of this trend and if you have to drive, you MUST stay clear of any alcohol. Neptune leads many unaware people to jail with a DUI to deal with. If you were born under the sign of Leo, an Aries or an Aquarius person may give you trouble. A Sagittarius person will be wondering about you.

Environment: Venus will try to stop her violent brother from stirring the earth's entrails as Mars loves earthquakes, explosions, volcanoes and mass disasters. Sad news may come from the ocean, the Middle East and oil spills.

Famous Personalities: Some prominent people may be caught in a secret sexual or love affair. Their dependency on chemicals, drugs or alcohol will be made public. The lucky ones will promote a new movie. Under Neptune's power in May of 1997 — West HOLLYWOOD, California — Sheriff's deputies pulled over Eddie Murphy early Friday and arrested a transsexual prostitute who was riding in his car, authorities said. A spokesman for the actor maintained Murphy was just being a "good Samaritan" by offering the transsexual a ride.

Events: Cairo, Egypt — A powerful sandstorm tore through southern Egypt Saturday, killing at least four people. The storm comes a day after the worst sandstorm in 30 years blasted across the country. With Mars' aggressive nature, expect this type of news again. Villains to be active during this trend; do not trust strangers and do not put yourself in any situation that could make you a potential victim. Avoid dark streets and keep your personal alarm (intuition) on all the time.

Shopping: Try to participate in volunteer work to provide love and help to the needy. Shop in places promoting a good cause; they need your financial support. Not a good time to invest in prescription drugs or visit your spiritual advisor, unless you know him well.

SAT., SUN., MON., TUE. — JUNE 20th, 21st, 22nd, 23rd:
RULERS — Venus (love torn apart) and Mercury (meaningless chatter).

Work, Career and Business: The Moon is still waning; forget about making any progress now. This is a time where you'd rather get away from it all and enjoy quietness by the water. Maybe you should try it for a while; you will feel the music in your soul and you would enjoy the break. Keep your head out of the swarm of stress, let go for now and put a big smile on your face. People tend to react positively to a smiling face and a happy heart. Better times are on the way; the new Moon is not too far, just be patient.

Partnerships: Someone is upset. Perhaps you should apologize with a romantic dinner; don't expect it to be perfect, but it would help your situation. Mercury will pass on all sorts of news including some financial or sexual secrets. A great time to improve your cosmic consciousness and do some inside soul-searching. See what makes you so different and what can be done to make your lives better.

Family and Friends: Save a difficult relationship with a friend or a family member; now is the time to use diplomacy and understanding. Expect disturbing news with brothers or sisters and take the time to reply to the mail. Mercury rules communication and will help you pass on your thoughts deeply and correctly. Don't let the waning moon sap your faith; stand strong, tomorrow is always better.

Love Affairs: This trend may induce stress and may require both of you to control destructive emotions like jealousy and suspicion. Love Affairs started now could be stressful and unproductive in the long run; use your head, use Starguide knowledge. This energy will also force many unsuited couples to get out of their unhealthy relationships. The worst of both of these planets is to be expected mainly due to the fast dying Moon. Now is the time to use all the diplomacy you were born with to save your relationship before it's too late. If you are a Virgo, don't be too critical with an older or younger person born in January or May who is attracted to you.

Travel and Communication: Venus will help those willing to use her gentle touch of love in all they do. If you were born with a passionate Venus in Scorpio, you will be challenged by this celestial trend. A very high level of suicidal tendencies will be enforced upon many souls these days. Stay clear of chemicals, drugs and alcohol.

Environment: The police will be needed in some situation where nature will get out of hand. Let's hope Venus will slow down Mercury's windy nature and stop him from producing hard weather or tornadoes.

Famous Personalities: Nothing good will come out of this trend pertaining to the rich and famous. Scandals, sex, drugs and all the tools used by the "devil" will be made public. A very famous but unlucky person may also get assassinated.

Events: Many public servants will meet with their deaths trying hard to help those in trouble or in speedy chases and violent confrontations. Be aware, don't be a victim, use Starguide wisely and if you know someone involved in the Law Enforcement let them read this book. With Pluto (death) still cruising through the religious sign of Sagittarius, different agendas and passion will run high. A nasty confrontation with foreigners could be the outcome. Let's hope the diplomats will work hard to a common agreement before it's too late for some.

Shopping: You may purchase anything dealing with cleaning the environment. With Venus' desire for peace and love, buy flowers and give fresh love. Take serious precautions if you happen to be in the dating game with a stranger met in a public place. Make him invest in a sexual protective item.

New Moon — June 24th, in Cancer. With the Moon so close to the earth, this specific lunation will have an important effect on many of us. Expect the beginning or ending of important phases of your and other people's lives. This lunation could represent a very significant part of your destiny. You may be forced by the universe to let go of your past and forge into your new future. Whatever the changes are, go with confidence. Many will be affected and forced to move on and around you due to previous natural catastrophes or simply to further specific wishes.

WED., THU., FRI., SAT. — JUNE 24th, 25th, 26th, 27th:
RULERS — The Moon (shift) and the Sun (source of all faith).

Work, Career and Business: Examine all business propositions carefully and if they do fit your rational mind go for it. The Moon is now waxing, so much progress is to be expected soon. Some may be forced to relocate, start or finish a business. Many of the stars are on your side and you should be confident in the outcome. Invest now.

Partnerships: The beginning or ending of an important part of your life or a business partnership is a strong possibility within the next few days. As you know, nothing is made to last forever and somehow a wrong business partnership must end. Again a time where anything you really do need could happen if you trust in yourself. Be patient with someone responding to the Sun's desire for power. Good time to meditate by the ocean or the river about the high purpose of your joined fate, your relationship and how it fits in your life. The Sun will make these days particularly romantic and beautiful for some.

Family and Friends: The Sun rules the children and love. Take the kids out to the park, but keep your eyes on them as, sadly enough, some have disappeared under this energy. Some vampires out there regenerate only by dealing with children and they will do all it takes to satisfy their unhealthy hunger. Accept the upcoming transformation with faith as the changes will promote a better life. You may want to plan a special gathering with someone you are close to. A friend will have to move away soon and this could bring tears. The family circle will also be active these days and mother will be requesting your presence. Enjoy Mom's food at home in the security and safety of your own family if you are in a new area and do not know many people. Expect an element of surprise from friends.

Love Affairs: Romance is on your mind more than ever and a meeting with some playmate can lead to an exciting love affair. You may feel comfortable with the person involved and sense that you can succeed; with the New Moon on your side you may end up with a form of commitment. If you are a Libra, someone born in April, June or February may give you the opportunity to experience real love.

Travel and Communication: Surely an interesting trend full of changes and surprises. Still, be careful in all you do and don't take chances. Visit or call your friends; they need to share interesting news. Great time to plan for future trips to Europe; you may also use the creativity of the Sun to start or finish a book. With the Sun (life) in charge, much of the destructive news will be seriously altered. Flying is also under his protective power. Use a positive approach in all your words and you will attract more luck.

Environment: Much work will be done to further life and security these days and nature will be radiant with life. If you are out in the wilderness and you plan to cook, beware. Some accidental explosions could still happen, as some of the propane gas containers might have been purchased under a vicious energy or under the bad Moon.

Famous Personalities: On the negative side expect weird news and dramatic ending of relationships. On the positive side, news of births, marriages.

Events: This will be an important time for your company or your local government to make decisions about a situation which needs to be dealt with. Thousands of people may be forced to relocate and start a new life due to new construction plans or previous natural catastrophes. Expect some stubborn conservative groups to make the news about abortion and religion.

Shopping: Investing in real estate or any expensive items will bring great joy to the owners. Great opportunities are to be found also at the swap meets and antique shops. Shop for anything that will further life and happiness. If you need to invest in something dangerous such as gas propane, cookers or sharp and dangerous items to take out to the wilderness, you can do it now.

SUN., MON., TUE. — JUNE 28th, 29th, 30th.
RULERS: — Mercury (action in words) & Venus (feelings of love)

Work, Career and Business: Time to reorganize your strategy and a few things around you. Use the new Moon and look for a better way to develop a better business. The new Moon in Cancer will make everyone very sensitive, so be gentle with the staff if you are in charge. Your boss or your employees are going through some changes and you must be patient with them. With the New Moon upon us, soon all will be fine again.

Partnerships: Important people are watching you; present an attitude of brightness and courage in front of difficulties. Some of your partners can only admire your inner strengths and will follow your example. Don't let anyone create a negative energy with uncontrolled disturbing thoughts. You are the example.

Family and Friends: Keep busy with the children as speedy Mercury will give them tons of energy. Let them spend time outside the home. Watch them closely and see yourself as a child doing exactly what kids do best, playing! A great opportunity to burn calories if you can keep up with them. One of them may need specific attention.

Love Affairs: Expect interesting surprises coming your way. With Venus around, love may enter your life without much notice; however, this world is a physical one and you must participate in the activities if you have any chance to succeed in finding what you're looking for. Do not stay home now as anything great could happen to you. Use that great New Moon to enjoy nature and the sea. Keep in mind that Venus rules love and romance, and if you are single you must take a chance. If you are a Scorpio, a Cancer or a Pisces will find you irresistible. A Taurus might get you down to your knees.

Travel and Communication: We are still in the positive Moon, and a strong desire for changes will be felt all over. Go on the road and make the most of this lunation. With Venus also there, some may drive to or find the love they are looking for. The month of June is about to end and with it a portion of your life.

Environment: Expect progressive news pertaining to concerned groups warring for the environment. They are after those wealthy executives who make money destroying the earth. They share the selfish attitude of that long-gone French King, Louis the 15th who use to say to his servants, "apres moi le deluge," after me the deluge.

Famous Personalities: Great news is also ahead with some famous personalities endorsing and supporting great community acts. New and beautiful love partners are in the air for some.

Events: Nature should be quiet during this great trend where love, romance and communication will reign. The only trouble I expect is with Mercury winds; he may decide to blow his own horn and create tornadoes in parts of the US.

Shopping: Satisfy Venus' desire for beauty. Invest in a fitness program or a diet; the results will amaze you. If you need a checkup now, the stars are in your favor as your physician will be accurate in his prognostication. Surgery is also fine and you can add anything to your body; cutting is permissible with those stars. Control your imagination as Mercury could get your mind going wild with all sorts of silly fears about your health.

Welcome to Your Day-to-Day Guidance For July 1998

July 1st, 1998 — Mercury enters Leo: Because of the impact of Pluto (decay and rebirth) this intense trend promise is loaded with a mixture of drama and statements related to love, creativity and children. Lots of thoughts will be geared towards an immense feeling of despair and true love. On a more positive note, souls born with Mercury in Leo will be gifted with a natural managerial disposition. Many of them will be born shrewd in business and attracted to the professions offering fame and fortune. Artistic talents involving music, dancing, painting will lead these souls toward the great fame and security they seek. This position makes for one of the most mentally domineering signs of the Zodiac. As with Venus in Leo, this Mercury position will lead the soul toward success in many artistic endeavors. An opportunity to experience mental fame is also offered to the soul.

Note: Attention — Pluto is back with us — Expect dramatic happenings all over; control is a must. Don't be a victim; be aware of Pluto's destructive power. Anything you say or do under his power will follow you for the rest of your life. Time to use extreme caution even in time of a waxing (positive) Moon. Happy July 4th to all. Please be aware as Pluto could ruin this holiday for you. Watch the children and avoid giving them explosives now. Many of them did lose their sight or their fingers playing with firecrackers. Time to make good use of my work.

WED., THU., FRI., SAT., SUN. — JULY 1st, 2nd, 3rd, 4th, 5th:
RULERS — Venus (enticement) & Pluto (fatal attraction/sex).

Work, Career and Business: You may be forced to realize the end of an era and the beginning of a new section of your financial life. Your wishes for a better business may not match your situation, Pluto will see to it and force you into a rebirth. Because of the New Moon involving the drama, it is all for your benefit in the long run; be at peace with yourself.

Partnerships: Time to enjoy good food, red wine and real sex! If you are in the wrong relationship, Pluto will free you soon. The opportunity to find real love will finally be given to you then. Better use diplomacy in all you say and do; you may end up sorry if you don't. Some secrets may come your way; keep them for yourself and respect Pluto's desire for privacy.

Family and Friends: Expect dramatic news from all over within the next few days; be ready to take care of some friends in trouble, but realize your limits. Everyone will have a short temper; don't let Pluto affect your psyche. Use the New Moon and beautiful Venus' diplomatic power with everyone around you.

Love Affairs: The great planet of love will make you feel good about yourself and will give tons of charm and beauty. Be aware of mysterious Pluto and his sensual magnetism. Accompanying Venus he could transform you into an irresistible sex magnet. Trouble may come your way if you fall for passion in unprotected sex activity. Fight insecurity and jealousy, avoid stressing. A love relationship started under this trend will be passionate and long-lasting. If you were born in December, a Gemini or a Leo will get your heart. An Aries person could prove difficult around you.

Travel and Communication: Pluto tends to choose the weakest or the strongest members of our society and play with their emotions. Whatever you say or do now will have incredible consequences; be diplomatic, stay clear of trouble. Do not stop for anyone on the road; let the police deal with Pluto. If you are with the children, it's time to watch them closely; this celestial mixture is totally against the children and many will fall victims of abusers.

Environment: As always, keep in mind that Pluto couldn't care less about a New Moon in his honor and could do some serious damage with nature's devastative forces, just to remind us of his power.

Famous Personalities: Famous people will meet with their death in a secret battle against chemical abuse. Avoid large crowds where emotion and passion reign. Be aware of the destructive power of Pluto; do not take chances.

Events: Do not trust strangers and avoid unfamiliar places. Pluto stirs man's animal tendencies. Pluto rules the crooks and the Cops, or the infinite forces of good and evil constantly teasing each other. The crooks will become more active and the police will try hard to cope. If you are a Police officer or a security guard on duty now, don't take chances, as the worst could happen to you. Some children will make sad news.

Shopping: Invest in your soul and your reason to be on earth. Time to visit your psychic friend and ask for direction. If you are into kinky stuff (smile) anything involving sexual toys will do the trick now. This sexual behavior and interest is produced by a mixture of Pluto (power/leather/sex), Venus (sensuality/enticement/beauty), Uranus (weird/freedom/original), and religious Neptune's vibration (deception/guilt/hidden).

July 6th, 1998 — Mars enters Cancer: The planet of danger is entering the sign regulating home and family. Mars is called the Lord of war for good reasons, so do not let his temperamental spirit produce war at home, and insure your home against fire. Much of your desire will be geared towards securing yourself, and this celestial manifestation may induce selling or buying a new home. Souls born with Mars in Cancer will spend much time working on improving their home environment. Beautiful gardens, restorations of cars, real estate endeavors, construction and business involving the Cancerian security and food principle are part of this astrological position. Be aware around the house as Mars regulates sharp instruments and tools. On a negative aspect, Mars regulates war, and in Cancer (home) the soul may lose his life for his country. Mars and Pluto are both destructive planets, so beware. Note: Millions of people all around the world lost their precious lives when Pluto (death/masses) passed through the home and family-oriented sign of Cancer. America, July 4th 1776, a Cancer country, lost many of her children in the many deadly conflicts.

Full Moon — July 9th, 1997 in Capricorn: Expect some serious career or personal developments to take place. Some will be starting a new job, and others drop one, this could also include a business relationship. Promotion or deception, whichever happens to you (or others), will mark an important part of your life. Just be ready to accept the upcoming changes with faith in your new future. Be ready to provide a supportive shoulder to the victims. Nature can also decide to do nasty tricks on some states, promoting destructive weather or earthquakes in the very near future. The government will have to make serious steps to promote peace in the world.

MON., TUE., WED., THU., FRI. — JULY 6th, 7th, 8th, 9th, 10th:
RULERS — Jupiter (philosophy on life) & Saturn (career demands)

Work, Career and Business: With Pluto's dramatic experiences behind us, many will keep a low profile and must accept the intense transformation. With benevolent Jupiter, the future has much better to offer and now you should be more confident in all your dealings. Jupiter, "the Lord of Luck," will make this transition easy and may even decide to throw you some luck; listen to your intuition and keep a positive attitude. A new career or a new beginning is on the horizon.

Partnerships: With Saturn's touch expect to work harder to organize or rebuild it all. For the hard-working souls, a promotion of some sort is coming your way. Money will also be on your mind, and serious decisions will have to be made soon. Nothing comes easy; one must strive and plan if he is to succeed. You might have to let go of someone or a portion of your business life soon.

Family and Friends: You may receive or give presents to the deserving family member or dear friend. With the new Moon, take the time to enjoy the week and the good food offered to you and if you decide to socialize during the night, expect interesting developments. A foreigner could make you happy and further an important wish.

Love Affairs: Someone much older or much younger could surprise you — Don't be shy with life; take a chance with someone you care for; there is plenty to gain in the long run. This endeavor may lead to an opportunity to further your career. If you are single and born under the sign of Capricorn, a Virgo or a Cancer will be getting closer to you. Listen to a friend born in November.

Travel and Communication: Expect your telephone to be busy and interesting mail to come your way. Don't try to be in so many places at the same time, and if you have to drive, take extra time to get there; don't rush as the police could spoil your day. A brother or a sister needs to talk to you. Keep a positive attitude; remember, positivity attracts positivity.

Environment: Close to a Full Moon, mother nature may decide to stretch herself and surprise some. Environmental groups will get active and will receive support from the media to save the earth from uncaring corporations. The earth will be active soon; stay clear of bridges as much as you can.

Famous Personalities: The great loss of an old and eminent political, religious or entertainment figure will plague the media soon. A group of people will work hard to help those starving in an area affected negatively by nature.

Events: March 28 under this energy 80 people were killed in a fire that gutted a shopping center in the West Java town of Bogor, about 40 miles from the capital, Jakarta. June, 1996 HOUSTON, Alaska — Fueled by gusty winds, a wildfire swept "out of control" in south-central Alaska, where it engulfed 7,000 acres and destroyed as many as 100 homes. Some terrorists groups could also get really ugly, and surprising destructive explosions are on the way.

Shopping: Surely a good time to spend outside before the upcoming Full Moon as Jupiter will replenish you with fresh air and a new approach to life. Good time to experience Las Vegas for the gamblers; however, keep it in control. The Moon is still waxing (positive) until the 8th of July; make the most of this interesting time. Don't waste this positive trend — get going after your desires.

SAT., SUN., MON., TUE. — JULY 11th, 12th, 13th, 14th:
RULERS — Uranus (amazement) & Neptune (trickery)

Work, Career and Business: Combined with the Full Moon, Neptune may make you feel depressed and overemotional at work on Monday; this could lead you to think about a new job. Keep your eyes and ears open; with Neptune's "dreamy" nature, you are prone to make serious errors or forget to do something important. Do not sign any contract now; in the long run, you will be sorry if you do. Be patient until the next New Moon.

Partnerships: Crazy things may happen now; do not make a fool of yourself in public. Things done or words said without forethought might bring trouble later. Use your will; be positive in all you say. Expect disturbing news by mail or telephone, but avoid fears as insecurity could take over your common sense; all will be fine, there is a Divine plan for you. This timing is ideal for meditation and renewing your faith in each other and the universe. You must control negative thoughts, even if many things around you do not seem positive.

Family and Friends: Spend some valuable time with your family. Do not expect the affairs of the heart to progress or get better for a while and teenagers may get themselves in trouble. Give them solid direction and be ready for some friction. Depressed friends may call you asking for spiritual support or direction. Confusion and deception is in the air with Neptune and if you socialize during the night hours, keep your eyes on your possessions, as they may disappear. Don't misplace your keys. Avoid complaining about life problems to those who care for you.

Love Affairs: Love and romance may suffer as during a Full Moon, Uranus' erratic emotions may take over and disturb your relationship. Be patient with the partner and use diplomacy to save trouble. However don't let someone else's problem get to you and affect your feelings. If you are single and born in February, a Gemini and Leo will be strongly attracted to you. A friend from a foreign land will bring you surprising news.

Travel and Communication: If you can, avoid flying during this trend unless you made your reservations before the waning Moon. Protect yourself against aeronautical accident; use "Moon Power" and your knowledge, take no chances. Perfect time to pass on the light and talk about Starguide guidance. Avoid drinking and driving at all costs; many accidents happen under Neptune's and Uranus' iniquitous energy. If you have to play or travel, avoid the ocean or the river these days.

Environment: Expect bad news about quakes and the possibility of sea/air accidents. Many naturalists will be upset and some groups will make a dramatic decision followed by dangerous actions. Nature will start to go berserk and may throw a bunch of negative weather patterns such as tornadoes or earthquakes in the near future. The Titanic sank under this energy; when Neptune, "Lord of the seas," gets angry, he likes to create huge waves and sink ships. This phrase was printed in the *1993 Starguide Moon Power* and gave the exact date of January 6th, 1993 for the following disaster. On Thursday, January 7th, 1993 The New York Times reported: "The Liberian oil tanker Braer sank yesterday off the Shetland Islands. Rough waters prevented the containment of what officials said could be an environmental disaster."

Famous Personalities: Many unaware famous daredevils will lose their lives because they have no knowledge of the stars' impact on human affairs. Do not take chances after the Full Moon, ever, and all will be fine.

Events: Under Uranus' powers following a post on the WWW.
Return-Path: mary41@ix.netcom.com
From: mary41@i.com
Date: Thu, 1 May 1997 To: drturi@pacbell.net-
Subject: Earthquakes

Dear Dr. Turi — I posted a note on alt.astrology that cited the 6.7 quake off the coast of Mexico in the Pacific Ocean. I included it under the rather "nasty" piece of mail that someone sent indicating that they believed your window of probability for April 30 to be invalid. Not that I think you need defending, as I have found your work very compelling. I just thought I'd let you know — in case you didn't — that you were "right again." On the late night of April 30, the 6.7 quake took place. Mary

Shopping: Provide spiritual guidance and support to all in need. Many will fall victim to Neptune's deceiving and Uranus' eccentric will. Do not invest in alcohol now; you would further a disaster later on. Some people out there are not aware of the stars' impact on their lives and may decide to jump from a bridge or a plane; good luck to them. You may invest in my work for them, mention or offer them 1998 Starguide, this can and will save them trouble. Avoid investing in any form of electronics; a nasty virus may get to your compueter.

WED., THU., FRI., SAT. — JULY 15th, 16th, 17th, 18th:
RULERS — Mars (desires/men) and Venus (love/women):

Work, Career and Business: The Moon is waning (negative); think twice before committing to an investment program. A hunch might save you trouble if you are unsure about a scheme. Don't let Mars affect your judgment; be patient with everyone around you. Expect upsetting financial news; don't let it get to you, you can only do so much. The future will offer better opportunities. Just wait patiently for the next New Moon; do some clean-up and reorganize around you.

Partnerships: As usual with Mars' aggressive personality, expect all sorts of trouble with partnerships. As always with the

Lord of war around these days, you are seriously advised to use discretion in all you do or mention to avoid serious complications. Keep in mind that the Moon is waning (negative) and not to expect much progress in any of your endeavors for now. Finish up a project or re-evaluate a situation.

Family and Friends: A difficult trend is taking place; do not let it get to you. Use your will and look for happy people. Starguide is preparing you for this type of celestial affliction; take a passive attitude and all will go your way. Use Venus' loving touch to provide spiritual help to those you care about with practical advice, but realize your limits. You need your own spiritual strength to face those tough stars.

Love Affairs: Expect some secrets to be divulged, especially the ones related to sex or financial scandals. Venus' gentle nature will reward you if you use her diplomatic, loving powers to smooth things out. Better stay home and enjoy good food during the late hours. A great movie with the one you care about this weekend is your best shot. Many will fall prey to con artists and weird sexual endeavors. If you are single and born in March, a Taurus or a Scorpio could be looking for you. A Cancer friend will give you good advice, but do not complain too much if you want to save your friendship. Stay clear of alcohol consumption.

Travel and Communication: After the Full Moon try to stay or deal with the people you know and avoid dangerous dark alleys. Keep your eyes open and your personal alarm (intuition) on all the time. Mars rules man's animal instincts and he could stimulate one of his aggressive children (Mars in bad aspect) to hurt you given the occasion. With any trouble on the highway, stay inside your car with the doors secured. Many violent crimes have been reported during this type of energy, especially when drugs or alcohol are involved; take no chances.

Environment: Soft Venus will try to stop her violent brother Mars from stirring the earth's entrails and producing earthquakes, explosions, volcanoes and disasters. In time of a waning Moon she might not have much influence on her turbulent brother, so be ready for destruction from the red planet, Mars, "The Lord Of War."

Famous Personalities: This same type of energy has taken the lives of many famous people, sometimes dramatically. Drama, sex, scandals of all sorts will go public and may induce a suicidal tendency in some prominent people. Stay clear of any chemicals and be aware around the water.

Events: Mars will stimulate the villains; expect them to be active during this trend. Again, do not trust strangers and do not put yourself in any situation that could make you a potential victim. The police will make disturbing news and many officers will be dispatched to cool off many situations, especially domestic violence. If you are in law enforcement, beware; Mars could hurt you; don't take any chances.

Shopping: Do not deal with finance these days. Avoid investing in tools or sharp instruments. Some will get bad news from their creditors and bank accounts or credit cards will be a source of trouble. Do not open a bank account now; the negative energy will induce unneeded financial stress in your life.

July 20th, 1998 — Venus enters Cancer: Wait for the upcoming New Moon of July 23rd, then it will be a perfect time to concentrate on launching any real estate endeavor. Home improvement, buying or selling a beautiful house is on the agenda for some. You may also invest in anything beautiful for your house; again, wait for the upcoming New Moon to do so. Souls born now will be soft and emotional in matters related to love and family. They will make money with business endeavors involving hotels and restaurants. Many of them will strive to find a partner willing to exchange deep emotions and spiritual research. Some will have to learn to let go of wrong relationships. This position makes for one of the most sensitive signs of the Zodiac. Usually a gift in cooking is present with this position. Those souls are born to feed the world with food and love. A top position involving financial security, communication and success in any real estate, sales and the artistic field.

New Moon — July 23rd, 1998 in Leo: This sign is ruled by the Sun, thus affairs of love and romance will be on the rise. Expect some surprises this month; the stars are giving you the possibility to reach one of your important wishes if you try hard after the upcoming New Moon of July 23rd. This lunation could play an important part in your love life and will surely your relationships. You may also be forced to let go of a deteriorating love association and experience a new one. This month promises to be very interesting for many of us. Make the most of this incredible time; don't waste it.

(* Means refer to this section when you see the star sign.)

Second Supernova Window July/August 1998

From Tuesday, July 21st through Thursday, August 27th, 1998.

Specific dates of extreme caution:
July 13th, 21st, 31st, August 7th, 13th, 18th.

July 13th, 21st & 31st, 1998 — Large quakes, tornadoes, loss of power, blackout, electronic disturbances/aeronautical and sea accidents.

August 7th, 13th & 18th, 1998. Thousands of people to relocate — Concentration of natural destructive forces and a succession of earthquakes, hurricanes, flooding and tornadoes. On those days, expect loss of power and blackout.

Be extremely prudent in driving, and expect chain-reaction accidents. Be prepared for delays, strikes, nature producing awful weather, including hurricanes and tornadoes. The same energy that produced both the Northridge, Los Angeles, and Kobe, Japan, earthquakes is approaching us again. Double-check all your appointments, and if you can, postpone traveling and flying during this Supernova "window." Communication and electricity will be cut off; general loss of power is to be expected. Appliances, computers, telephones, planes, trains, cars — all of these "tools" will be adversely affected by this energy.

They will be stopped in one way or another. The people of the past will make the news, as people from your past will reenter your life. Expect trouble with the post office, education, students, prisoners, newspaper, broadcasting industry and computer viruses may bother us again. As usual NASA, which is not aware of the science of astrology, will waste our tax money with a failed mission due to bad weather and/or electronic malfunctions.

All these malevolent predictions do not have to hurt or touch you as they unfold. Instead, they are printed to prepare you for setbacks and frustrations, thus advising you to be patient and prudent during this trend. Smile, it's just a short time really.

SUN., MON., TUE., WED., THU. — JULY 19th, 20th, 21st, 22nd, 23rd.
RULERS — Mercury (notification) & the Moon (new beginning).

Work, Career and Business: Great news is to be expected soon in the work and career scene, and progressive changes are on the way. Make the most of Mercury's intellectual powers to review your business life and do some financial planning. Concentrate on everything important, then go for it with faith. Lots of progress ahead; make the most of this progressive trend.

Partnerships: The Moon will be up and happy soon; prepare to do all you can to further your partnerships and if you have to, look somewhere else. There are plenty of great souls walking this earth; just ask for your happiness and let go of the past. Use Mercury's strength to fight against moodiness and depression. Give spiritual help to those who have been touched by the bad Moon.

Family and Friends: Your maternal instinct will show itself to your children. Share your knowledge with friends; help them to understand some of the secrets of life and make them understand their emotions which are regulated by the Moon's passage through each and every sign of the zodiac. The subconscious response to the moon's fluctuations upon humans is referred as "lunatic behavior or moodiness" and right now you may realize and understand the full impact of its meaning. Expect the beginning or ending of important parts of your or others' life. Expect some surprising news from the children. A close friend needs your attention to deal with an emotional situation.

Love Affairs: realize your limits, be honest with your feelings and make the needed changes. Your own future, positive or negative, is mostly based upon your decisions. An old friend who lives far away may need to communicate with you; use Mercury and write those letters. Don't expect great news until the next new Moon, and provide support as long as you not being used. A love from the past could bring you more trouble than anything else. Time to let go. If you are an Aries, a Leo or an Aquarius could fall for you. Someone born in December could be a bit of a problem sometimes.

Travel and Communication: If you have to travel for a business purpose, make sure to structure your trip during the upcoming New Moon. Don't let ignorance stop your progress, but do not promote important business just yet. Expect the mail and your telephone to bring you unwanted news. Some of us will experience communication problems and trouble with appliances or the car.

Environment: The Moon's waning energy could induce stress on the faults, so that many people will be forced to relocate soon following natural disasters. It's time for her to stretch herself and restructure her inside. Mars is still in Cancer; be aware of fires.

Famous Personalities: The rich and famous will be planning a reunion to feed the children of the world. Their artistic gifts will benefit many generous organizations. Some other crazy famous people may make surprising news trying to use Mercury (press) power to gain free publicity.

Events: You could hear about the military performing deeds that will aid the general public and save lives from a disaster area. Under this celestial manifestation on August the 8th, 1996 — Wildfires burn in 6 Western states — Wildfires that had burned nearly a quarter-million acres in the Western United States remained out of control Thursday in at least six states. The same energy was active on June 17, 1996 SIDON, Lebanon — Five people died and 15 were wounded Monday when explosions sparked by an electrical fire ripped through a house used as an arms depot, Lebanese security sources said. Seven other houses also were destroyed.

Shopping: Anything that needs to be replaced in the home or the garden. Avoid signing anything related to real estate endeavors until the next New Moon. Beware of food poisoning; buy and consume food right away. The negative Moon may induce troublesome bacteria in some items.

FRI., SAT., SUN., MON. — JULY 24th, 25th, 26th, 27th:
RULERS — The Sun (Light and life) and Mercury (sparkling genius):

Work, Career and Business: Don't let the burning power of the Sun take over your management skills. Keep in mind that we are still human and have egos that sometimes get out of hand. Make the most of the Sun's and Mercury's revitalizing energy to further your business life. Interesting surprises and progress are on the way. You've been waiting for this new Moon long enough; push now.

Partnerships: We are under a waxing Moon and you can feel the valiant Sun's power light up your relationships. Time to offer presents or flowers to those you care about. You should nurture happiness and feel rejuvenated; your spirit is free and happy. Use this long-awaited new Moon to your advantage; get active with life.

Family and Friends: The emphasis is on the children, love and creativity for the next few days. A trip to the wild or the zoo would be rejuvenating for the entire family; get your camera as those laughs and sincere smiles are priceless. With Mercury's speed affecting the kids, watch over them carefully around the water. If you feel sorry about a situation, Mercury will help you to find the perfect words to heal emotional wounds in the form of apologies. Expect interesting surprises coming your way via telephone, mail or social activity. Use this powerful lunation to your advantage; get yourself in shape and do something different this weekend.

Love Affairs: Love can be found practically anywhere, especially if you set your mind to it and participate in all the activities. Throwing a party will pay off for some, and love may just enter your own home by chance. Again, don't stay home this weekend if you are invited; the Sun may reward your heart's desire. One of your important wishes is in the hands of a friend; don't miss the party. If you are single and born in May, a person born in November or March will be strongly attracted to you. A friend born in September or January may be too critical or too distant.

Travel and Communication: use all the beautiful words you can think of. Everyone will sparkle with the Sun's power. Make plans now for a trip close to the water. Let those you care about know that you miss them and you'll be there soon. Travel is under the protection of the Sun.

Environment: The Sun in Leo will oppose Uranus these days, and this aspect could remind us of our vulnerability against the shocking destructive forces of nature. With the new Moon with us, let's hope that no earthquake will come and remind us that the earth is still very much alive. Trouble may be coming from an accident involving children. Keep your eyes open, especially close to the water.

Famous Personalities: Many new figures will show up on the entertainment field and much work will be done to produce the best of the best in the arts. Great movies are being made and expected in the fall. Some famous actors will get in or out of business and love relationships.

Events: Are you into the extraordinary? If so, bring and use your camera all the way to the wilderness as UFOs have been active under this energy. The Sun's light brings the undiluted truth to whoever wants to see or experience the incredible power of the divine.

Shopping: Anything expensive, gold, cars, electronics for the children. Presents bought and given now will bring luck to both of you. Invest in all that show true love and you will win the heart of that person later.

> **Note**: Attention — Pluto is back with us for a few days — Expect dramatic happenings all over; control is a must. Don't be a victim; be aware of Pluto's destructive power. Anything you say or do under his power will follow you for the rest of your life. Time to use extreme caution even in time of a waxing (positive) Moon.

TUE., WED., THU., FRI. — JULY 28th, 29th, 30th, 31st:
RULERS — Venus (Caring) and Pluto (rebirth):

Work, Career and Business: The Moon is waxing (positive) and much can happen as long as you understand how to use Pluto's and Venus' energy positively. Promote your business life now, advertise, reach the people, travel. If you do, soon your telephone will be busy and the mail will bring awakening news. You will be soon be forced to realize what is wrong in your career, and the changes are on the way.

Partnerships: A new plan is needed to succeed in your endeavor; use this trend to get rid of what or whom is bothering you. Expect some secret to resurface soon. Nothing can really go wrong if you use Venus' diplomatic gift to deal with others and aim high with them.

Family and Friends: Expect news from your brother or sister; you might get in touch with some of your friends for a good chat. Do not fall for gossiping; you may end up trapped in a sandwich.

Use the positive Moon and Venus kind-hearted nature to promote your life. Surely a good time to appreciate your loved ones or plan a dinner at home or maybe just see a great movie. Avoid Pluto's sarcastic remarks or you might be sorry later.

Love Affairs: Combined with Venus' sensuality, Pluto will give you the power to "stimulate" your partner in many ways. Candlelight, soft music and words of love will pay off big. A trend loaded with powerful emotion and good energy where nothing wrong can happen if you play your cards right. A foreign person could play an important part of this trend and later on your future. If you are single and born in June, a person born under the sign of Libra or Sagittarius will be strongly attracted to you.

Travel and Communication: The call of nature will be strong for many. Enjoy the wild and water and make plans for a fishing trip; the river or the sea has a lot of fish to give away and for some magical reason they will all bite the bait. Drive slowly; don't spoil your day with a speeding ticket. Watch over Pluto's destructive communication ways and use Venus' diplomatic manner instead.

Environment: Many mother earth supporters will march to be heard by government officials and they will succeed in their request to save the environment. Pluto is about to show his power and will induce some disasters. Dramatic news for some unlucky souls is to be expected.

Famous Personalities: An important legal action pertaining to an engagement will be taken by a famous entertainer. Another famous figure may have to leave this world. Large corporations will find strength in their new association.

Events: The government will make important decisions to change or establish laws against criminals. The police may make some disturbing news as Pluto will pick on the weakest members of our society to disturb the rest of us. Expect nature to get out of hand and accidents to plague the media.

Shopping: Cameras bought now will take dramatic pictures or will be used against criminals. Invest in anything that will be used to clean up your environment. Good metaphysical books can also be bought and used for your own mental progression. Spruce yourself up by brightening up your wardrobe. Purchase or wear black or red garments; it will bring magic to you.

Welcome to Your Day-to-Day Guidance For August 1998

> **Note**: Attention: Pluto doesn't care much for the waxing Moon; he is still with us — Expect dramatic happenings all over; control is a must. Don't be a victim.

SAT., SUN., MON., TUE. — AUGUST 1st, 2nd, 3rd, 4th:
RULERS — Pluto (drama of life and death) and Jupiter (foreigners)

Work, Career and Business: With Pluto in charge these days, if you are a law enforcement professional, be aware and do not take chances out there. Some large organizations will be forced to deal with the law and this may affect your own business on a later date. Time to rebuild and plan a new strategy to improve your public standing. Use your intuition and with Jupiter's benevolence you could get a lucky break.

Partnerships: As always with the Lord of Hades around, be aware of the energy surrounding you. Remember, now is the time to socialize or deal with strangers with caution. Even within a good moon, do not trust anyone as Pluto triggers man's killer instinct. Like wild animals, villains, rapists, psychopaths will be looking for their prey in deserted areas. You may find things out that help you settle your fears about a business proposition. Avoid the restless crowds and keep away from trouble or any lunatic's promise for another world.

Family and Friends: Secrets will be uncovered as friends will readily communicate with each other. Brothers and sisters may also get in touch with you for help or spiritual guidance. Better stay in the security of your home and communicate by telephone if you don't know the person in question. Avoid sarcasm and use diplomacy; do not let Pluto upset you.

Love Affairs: Again, be especially careful in dealing with strangers, and take precautions against sexually transmitted diseases. Pluto has a strong drive for sex, and his passion for action is very strong. Be ready for secrets to surface and remember to use these secrets to your own advantage. If you are single and born in July, a Scorpio or a Pisces will be strongly attracted to you. Listen to the advice of a friend born in May.

Travel and Communication: The police will be extremely busy trying to cope with the madness of these nights, as the blood of innocents and ignorant will stain the dark streets of our cities. Some people will be forced to realize the hard way the full word of diplomacy and its consequences when omitted.

Environment: Pluto won't stay quiet; watch the drama unfold with mother nature and mankind becoming the victim of his awful passionate and shattering nature.

Famous Personalities: Unaware of Pluto's power, sex scandals, murder, secrets, drugs, etc., all is there. There is no room for ignorance in Divine Astrology even for the wealthy. Some will pay the price and will make sad news. A famous person will be called to God and many will be saddened by the news.

Events: Keep in mind that Pluto does not care much about the New Moon and chances are that he will disturb the earth's belly, producing a bad quake. Pluto rules ultimate power, the Mafia and the police force. Dramatic news pertaining to the police force confronting the villains is to be expected.

Shopping: Finances will play an important part of this trend, and you are strongly advised to avoid financial discussions, committing yourself or signing important documents until this nefarious energy goes away. Use your intuition in terms of shopping and be aware of your decision to purchase any items of destruction.

Full Moon — August 8th, 1998 in the explosive sign of Aquarius: There will be an Appulse Lunar eclipse on this day. "Appulse" means a penumbral eclipse where the Moon enters only the penumbra of the earth. (*) — Expect some serious surprising developments to take place in the near future. The same energy produced the Middle East "US surprising bombing attack" on Saddam Hussein's forces in Iraq. This energy can affect sophisticated electronic equipment and produce a bad aeronautic accident. Unlucky children could suffer this disturbing dramatic lunation; keep an eye on them as they are accident-prone for a while. Just be ready to accept the upcoming changes with faith in God's desire to restructure the earth's entrails. Be ready for nature's devastating forces producing destructive weather, tornadoes, earthquakes and volcanic eruptions. Expect anything surprising, even incredible to take place soon and see the real power of Uranus, the planet of sudden release of energy, in action.

WED., THU., FRI., SAT. — AUGUST 5th, 6th, 7th, 8th:
RULERS — Uranus (destruction) and Saturn (rebuilding):

Work, Career and Business: * — Do not expect to make much progress for a while; many of your plans will fall apart. Listen to other people's stories; the stars affect everybody and they may come up with interesting, even surprising news. Be ready to invest in some appliances or equipment. Saturn will help you to make some great adjustment after a careful planning.

Partnerships: With Uranus in charge, anything and everything unusual can happen and with a waning Moon (negative) upon us, do not expect great news. Restaurants will be busy; better make reservations if you don't like to be turned down. However, any changes should be accepted with faith in yourself and the new future. Be patient with everyone around as Uranus may make them eccentric.

Family and Friends: An opportunity to meet with some family members you have not seen for a while will be given to you by this lunation. The past will come alive again and an old friend will reappear soon. A person who owes you money sincerely wants to repay, but may be in such a difficult set of circumstances that he or she can't. Be patient as he/she may repay you in a different way. A friend who has invited himself and who has been a house guest for a while may need a little push to get him/her out of your domicile. Providing help is great, but let people know your limits.

Love Affairs: Be ready for the incredible to happen; if you are in a karmic relationship, changes are needed. Friends may fall in love with other friends or mistake love for friendship. An old love or an old friend long gone will reappear in your life soon. If you are single and born under the sign of Leo, a Scorpio could give you trouble and a Sagittarius may be attracted to you. A friend born in June has a lot to tell you.

* See page 198

Travel and Communication: A business trip or an invitation may lead you to many good contacts from the past. However, you might have a problem getting to the given address and will get lost a few times. Be patient as you will still have plenty of time to play and enjoy yourself with various and unusual people. For the UFO investigators, now is the time to look for them in secluded places; don't forget your video camera; you may be sorry if you are not ready when Uranus is willing to display the secret of an extraterrestrial intelligence. Stay clear from tall trees and posts to avoid lightning; many people met their death within a stormy Uranus trend.

Environment: Expect this type of news to happen: Australian wildlife officials made repeated attempts to prevent up to 300 long-finned pilot whales from beaching themselves on a remote part of Australia's west coast. Mammals' and birds' navigational systems get confused when Uranus is in charge and many get lost.

Famous Personalities: Very surprising behavior or news will come from the rich and famous. Disturbing and sad news about a famous child could reach the media. Fire and electrocution are high on the list; be aware.

Events: * — Uranus loves accidents and explosions; under his power expect surprising and original pieces of news such as: Four people died when a Marine Corps electronic warfare plane went down in the desert. It was the third military plane crash in two days. Two teen-agers were killed when a butane pipeline broke and exploded in northeast Texas Saturday.

Shopping: Not a time to purchase new electronic equipment or plan a long voyage by air to a foreign land. As always, Uranus rules the future, and his psychic powers can be used through your trusted local psychic or astrologer. Second-hand shopping will pay off for some.

* See page 198

SUN., MON., TUE., WED. — AUGUST 9th, 10th, 11th, 12th:
RULERS — Neptune (deception/illusion) and Mars (battle).

Work, Career and Business: Use Neptune's intuition and meditation as a great tool to face setbacks and difficulty. Don't let the waning Moon bring you down; reevaluate your business venture. You may need to take more time to focus clearly on your future and create a vision that will become a blueprint or a pathway. New goals require some hard work, but you have all the needed tools to make it happen. Be confident of your abilities and be steady in your efforts. Do not give up on your dreams but be practical.

Partnerships: Gloomy Saturn is in the sign of Taurus and may induce insecurity or financial worries. He may force many of us to find a practical way to restructure our finances and experience a form of rebirth. A word of caution about Saturn's depressive nature: be patient and use his structural power to your advantage. You must get rid of insecurity feelings or they could seriously affect your partnership. You'd better invest in financial planning to promote your business sense. Under his rulership you could also improve your natural artistic abilities. With Jupiter (traveling) in Pisces you may be able to regenerate your spirit by traveling to an exotic place. Complete or start a spiritual study and you will experience the realization of an important wish.

Family and Friends: Take care of your health without being too overconcerned with it; Neptune may produce melancholy and vivid imagination that could affect the "Temple of God," your body. You and those you care about will feel a lot better after the New Moon; be patient until August 22nd. Eat right and get plenty of exercise, and a better attitude will help you through this negative lunation. Keep away from alcohol as Neptune may depress some of us. Use plenty of words of support for the victims of Neptune's depressive mode.

Love Affairs: With Lovely Venus residing in the sign of Leo you may have an attraction for an interesting happy person, or you may be asked to take a trip soon. Some will start a secret love affair that will bring deception in the long run. Love can be found close to the water this weekend, but don't count on the promises you may hear. If you are single and born in September, a Pisces or a Capricorn (much older or younger than you) will be strongly attracted to you. A movie at home is your best shot; be patient with life.

Travel and Communication: Stay clear of alcohol consumption if you have to take the road. You might have to go back in your past and enjoy some old friends soon. Take plenty of rest if you decide to take a long trip; Neptune may sap your energy and make you feel sleepy on the highway. Chew gum if this happens to you, Neptune hates it! you may not be able to arrive on time but you will be in one piece. Be patient and courteous with others as Mars may make them aggressive and impatient. Check your wheels before leaving; lots of people will fall for Mercury retrograde and will be stuck in the airport and along the side of the road.

Environment: Many devastating oil spills have happened under Supernova windows. Let's hope I am wrong this time. The weather will turn out really nasty and may stop you. You might have to reschedule some of your plans. Be patient.

Famous Personalities: Prominent people will make sad news pertaining to drugs and alcohol. Some water sports figures are in serious danger now. Eminent religious or foreign figures will make the news. Bad news for the Pope or religions in general.

Events: Mars is getting stronger towards the end of the week and may decide to create serious trouble with nature's forces. Expect devastative news of earthquakes, tornadoes and very uncooperative weather. This trend with Mercury retrograde won't be an easy one as death will catch many unaware souls. Better stay home these days or be extremely prudent in your words and action.

Shopping: Great time to conclude artistic projects, but avoid starting a new class involving the arts now. Don't invest in your future now and stay away from psychics. Their caring spirits will suffer Neptune's illusion and deception. Mars (desire) is now in the sign of Leo (Children). Much depends on your awareness of his dangerous temper to save children from trouble. On a more positive note, Mars will deepen your creativity and may lead you to invest in a new artistic study. Spend on candles and do a cabalistic candles ritual. Burn white, blue and green candles and use incense to purify your environment and your spirit.

August 13th, 1998 — Venus enters Leo: Perfect time to concentrate in launching any artistic endeavor. Giving and receiving expensive items is on the agenda for some. You may also invest in a car or gold; however, wait for the upcoming New Moon to do so. Souls born now will be very magnetic and dramatic in matters related to love. They will make a good living and will attract money in artistic endeavors. Many of them will strive to find a beautiful, rich and famous partner willing to exchange a deep zest for life. Some will have to learn to let go of Mr. Pride and Mrs. Ego to save true love. This position makes for one of the most dramatic but lucky signs of the Zodiac. Usually a gift in acting or other great talents is present with this position. Those souls are born to experience a flamboyant and busy love life. A top position involving fame and fortune for those involved in the artistic field, creativity or children.

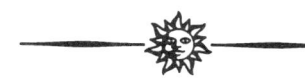

THU., FRI., SAT., SUN., MON. — AUGUST 13th, 14th, 15th, 16th, 17th:
RULERS — Venus (softness) & Mercury (meaningless gibberish).

Work, Career and Business: The worst of both of these planets is to be expected mainly due to the waning Moon (negative) and the pessimistic trend of Mercury retrograde until August 27th, 1998. Do not fall for depression and self-defeating attitudes. You may communicate your feelings but avoid uncontrolled imagination. The stars have a specific role to play in your life and you are the actor. Go with the trend, do not force issues, be patient and further your business life after the New Moon. At work keep a low profile, your co-workers or your boss may not be aware of the work of the Moon on their psyche and could become "lunatic" with you. Keep busy on Monday and rearrange your desk or your paper work.

Partnerships: If you want to save a difficult business relationship, now is the time to use full diplomacy and understanding. Using Venus' love touch, you could apologize with some flowers or a romantic dinner. With Mars still in Cancer expect some action in the real estate area. Take serious precautions if you happen to be in the dating game as Mars, Venus and Mercury could mean impatience and speed.

Family and Friends: Expect disturbing news involving friends, brothers or sisters and take the time to reply to the mail. If you get caught on the telephone, mold the discussion towards a positive note. Mercury rules communication and will help you pass on your thoughts deeply and correctly. Again, provide a helping hand, but do not let abusive or depressive friends take the best of your own spirit.

Love Affairs: With Venus in Leo, many will feel the passion, and secret love affairs may be started with someone from their past. However, do not expect this undercover relationship to stay a secret for long. Love affairs started now could have a dramatic impact in your life. Many unsuited couples will also be forced out of their unhealthy relationships and realize the end of a section of life. Mars in Cancer, danger may come from the home, and the emphasis these days will be on destructive behavior and violence. If you are single and born in October, an Aries or an Aquarius could be difficult just now. Listen to a Leo friend for advice.

Travel and Communication: (*) Mercury will pass on all sorts of news including some of a secret nature. A great time to improve your cosmic consciousness and do some "deep" reading concerning life and death or metaphysics. Great time to finish your book if you are into writing. Drive slowly and be ready for obstacles on the road.

Environment: (*) Tornadoes, hurricanes, earthquakes, chain-reaction accidents due to bad weather are very high on the list. Stay safe and be aware of mother nature's destructive forces. She is alive and she needs to stretch herself now and then.

Famous personalities: A famous personality from a foreign country will see the end of his life. Many will miss his message and his great spirit.

Events: With Mars in Cancer at home, the US, acts of terrorism could produce devastative explosions. Stay clear from crowds and listen to your intuition at all times. Avoid crowded places and beware of foreigners.

Shopping: Electronic equipment, car, telephone, computers, etc., may decide to give up on you. This is only Mercury retrograde in action. The purpose behind this disturbing energy is to give work to those who build moving parts (cars, etc.) and rely on your future trouble to survive. Fix it or rent it but do not buy anything new now. Take care of your car as the machine may decide to let you down at the wrong time and in the wrong place. Be cautious and be patient.
* See page 198

TUE., WED., THU., FRI., SAT. — AUGUST 18th, 19th, 20th, 21st, 22nd.
RULERS — Mercury (transmission) and the Moon (endings).

Work, Career and Business: You may find it difficult to concentrate on your duties as your mind will wander about everything at the same time. The deserving hard-working souls will benefit with well-deserved bonuses or a new opportunity to promote their career. Some may face the ultimate end of a portion of their business life. Whatever happens, you must accept the changes with faith. Your desires or dreams may not fit your present situation and the stars may decide to shut you down. It's for your best interest.

Partnerships: Some of the people you know will have to move away from you or you may decide yourself to relocate to a better place. Expect the beginning or ending of important phases of your life and others too. Watch the drama of life taking place as old people must be replaced by new ones in many aspects of the human experience.

Family and Friends: You may receive an invitation to socialize with some faraway dear friends or family members; use this opportunity to get closer to them. This waning Moon trend (negative) may prove to be sad for many. You and some friends get together to socialize; you may be the one doing the entertaining. Keep in mind that the Moon is now waning and you can always do better when she turns new again soon. A family member or a child needs your advice. Be willing to consider the issue from their point of view; avoid emotional involvement or forcing your opinion on others. Most of all provide spiritual support.

Love Affairs: With a waning Moon upon us do not expect much progress in the area of love. The people from the past will become heavy and could produce stress in your life. If they bring good memories, have fun, but don't get too caught up in the nostalgia. If they were negative in the first place, stay far away from their charms the second time around. Nobody really changes. If you were born in November, stay clear of alcohol. A Cancer or a Taurus may find you too depressive lately. Listen to a friend born in September; you may learn something. Don't let guilt drag you down; life must go on.

Travel and Communication: Local errands keep you busy and bring you in contact with interesting people. This trend brings difficult mail and reminds us of our responsibility. Mostly, be cautious and prudent in your driving as people may not see you. Drive slowly and go visit your past.

Environment: Nature will go berserk and like last year on May 10, 1997 earthquakes could be devastative. TEHRAN, Iran — A powerful earthquake jolted Iran's rugged Khorasan province Saturday, killing nearly 2,400 people and injuring an estimated 6,000. The U.S. Geological Survey told CNN the quake had a magnitude of 7.3. Nature may also show her power with shocking weather. Thousands of people may be forced to relocate. Many unaware daredevils or unlucky souls will lose their lives because they have no knowledge of the stars' impact on human affairs. You may suggest or offer them a copy of *Starguide;* a little information is better than none, and that is the purpose of this publication. They will probably love you forever because of this practical, thoughtful gesture.

Famous Personalities: A famous person (or their children) could make dramatic news traveling around. Lots of interesting news about many famous people who left us a long time ago. Some will work hard to provide housing or clothing to the world at large.

Events: Uranus rules aviation, and with Mercury retrograde, he could alter electronic equipment and this could produce another dramatic air crash. Not a time to fly or take any risks. Blackout, tornadoes, volcanic eruptions, including rough weather are high on the list

Shopping: Don't overspend, no matter how glittery the gift in question is. You can find a good deal on a big-ticket item by comparison shopping. Not a great time to visit Las Vegas' casinos as the waning Moon (negative) may make you unlucky. Better make all your plans in the New Moon, starting very soon to enjoy the best of what life has to offer you. Don't stress; understand and use the stars; they are there to be used and make life easier.

New Moon — August 22nd, 1998 in Leo: This sign is ruled by the Sun, thus affairs of love and romance and children will be on the rise. Expect a couple of large surprises these days and the possibility one of your important wishes. This lunation could play an important part in your love life and will affect your relationships with children. You may be forced to let go of a deteriorating love association and move into a new one. Some will give life to beautiful children. This month promises to be very interesting one for many deserving souls where fame and fortune will be offered to the deserving.

SUN., MON., TUE., WED. —AUGUST 23rd, 24th, 25th, 26th: RULERS — Mercury (smart-aleck) and Venus (elegant):

Work, Career and Business: The Moon is finally waxing (positive) and much can happen as long as you understand how to use her energy constructively. Promote your business life now, advertise, reach the people, travel and participate in the universal growth. If you do, soon your telephone will be busy and the mail will bring promising news. Get going in all your communications, use Mercury's wit to find a solution to your problem.

Partnerships: A plan is needed to succeed in your endeavor; use this trend to acquire new equipment for your office and reorganize your environment. Nothing can go wrong if you aim high and do something about it. Use Venus' "tact" to get what you need from others. Enjoy the evening with a romantic dinner talking about a potential business venture.

Family and Friends: Expect news from your brother or sister; you might get in touch with some of your friends for a good chat. Don't let Mercury get out of hand; avoid gossiping, you may end up trapped in a sandwich. Use the positive Moon to promote your life and try to excel in all your wishes. Surely a good time to appreciate your loved ones or plan a dinner at home or maybe rent a great movie. Kids need attention; give them some time especially if they ask for help.

Love Affairs: With Venus in the air these days, candlelight, soft music and words of love are pretty much on your mind. A trend loaded with good energy where nothing wrong can happen if you know how to play your cards right. A foreign person will play a considerable part in your future. If you are single and born in December, a Leo or a Gemini wants to know you. Listen to a Libra friend's advice.

Travel and Communication: Driving away from the city would be a good idea. The call of nature will be strong and the fresh smell of the out-of-doors or seascape will regenerate your soul. Enjoy the water or make plans for a fishing trip, the river or the sea, but keep an eye on the young ones. Drive slowly, don't spoil your day with trouble.

Environment: Many mother earth supporters will march to be heard by government officials and they will succeed in their request to save the environment. Nature may surprise some of us with a volcanic eruption.

Famous Personalities: An important legal action pertaining to an engagement will be taken by a famous entertainer. Large corporations will find strength in their new association. Much work will be done by concerned groups to further children's welfare in a foreign land.

Events: France or Japan may make interesting, even surprising news soon. The government will make important decisions to change or establish laws that will benefit children.

Shopping: You may invest in anything that will further your education or the arts. Cameras bought now will last long and take incredible pictures. Good books can also be bought and used positively for your own progression and mental exploration. Spruce yourself up by brightening up your wardrobe or, if you can afford it, invest in expensive jewelry.

August 23rd, 1998: Neptune in retrograde enters the sign of Capricorn: Located in the down-to-earth sign of Capricorn, Neptune, the planet of illusion, will advocate a form of deceptive energy to the world. In the practical sign of Capricorn (structure), Neptune's creative energy is being utilized to the maximum. Responding to the deceiving Dragon's Tail in Pisces, another wave of reborn evangelists will take to the bullhorn, using the "last days" of the Apocalypse, making fortunes in deceiving the uninformed, God-fearing religious masses. On November 28th, 1998, Neptune will return to the sign of Aquarius where he will stay for several years to come. On the artistic side, combined with Uranus' electronic ingeniousness in Aquarius, Neptune (movies) in Capricorn (structures) will promote a serious increase in creativity and a solid restructure within the cinematography industry. On a spiritual side, more spiritually elevated spiritual leaders will began to transform Neptune illusive/pious vibrations into an advanced Uranian astrologically oriented generation.

> **Note**: Attention — Pluto doesn't care much for the waxing Moon, he is back with us — Expect dramatic happenings all over; control is a must. Don't be a victim; be aware of Pluto's destructive power.

THU., FRI., SAT., SUN., MON. — AUGUST 27th, 28th, 29th, 30, 31st:
RULERS — Pluto (wake-up call) and Jupiter (sanctuary):

Work, Career and Business: Hopefully the New Moon energy will make all of those changes positive in the long run. Push forward for the next few days; make the most of this lunation. At last the negative Supernova trend that has plagued many of us is now over. You may also find out why you had to go through so much stress. Be ready for a form of rebirth and accept your limits. A new business proposition may further your entire business life. Time to review all your accomplishments and the reasons for your failures. Meditate on improving your future and if you feel you need to educate yourself in some area, do it now; there is no time like the present!

Partnerships: Money will play an important part in your life now, and you are advised to keep a close eye on your bank account. You may inherit a few expensive items, and this will help relieve a form of stress you had to experience. Commitments made now could become very fruitful in the long run. You may also make a commitment on paper as we are still under the blessing of the New Moon. You may decide to spend some time in nature or to visit an old Church in response to Jupiter's religious nature. Some may decide to go to the desert and "see" the creator displaying his lightening face in the universe. We will all receive God's full support from the stars.

Family and Friends: Many will be enjoying foreign places and the different cultures of these people. Expect news from brothers and sisters from afar and let yourself be immersed in this great summer season. The circle of friends will be extremely busy as we are all enjoying the best of what life has to offer. Children are very excited and will be enjoying the festivities. Uranus may make them restless, and a trip out of the house is in order. Watch over them, especially close to the water. Use diplomacy at all costs; Pluto will make everyone around you very susceptible to your comments. Control emotion and watch what's going on in the house, especially if children are around. A great time is ahead of you if you listen to your intuition. A friend may bring a stranger in your house; watch the young ones closely. Be aware of Pluto and don't let him upset your life. Enjoy it all.

Love Affairs: Expect secrets of a sexual nature to surface to the light and new secret affairs to be born. The planet of passion will make you feel good about yourself and will give tons of charm. Be aware of mysterious Pluto and his sensual magnetism. Do not drink too much during the evenings. Accompanying Jupiter could transform your life with a passionate foreigner into an irresistible sex magnet. The Moon is still waxing, but trouble may come your way if you let your passion express itself with unprotected sex. If you're born in January, a Cancer or a Taurus could mean love.

Travel and Communication: Pluto rules ultimate power, the Mafia and the police force. News pertaining to the police force will always appear during his ruling days. I can hear Police Executives of the future, in the training Academy warning their officers of the impact of the power of Pluto and how vulnerable they all are under his destructive jurisdiction. I can also foresee the use of Astrology to pinpoint who the bad guys are, using their natal profile and the impact of Pluto in a sensitive house predisposing him for murder. Then many brave public servants won't have to waste their precious lives because of ignorance or fear of ridicule. Time will tell.

Environment: Keep in mind that Pluto does not care much about the New Moon and could disturb the earth's belly, producing a bad earthquake. As usual with Pluto in charge, be ready for many interesting secrets to surface and remember to use these secrets to your own advantage.

Famous Personalities: A famous personality will be called to God and many will miss the soul. A reminder of our own mortality.

Events: Do NOT TRUST any strangers now, as Pluto stirs man's animal tendencies. Pluto rules the crooks and the Cops, or the infinite forces of good and evil constantly teasing each other. Thus the villains will become more active and the police will be busy trying to stop them. Of course if you are a Police officer and on duty now, don't take chances.

Shopping: Invest in anything that can kill pests and use Jupiter to find a great traveling bargain.

Welcome to Your Day-to-Day Guidance For September 1998

TUE., WED., THU., FRI., SAT. — SEPTEMBER 1st, 2nd, 3rd, 4th, 5th:
RULERS — Uranus (surprising wish) & Saturn (responsibility):

Work, Career and Business: Expect this trend to promote surprising changes pertaining to your career. The lucky ones will benefit from the New Moon trend and get rewarded for their long and enduring work. Make the most of the waxing Moon and get your wishes. Saturn may force you to realize what needs to be done to further your career.

Partnerships: Time to socialize as Saturn's children (CEOs) will be out in public places and many of them can further your career wishes. This trend will induce serious changes and interesting surprises in your partnership also. A business trip or an invitation may lead you to many good contacts that could prove to be rewarding in the long run You must take the time to play and enjoy yourself with unusual people.

Family and Friends: A friend may request some money from you or another one who owes you money sincerely wants to repay, but may be in a difficult set of circumstances. Be patient; they may repay you in a better way. A friend may surprise you and may decide to come closer to you. Providing help is great, but let some of your friends understand their limits. Keep in mind that Uranus rules friends and wishes; do not turn down an invitation for a party or throw your own. With Uranus, anything can happen and with a waxing Moon (positive) the changes should be positive.

Love Affairs: As usual with Uranus be ready for nice surprises brought by friends bringing new people into your life. The Moon is still up, so those surprises should be of a positive nature. Many lucky souls will find love, and this new relationship may lead you to a rewarding future. Remember, serious Saturn is also part of the festivities and you must not overindulge. If you were born under the sign of Aquarius, a younger or older Leo or a Gemini will find you irresistible.

Travel and Communication: Your telephone and your mail will bring you all sorts of news and invitations. The lucky ones will enjoy or plan a faraway trip close to those they love. Expect news from many people around you and get in touch with some of your friends for a good chat. However, do not fall for gossiping about other friends as sooner or later you will have some explaining to do. Use the positive Moon to promote your life and excel in your mental capacity.

Environment: As always with Uranus with us, a volcano could erupt soon; be ready for surprising news about the weather. Stay clear of lightning.

Famous Personalities: Famous people will offer the best of their performance and the money will be offered to organizations supporting the very old or the very young.

Events: Saturn (structure) still reside in Taurus (money) and could induce some worries about your finances. Don't let it get the best of you. Financial affairs will be a concern for many as the government will make very important decisions about other countries in the world. With the New Moon trend on us (positive) nothing seriously wrong could affect you now. Uranus rules the incredible, UFO investigators; now is the time to carry your camera and look for them in secluded places. A blackout could plague some parts of the US.

Shopping: Great time to purchase electronic equipment or plan a long voyage in a foreign land. As always Uranus rules the future and his psychic powers can be used. Don't waste those days; do something original as your wishes depend on your interaction with others.

Full Moon — September 6th, 1998 in the sign of Pisces: There will be an Appulse Lunar eclipse on this day. "Appulse" means a penumbral eclipse where the Moon enters only the penumbra of the earth. This sign is ruled by Neptune, thus religion, the abortion dilemma, fear of the apocalyptic end of times, deception, illusion and secret affairs are on the agenda. Bad news ahead for any and all denominations where religious figures will "pass over." Expect negative developments pertaining to oil spills and the Middle East to take place in the near future. The same Neptunian energy produced the Valdez disaster and the sinking of the Titanic in 1912. Sad news is to be expected with drugs affecting the young generation and many souls will suffer this disturbing lunation. Just be ready to provide as much help as needed and do not lose faith in the future. More devastating forces producing destructive weather and flooding in the very near future. Expect a general feeling of hopelessness plaguing the media and the church authorities. Deceiving news will take place and affect many of us; some desperate souls will fall for Neptune's suicidal tendency and some will end up in jail or a mental institution. This trend will be very difficult for some, but do not lose faith in yourself and trust the Universe; get all the help you can to fight Neptune's depressive tendencies; amuse yourself, keep busy and let go of the past. Life must go on.

September 7th, 1998 — Venus enters Virgo: Perfect time to concentrate on your health and launch an exercise program or a diet. Giving and receiving plants or flowers is on the agenda for some. You may also decide to invest in some good deal in clothing. Souls born now will be quite critical in matters related to love. They will concentrate and achieve perfection in many of their artistic endeavors. Many of them will strive to find a "perfect" and hard-working partner willing to exchange a love/career relationship in their life. Some will have to learn to be less critical of the world around them in order to avoid loneliness. This position makes for one of the most practical and enjoyable joint endeavors. Usually a gift in dealing with details and an interest in health matters is present with this position. These souls are born to experience love on a practical level. A top position for involvement in the medical or the clothing field. Plants are needed around those souls.

September 8th, 1998 — Mercury enters Virgo: A trend loaded with communication related to work, health and service to the world. Lots of thoughts will be geared toward finding a better job or working on improving health. Souls born now will be gifted with a natural ability for details and the opportunity to learn everything they can about health. Many of them will be born with an aptitude for investigation and literary powers. Some will be attracted to the professions offering mental work; rewards of fame and fortune will come to the writers. The artistic talents of editing, dancing, writing, photography, painting and general health will lead these souls towards the body and mind security they seek. This position makes for one of the most critical signs of the Zodiac. Souls born with this Mercury position will have to learn to avoid criticism as the soul is looking for a perfect mate, with a perfect attitude and a perfect job. The problem is that no one is perfect and the soul may suffer long periods of time alone. However, an opportunity to experience mental fame is offered to the advanced soul. A great position for writers and editors.

SUN., MON., TUE., WED. — SEPTEMBER 6th, 7th, 8th, 9th:
RULERS — Neptune (deception) and Mars (offensive):

Work, Career and Business: We are now into the Full Moon (as of September the 6th). Listen to intangible impulses from a different plane than the physical before making an important decision. Avoid insecurity and imagination to blur your vision or your faith during this trend. Neurotic tendencies and depression come from a heavy Neptune in anyone's chart; use your will and see the bright side of your business life. You may find it hard to concentrate at work on Monday or Tuesday, but everything will be clear again in a couple of days. Keep emotions in control; use plenty of patience and diplomacy with co-workers or the boss if you happen to work on Sunday. Try to concentrate on the future.

Partnerships: Mars is called the "Lord of war" for good reasons. Do not let him aggravate a situation, as this could hurt a friend or a loved one. The purpose of Starguide is to teach you firm control over the stars and to manage positively the outcome of any situation. If you know someone who needs help, offer it as a birthday present. Mars also rules cars and machinery, and with deceiving Neptune around, avoid drinking and driving (you should never do this but right now, even a little could hurt you). Danger could enter the lives of those ignorant of the celestial rules just now; beware. You will be given energy from the red planet; make good use of it by channeling the power constructively. Still, Mars' energy can help you to start a new project, new business even a new relationship. Keep a positive attitude.

Family and Friends: Help some family members see through the veil of self-deceit. Some of your friends may need spiritual support; work with them without getting emotionally involved in their problems. Keep away from alcohol after dark if you decide to meet them. A trip close to the water or Sea World will be rewarding. Keep a vigilant eye on the kids and your pet as impatient drivers could hurt them. Be prudent, be patient but firm and confident. Spend some time with the children, teach them love and harmony as Mars may make them play rough. Be aware around water. Remember my prediction about children playing rough with Mars. (Moon Power 1997 page 116) Memo: Water slide collapses kills one, injures 32 — An amusement park water slide collapsed Monday June 2nd, 1997 after a group of high school seniors on a graduation outing ignored a lifeguard's warning and went down together. One student was killed and 32 were injured, six critically. Be aware; watch the kids around water.

Love Affairs: Come right out with what you feel and don't be vague in love matters. Secret love affairs will start under Neptune's deceiving power and many will end up deceived; beware who you tell! Avoid drinking heavily and enjoy a great walk by the sea or any watery area. If you are single and born in March, a Cancer or a Scorpio will be strongly attracted to you. In any rate do not expect much with love now; you'd better wait for better auspices.

Travel and Communication: Some of us may have strange experiences in unfamiliar places or find themselves with weird people. Keep an eye on your personal belongings and learn to rely on your gut feelings. Nevertheless, you can expect heavenly intervention in a dangerous situation. For those at sea, take all precautions as the weather could turn nasty without much notice. Plan a trip to Hawaii or any exotic islands now and try to go after the new Moon.

Environment: Disturbing news from the sea, oil and flooding is still coming. News about medicine and chemical explosions and broken dams can also be expected.

Famous Personalities: Sad news regarding alcoholism, drugs and incarceration will come about the rich and famous. The release of a new movie will make some of them very happy. Some famous people will suffer incarceration or hospitalization.

Events: Interesting news will come from the Middle East — Oil prices may rise due to another oil spill. The sky will pour a lot of water, tornadoes, typhoons, hurricanes etc.

Shopping: Great time to invest in anything related to the spiritual arts. Musical instruments, painting and spiritual materials should be bought before the upcoming Full Moon.

THU., FRI., SAT., SUN. — SEPTEMBER 10th, 11th, 12th, 13th:
RULERS — Venus (diplomacy) and Mercury (conversation):

Work, Career and Business: Fight the depressive mood; you need to reach out to new people and expand the various social networks in your life. The moon might be against you, but you can still make significant progress; reorganize it all. Business started now won't bring much financial security to all parties involved. Not a time to ask for a loan from your bank or a financial favor from a friend or family member. Money and security will play an important part of this trend and you might find yourself investing in a good deal from the past that you missed earlier. You should be confident no matter what, as your will is still stronger than the Moon.

Partnerships: Candlelight, soft music, courtship and social gatherings for the upcoming weekend are on the agenda for some. The soft Venus energy will tone down the aggressiveness of many people around you. Time to make peace and to apologize for your mistakes. You need to reach out to the people you know, but avoid expanding the various social networks in your life. Use finesse in all you do; you can't miss. Under Venus' blessings, you must keep in mind that whatever is offered with true love will bring luck to the giver. Abusing her kindness will bring back heavy karma and will be paid in full. Let your partner know about your deep feelings and see the good side of life.

Family and Friends: Do not turn down an invitation or a chance to socialize with old friends; weird new people will be there waiting for you. Communication is on the fore; don't hesitate to participate in it; everybody will listen to your comments. However, avoid falling into useless gossiping over the telephone — only "Ma Bell" will benefit from that! You may hear distressing news about brothers or sisters. Use Mercury's power of expression to write those long overdue letters.

Love Affairs: Some will happily give, some will gladly receive presents that will last forever in their hearts. Promote words of love and be aware of the feelings of others; lovely Venus will change uneasiness into love, attention and respect. You and a long-standing friend may discover that your relationship is growing towards romance and both are surprised. A dual situation may force some to make a decision; use your intuition, keep a cool head. The lessons of the past should be remembered. If you are single and born in April, a Leo or a Libra may make your life a misery. Be patient with all the people around you.

Travel and Communication: Do not expect interesting news as your telephone might be full of distressing messages. Not a time for traveling, however; avoid the impulsive Mercurial need for speed. You might have to deal with high winds or water. Time to express yourself, write letters, start (or finish) a book.

Environment: With the waning Moon, nature may get out of hand with a bad earthquake, or a monetary scandal could make the news. A famous personality will pay a heavy price for a stupid act.

Events: A financial scandal or some secrets may reach you. Foreign affairs could be distressing, forcing some interaction soon.

Shopping: Take care of your wheels and shop around for things for the office. If you decide to purchase a second-hand car, you could strike a good bargain; don't be afraid to barter aggressively. Mercury loves mental stimulation and your wit will help you to save money. Be happy and alert — don't be afraid to use your communication powers.

MON., TUE., WED., THU., FRI. — SEPTEMBER 14th, 15th, 16th, 17th, 18th:
RULERS — The Moon (changes) and the Sun (shocking):

Work, Career and Business: You may find yourself discussing goals for the future with someone close to you. Some will even sell their houses or move to a better location. Life is a process of constant change and this lunation will touch you or someone close to you. Make the most out of this change and trust the upcoming future. Not exactly a time to promote any endeavors, sign contracts or travel; wait for the next New Moon to move or deal with important matters.

Partnerships: Time to promote only faith and confidence in all you do. This type of energy will be difficult for some as they might be forced out of a business relationship or a job. Accept those changes as your personal wishes might not match your present situation. Thus before building a new house you must destroy the old one. You might be going through a hard time now, but the Universe will pay you back in spades if you learn from your experiences and keep faith in yourself.

Family and Friends: Listen to your friends' stories and be ready for the beginning or ending of an important part of their lives. Keep in mind that the Moon is waning (negative) and those unexpected changes must be faced with courage no matter what. Give special attention to the children these days and provide them guidance if needed. Their young and fragile spirits need constant reassurance and appreciation. Also, with the Sun in charge you might stimulate their creativity and enjoy their youth and boundless energy. This energy will be against them and some will be accident-prone.

Love Affairs: Some people might surprise you; however, don't dream or hope for a long-lasting lost love found now. Be ready for the beginning or ending of an important part of your (and others') life. If you are stuck with the wrong relationship, this lunation will force you out of this stressful situation very soon. Accept the upcoming changes with grace and have faith in the future. Those changes will bring someone worthy of your feelings. Wait for the next upcoming New Moon to get active in your social circle again. Your friends possess all your wishes and you should spend more time with them, especially if you are single and looking for love. For those born in May, Pisces and Virgo will be strongly attracted to you. Enjoy a great show when possible; you need to forget a few things in your own life.

Travel and Communication: With the waning Moon affecting our psyche, depression might be a problem for some. Keep busy, avoid negative thoughts of the past and look for positive endeavors. Free yourself from pessimistic people or stressful situations; use your will and surprise others with a formidable optimistic attitude. Be a defensive driver ever ready to give way to the crazies of the freeway. Make plans to travel far now.

Environment: The weather will turn very nasty in many states and many will lose their lives and possessions. Thousands may be forced to relocate due to dramatic experiences with nature. Loss of power is part of this trend; don't take any chances, stay safe.

Famous Personalities: An important figure could suffer a heart attack or surgery! A naughty love affair may end up dramatically and some unlucky children could be involved in an awful accident.

Events: On a large scale, many governments may also make news that will affect all of us. Disturbing news may be coming from France or Japan. Stay clear of traveling by air.

Shopping: A perfect time to give old toys or clothes to unlucky children. Avoid spending money on expensive items for your own children. Now is not the time to find great deals by visiting your local flea market. Spend time doing something creative; it doesn't have to be a masterpiece, just something to ease your spirit. We are getting closer to the New Moon and all will be soon much better.

New Moon — September 20th, 1998 in the practical, health-oriented sign of Virgo: Much progress is ahead of you in term of employment. This critical sign is ruled by Mercury, so affairs of work and health will be on the rise. Expect an overwhelming feeling of perfection and unusual worry about health and work to take over your psyche; do not let this lunation overstress you. This trend will play an important part in your health and working life and in some ways will affect your environment. You may be forced to let go of a deteriorating working situation and forced into a new one. The emphasis is on the body (perfect health) and the mind (education) to perform efficiently in serving the world at large. All changes you may be forced to experience are positive in nature and will further much of your deep desire for a better situation in the long run.

SAT., SUN., MON., TUE., WED. — SEPTEMBER 19th, 20th, 21st, 22nd, 23rd: RULERS — Mercury (thinking) and Venus (commitment)

Work, Career and Business: You may find yourself in an awkward or difficult situation with a co-worker, and something must be done soon. Don't let this stressful situation in your working life become a major problem for you and others; handle your affairs with discretion and dignity. Meditate for insight; use your intuition and be patient; the right opportunity is on the way. Use the new Moon to push forward.

Partnerships: With the new Moon upon you, much transformation will take place soon. However, avoid getting into a heated argument with a friend or an acquaintance who will challenge you about your politics at work or your personal philosophy of life. Be patient and tolerant.

Family and Friends: Expect interesting news from close friends or family members and provide them with some spiritual support. Avoid gossiping and make sure that you are saying what you actually mean today, as others could interpret it the wrong way. Nothing really can happen to you now; have faith in the stars and your new future.

Love Affairs: Romance is on your mind and therefore you may consider a trip with your special someone. Someone close to you may be a challenge for you to understand; just realize that none of us is perfect. A desire for a permanent commitment from a lover or the chance to find love this weekend has a good chance of working out. You may find yourself focusing on personal relationships; you feel better with others' approval. Don't be tempted to let sadness or depression or the ending of a situation to get the best of you; this emotional approach to decision-making can be the source of strife; use diplomacy and coordinate your efforts with your mate's. If you are single and born in June, an Aquarius or a Sagittarius (foreigners) could mean love to you. Make the most of this New Moon; with Venus' touch you can't go wrong.

Travel and Communication: Take extra time in explaining yourself, as the possibility for miscommunication is high and ill will could ensue. Venus will see to it that there is harmony these days. Emotions may also run high and could affect your words; make sure they are well thought out and supportive. Remember, Mercury rules transportation, and impatient drivers could promote accidents. Time to take care of your car's brakes, oil or anything else it may need as you might have to take a journey soon.

Environment: Expect sad news from the ocean or a chemical accident. News of medicine and hospitals may also come your way. The weather will not be too cooperative and many thousands of people might have to relocate due to nature's devastating forces.

Famous Personalities: News of hospitalization, drugs or alcohol may plague the media as the rich and famous won't be able to hide their dependency.

Events: Middle Eastern Leaders may surprise some; religion and many difficult topics will emerge (abortion, etc.), producing stress and trouble.

Shopping: Surely a great time to buy everything you need to make your home a better or safer place to live. You may also invest money in shopping for clothes, plants, food and a little surprise for those you care about.

September 24th, 1998 — Mercury enters Libra: A trend loaded with communication related to partners, contracts, legal activity, marriage and divorce. Lots of thoughts will be geared towards finding a better working environment or a new business partner. Souls born now will be gifted with a natural ability for diplomacy and "savoir faire." The opportunity to learn everything under the sun is offered to the soul. Many of them will be born with an aptitude for judicial investigation and psychology. Some will be attracted to the professions offering an artistic aptitude such as interior designing. Fame and fortune will come to the writers and teachers. Artistic talents in harmony and mental health will lead these souls toward the balance they seek. This position makes for one of the most well-balanced signs of the Zodiac. The soul must avoid being too diplomatic with others and may be suffering a lack of expression and direction. However, an opportunity to experience justice, real love and harmony is offered to the advanced souls.

> **Note**: We may be in a new Moon period, but be alert of Pluto's power upon us for a few days — As always with the Lord of Hades, expect dramatic happenings all over; control is a must. Anything you say or do now will have repercussions in your future. Be aware of Pluto's emotional and dramatic nature.

THU., FRI., SAT., SUN. — SEPTEMBER 24th, 25th, 26th, 27th:
RULERS — Pluto (netherworld) and Jupiter (law enforcement):

Work, Career and Business: Don't be Pluto's victim; avoid all confrontations. Emotion, destruction, hate and crime are all part of Pluto's signature. You are aware of Pluto; many others are not! Compromise in the office and don't let the stinger of the beast get to you. Sarcasm is the last thing you need to use just now. You will be forced to recognize many of your errors and your limits. A wake-up call for some dreamers is ahead.

Partnerships: The crooks and the police are going to be busy; avoid the unsafe or unknown. Pluto's power is not for unity but discord and will affect the mass, including your very own relationships. Do not participate in large gatherings, as death may strike anytime anywhere against the unaware. Secrets like the Whitewater, RTC's allegations, sex scandals, police, CIA, FBI's wrongdoings will be divulged to the public. Expect news pertaining to AIDS, abortion and religious groups to make the news once more.

Family and Friends: The influence of benevolent Jupiter should tone down Pluto's desire for drama. Participate in promoting cosmic consciousness among friends and family, and share your knowledge about Pluto's destructive energy. Build up good karma for yourself and let them know about the energies that control them — share your knowledge. The good thing about Pluto is that you, your friends and family members will all be forced to realize their limits and do something about any and all aggravated situations. Stay alert! Be patient and practice super diplomacy during this trend. Use the secrets you hear to your advantage and don't repeat them to others!

Love Affairs: The real you, the raw you and the plain truth around you and its impact in your life will force you to mutate or transform with your newly acquired knowledge. Expect secrets pertaining to sex and money, but most of all stay calm in your dealings. Take smart precautions if you are going to be sexually active. If you are single and born in July, a Scorpio or a Pisces can go crazy for or against you.

Travel and Communication: Better stay home, read a good book or watch a movie! Observe and listen to your intuition. The less you talk, the less chance you will have to get hurt. Control your own thoughts; don't fall for jealousy or depression. If you must take the road, be extremely prudent and don't trust any strangers. Watch the children; the vampires are out.

Environment: We are still in a waxing moon period, but let's hope that Pluto won't stir a tragedy with nature's devastative forces like an earthquake or a series of floods. Anything dramatic can happen now; let's pray for the victims of the planet of death. If you are a law enforcement officer or a security guard, be extremely cautious, as violent and dangerous karmic souls will roam the streets. Remember that the Rodney King beating took place under Pluto, and those who lost control over their emotions will forever pay the ultimate price. The legacy of this action that took place on that night transformed into the Los Angeles riots where disorder and fires exploded all over.

Famous Personalities: Many famous people die under Pluto's rule. The same energy may also take away a famous public figure in a secret way where drugs, sex and rock and roll are never far away. Pluto rules the police force and brings the hidden facts to life. A form of rebirth, a new part of life for the parties involved and for some million-dollar lawsuits!

Events: This is a particularly destructive time event in a good Moon and I want you people to be aware of everything around you and your loved ones. Under Pluto's power, May 1997 a brutal slaying follows a beer-drinking in Central Park, NEW YORK. Two teenagers stabbed a real estate agent at least 30 times and tried to chop off his hands so police couldn't use fingerprints to identify him before dumping him in a lake in Central Park. Both perpetrators, Daphne Abdela, 15, and her boyfriend, 15-year-old Christopher Vasquez, "gutted the body so it would sink." Both of those young souls are from the dramatic Pluto generation "The Death Wish Generation." See Pluto's impact upon generations or order ***The Power of the Dragon*** to learn more about this phenomenon. Some unlucky souls will have to undergo sorrow and loss. Be ready to help those in need as the favor may hit close to home. Expect the weather to be harsh and crime to be high!

Shopping: A great time to purchase anything related to metaphysics or look for a good attorney. Anything and everything related to checkup or investigation is under good stars. Do not invest in dangerous toys.

MON., TUE., WED. — SEPTEMBER 28th, 29th, 30th:
RULERS — Saturn (government news) & Uranus (astonishment):

Work, Career and Business: Better keep an eye on your attitude as eccentric Uranus could jeopardize your job or image. With the waxing Moon, some of your wishes may take place. Keep in mind that sometimes a full breakdown is needed if you hope for restoration. Be ready for anything to happen these days and accept the challenges with a sunny disposition. A beginning and ending of an important phase of your life is about to take place. Many ingenious ideas to rebuild or invest will come to fruition during this trend.

Partnerships: Like Pluto, Uranus is of a disturbing nature, so caution is also advised in all you do or say to others. Be patient or suffer the consequences of impetuosity. The light is green for friendship and hope, and so much can happen if you participate in life. Try something different this weekend; you'll be surprised by the payoff. Throw a party; you may bring a wish to you.

Family and Friends: Help a friend in trouble and meditate on the world around you, the more people think positively, the more definite things will happen to this world. Don't turn down any opportunity to socialize, but be responsible with children. Some of them need to burn off some energy and will be begging for a boisterous outdoor romp. A trip close to nature or to the nearest electronic attraction will do wonders for the entire family. Make the most of what is left of this New Moon trend.

Love Affairs: Absolutely anything can happen this weekend; stay alert and participate with the best of your social life. A chance to find love or reach a dream will be given to you if you try hard enough. You may encounter funny people or be involved in strange situations; make the most of it. If you are single and born in August, an Aquarius or a Sagittarius will want to know you.

Travel and Communication: Your desire to travel will become intense. Some will plan a very long trip by airplane; as always, try to travel after the New Moon. Be gentle with words and realize your inner mental power; promote your future. Remember, the future is the reincarnation of all your thoughts and you may use the universal mind to influence your fate. Knowledge is power.

Environment: I have noticed also that the sudden release of Uranus' energy has in the past produced serious explosions and terrible accidents such as the US shuttle explosion, so be aware of his discharging power. Both attacks on Iraq happened under his command and I wonder if our Presidents were just lucky or if they follow the advice of wise astrologers! Remember, Uranus rules the future, computers, avionics, atomics and aeronautics, and both wars were very much "electronics-oriented with the introduction of the Patriot missiles." Keep in mind that Uranus also rules earthquakes and volcanoes: Many surprising things take place on these particular days. Be ready for the ending of important phases of your life and expect the government to make serious decisions pertaining to other countries. Let's hope China will be our friend soon.

Famous Personalities: Many "crazy" souls will fall for Uranus' desire for originality and some will do all they can to make weird news. Famous people will be caught doing silly things, such as slapping a police officer or being caught making love in a car with a prostitute. Japanese and French personalities may also make the news. Some scientists will gain fame for their accomplishments.

Events: During Saturn's command Iranian voters stunned the experts and their country's conservative rulers by choosing as president a man who is considered open-minded, intellectual and tolerant. If you are into UFOs, now is the time to look for them. Uranus rules the incredible and extraterrestrials may need this sophisticated energy to manifest themselves in our dense physical world. Don't forget your video camera! Uranus also helps in the explosions, volcanoes, etc., so be prepared to hear about these kinds of situations.

Shopping: The futuristic spirit of Uranus rejects the traditional and promotes the new age. Uranus hates dogmas and needs to deals with the future only. Use his futuristic energy to tap into your own subconscious or visit your local psychic or astrologer; others of you may just want to update your stereo equipment or buy some of those flashy trendy fashions as seen on those famous runways in Paris.

Welcome to Your Day-to-Day Guidance For October 1998

October 1st, 1998 — Venus enters Libra: With the love planet in her own sign, the opportunity to concentrate on your partnership (business or emotional) will be given to you. The lucky ones will start a lifetime commitment blessed with love and happiness. Giving and receiving presents and lots of flowers for some. Souls born now will be quite gifted in matters related to love. They will concentrate and achieve perfection in many of their artistic endeavors. Blessed with such a positive location, Venus will grant them with a "perfect" and loving partner willing to work hard to promote their married life. Some karmic souls will have to learn to be more critical and stand up for themselves or suffer abusive partners and loneliness. This position makes for one of the most beautiful and loving partners. Usually artistic talent and an interest in beauty matters is present with this position. These souls are born to experience love on an emotional and intellectual level. A top position for those involved in the artistic or psychological field.

Full Moon — October 5th, 1998 in the warlike sign of Aries. This upcoming trend will be tough for many. Mars is very strong these days and will bring about serious confrontations, explosions, fires, and the possibility of war. Be ready for serious even fatalistic news in the near future. With Neptune's religious and deceiving tendency accompanying him in this dance, a disturbing development with the Middle East is to be expected. Expect a negative development pertaining to oil spills or explosions, even terrorist activity, to take place in the near future. Be ready for devastating forces producing destructive weather and flooding in different parts of the world. Do not lose faith in the future; we all must go on. The stars are a reflection of God and his Divine plan for all of us and we must go through with it. Do not lose faith.

THU., FRI., SAT., SUN., MON., TUE. — OCTOBER 1st, 2nd, 3rd, 4th, 5th, 6th:
RULERS — Uranus (wonderment), Neptune (thoughtful) and Mars (enterprises):

Work, Career and Business: Make the most of what is left of this waxing Moon. Be practical at work on Thursday; clean around the office and don't challenge authority. Don't hesitate to initiate actions for the next few days and slow down after the 5th of October. With Neptune in charge, many of your wishes to further your career may happen just by being at the right place at the right time. However, Neptune is sometimes deceiving, and you should be practical in your expectations of all the promises made.

Partnerships: The New Moon's uplifting energy will renovate many depressed spirits as hope and activity will once again lead the way to a better future. Neptune will sharpen your intuition and your creativity; many will ask you for direction in their personal life. Support your partner and build self-confidence. Peace of mind can be found close to the water.

Family and Friends: Give spiritual support to those you care about but don't get emotionally involved in their personal problems. Don't let them waste too much of your time talking or complaining over the telephone. If you feel blue yourself, know that it is Neptune's deceiving power and use your will to fight him. At home, stimulate love and attention to the ones around you and be careful of fire (Mars) or water (Neptune). As always, don't overindulge in alcohol as it will only make things worse. Narcotics can only further depressive thoughts of your past and promote accidents of all kinds. A trip to the local playhouse or movie theater may be just what your soul needs for inspiration. For those with a laid-back attitude, some good tunes and a walk by the ocean will do the trick. Get close to God and meditate about your life in general; Neptune may reward you magically.

Love Affairs: Under Neptune's auspices secret love affairs flourish. Whatever you do, make solid decisions about your own relationship and be aware of deception. Aggressive Mars may stimulate your desires for action; dancing and music would be a good outlet. Mars is far from being diplomatic; use "savoir faire" if you intend to have a smooth evening. If you are single and born under the sign of Virgo, a Pisces or a Capricorn needs your help. A Taurus will be forceful in his love for you.

Travel and Communication: Use Neptune's dreamy nature and consider spending time by the water away from the city's stressful activities. If you have to drive a long way, remember to take plenty of rest, because dreamy Neptune could make you sleepy. Some will have to take a trip to the hospital to visit a person, and others may hear deceiving news about a legal system decision pertaining to arrest and imprisonment. Come clear with what you mean these days and control your imagination.

Environment: Mars is an aggressive planet and with Uranus still with us he could put some stress on some faults, producing tremors terrifying the inhabitants above. This negative trend of calamities will be with us for a while, and caution is advised in all you do. Let's hope that Mars or Uranus will be tolerant for the people living on this earth and play somewhere else in those worlds above and below us. Let's hope the waxing Moon will stop those destructive gods from doing damage to us.

Famous Personalities: The cinematography industry will launch many great movies, and numerous actors and actresses will parade all over. Some will be caught doing the wrong thing at the wrong time and others will pay a visit to an "alcoholics anonymous" organization. Some unlucky ones will be caught doing something nasty and will pay a heavy price for it.

Events: With this powerful trio, Uranus (explosion), Neptune (ocean) and Mars (explosion) the worst that could happen is another devastating oil spill or chemical explosion. Mars is a warrior and favors accidents on the road. Be extremely careful when driving. Boating is something you should forget about, especially after the Full Moon.

Shopping: Use Neptune's sensitivity to further any artistic talent and become more creative. Dancing, music or a metaphysical study will favor this lunation. Visit your spiritual friend and enjoy a trip into your future; Neptune will sharpen his intuition. Bargains on alcohol and paint will be offered by Neptune and sharp tools by Mars before the Full Moon. Do not invest in any chemicals or dangerous tools during this lunation.

October 8th, 1998 — Mars enters Virgo: The Lord of action in the perfectionist sign of Virgo will induce much action in research for a better way to serve this world. Perfect time to start on a health program or diet. Medical study or surgery is ahead for some. Invest in your desire for purity, health, clothing and creativity. Don't let the desire principle of Mars stimulate criticism of all around you. Much of your thoughts will be geared towards work, health and organization. Souls born now will inherit natural gifts in the medical field, mechanics and computer programming. A top position to lead in any scientific or research field. Souls born now will have a strong desire to save or keep nature for future generations to enjoy.

WED., THU., FRI., SAT. — OCTOBER 7th, 8th, 9th, 10th: RULERS — Venus (laziness) & Mercury (meaningless chatter).

Work, Career and Business: The worst of both of these planets is to be expected due to the pessimistic trend of the Full Moon. Do not fall for depression and self-defeating attitudes. The stars have a specific role to play and you are an actor on the big stage of your life. Go with the trend, do not force issues, be patient for a few days. At work keep a low profile; your co-workers or your boss may not be aware of the work of the Moon on their psyche and could become "lunatic" with you. Keep busy on Wednesday and rearrange your desk or your paperwork. Time to use patience.

Partnerships: If you want to save trouble in your relationship, now is the time to use full diplomacy and understanding. Don't let the waning Moon make you "lunatic" or "moody." If you experienced trouble with the one you care about, you could make up with a romantic dinner at home. With Mars in Virgo, criticism is to be expected from everyone; don't take it too seriously, you know better. Use Venus as much as you can to uplift any difficult situation.

Family and Friends: Disturbing situations involving friends or a family member will come to the fore. Take the time to review all the reasons and find a way to make peace with the party involved. Mercury rules communication and will help you pass on your thoughts deeply and correctly. Provide a helping hand, but do not let abusive friends take the best of your spirit. Emotions will run high these days; keep a cool head.

Love Affairs: With Venus in her own sign, many will try to keep harmony at home. Love affairs started now won't stand much chance of living long. Many unsuited couples will also be forced out of their unhealthy relationships. Mars (the warrior) in Virgo (perfection) is running the show for a while. The emphasis will be on destructive behavior, even violence where you could be fighting for an ideal love or practical alliance. Many will be forced to realize their limits as Mars will destroy the old relationship. You cannot build a new house under weak or unsuitable foundations, so Mars may free you soon. If you are born in October, an Aries or a Gemini will drive you nuts. Virgos and Pisces are strongly cautioned to handle relationships carefully due to the destructive Mars Passage in their first (personality) and seventh (marriage) areas.

Travel and Communication: Mercury will pass on all sorts of news. Use his power to pass on your ideas to those willing to listen. A great time to improve your cosmic consciousness and do some "deep" reading concerning life and death or metaphysics. Great time to finish your book if you are into writing. Be aware on the road and take care of your wheels.

Environment: Following the Full Moon, tornadoes, high winds, earthquakes, and chain-reaction accidents due to bad weather are very high on the list. The earth is alive and she needs to stretch herself now and then. Stay safe and be prudent on the road.

Famous Personalities: A famous personality will see the end of his life. Many will miss the great spirit. Rumor of a strike could plague the media soon.

Events: As usual after the Full Moon, stay clear of the crazy crowd and listen to your intuition at all times.

Shopping: Rent anything; do not buy anything new now. Take care of your car as she may decide to let you down at the wrong time and in the wrong place. Be cautious and be patient.

October 12th, 1998 — Mercury enters Scorpio: A trend loaded with communication related to finance, sex, legacy, death and metaphysics for the advanced souls. Lots of thought will be geared towards finding the meaning of life for some or how to find the weakest part and revive an unproductive business for others. Children born now will be gifted with a natural ability for investigation and incredible staying power. The opportunity to learn anything hidden is offered to the soul. Many of them will be born with an aptitude for deep medicinal investigation or financial endeavors. Some will be attracted to the professions of danger such as the police force or emergency service where quick thinking and courage can make a difference between life and death. Fame and fortune will come to the ones involved in writing, teaching or those deeply involved in science, research, the medical or metaphysical field. This position makes for one of the most intense investigators' signs of the Zodiac. The soul must learn to use diplomacy in times of confrontation and may be suffering a lack of communication. However, an opportunity to experience cosmic consciousness and spiritual peace is offered to the advanced soul.

SUN., MON., TUE., WED., THU. — OCTOBER 11th, 12th, 13th, 14th, 15th:
RULERS: The Moon (big changes) and the Sun (expectation).

Work, Career and Business: The general mood will be depressive. You can expect the serious beginning and ending of important parts of your (and others') life. Be ready for those upcoming progressive variations. Keep in mind that life is a constant process of change and the stars are (even if you don't realize it) working for your benefit. With Mercury (communication) in Scorpio (directness), avoid sarcasm with others. Be patient with everyone around the office.

Partnerships: You will be forced to let go of negative people in your life and disturbing situations. You must take a chance on the new future with faith. Many will experience the closing of a destructive relationship and others may see the new beginning. Under these stars any new relationship is doomed to fail in the long run. Further the positive only and don't fall for the waning Moon.

Family and Friends: The Sun rules love, romance and children, but we are still under a difficult trend, so this energy won't bring you good news. The Sun gives life to children, but watch over them especially close to the water. On a more positive note he will put his undiscriminating light on many secrets. Friends will need spiritual support; give love and attention and build good karma for yourself.

Love Affairs: Be ready for new starts in love matters and provide a solid shoulder for the victims suffering a broken heart. The right partner might not be the one you were with; use the new-found freedom to look (after the New Moon) for someone who really deserves your love. Under the Sun's command, the lucky ones will find great happiness with true love relationships. A new arrival is to be expected by a young couple. If you are a

Scorpio, a Cancer or a Taurus could induce serious stress in your life. A Virgo friend has a good discernment for you; you must listen.

Travel and Communication: You may be asked to go home and see Mom. Be aware on the road; do not trust any driver and be ready for sudden action. Surprises are on the way as people from your past will come into the picture soon.

Environment: What was once built by man (cities/homes) or nature (forests) must be destroyed; what was once born must sooner or later die, and this is what life is all about. Recycling is the key word in nature and nothing is really wasted. There is nothing else to do than to accept the ultimate changes imposed by God, and usually the future offers better. Famous personalities: Expect interesting but not necessarily positive surprises with the rich and famous. Be ready for the unexpected in their words and actions. Don't take chances unless you know what you're in for and be prudent.

Events: Large quakes and nature forces may force thousands of victims to relocate to rebuild a new life. Blackouts and loss of power are on the way too. Terrible tragedies such as the Kobe, Japan earthquake and many volcanic eruptions have happened under this configuration and thousands of people were forced out of their homes because of nature's destructive forces.

Shopping: Anything for children as long as it is not new. Great time to get rid of the extra stuff clogging the house or the garage and a garage sale would not be a bad idea. Do not invest in silver, gold or expensive items. Anything to clean the house will do good.

New Moon — October 20th, 1998 in the diplomatic oriented sign of Libra: This sign is ruled by Venus, thus affairs of the law and politics will be on the rise. Expect an overwhelming feeling for peace and diplomacy instead of war to take over the world and your psyche. Stand firm on your decisions and do not let this lunation overstress you as balance and harmony will prevail. This trend will play an important part in the equilibrium of your physical and spiritual life. This trend will affect some of your business and emotional relationships. The upcoming changes must be accepted as the New Moon (positive) has a great plan that you may not understand just yet. Some will be involved in the signing of very important documents, contracts or the legal system. You may be forced to realize the importance of making up your mind about a serious situation and make painful decisions. The emphasis is on a balance and harmony in all, if we are to perform efficiently and live in peace with the rest of the world. Diplomats will be requested and busy in many places of this crazy world to preserve all of us to suffer future wars.

IMPORTANT NOTE:

October 20th, 1998 — The powerful Dragon's Head enters the magnanimous sign of Leo. The destructive Dragon's Tail enters the disruptive sign of Aquarius. The almighty Dragon will stay in these signs until April 9th, 2000. The upcoming predictions for the dawning of the age of Aquarius are somehow incredible and will be totally different from those presented this year. The 1999 "Moon Power" issue will be available to the public in September 1998 don't miss this copy. Rest assured, California will not fall under the ocean and New York will not be attacked by missiles. A new consciousness for the entire world is slowly but surely taking place where ignorance, fear and dogmas will be replaced by a higher knowledge based upon the study and understanding of God's celestial tools. The incredible is around the corner and will involve the incredible UFOs phenomenon. Have faith, be happy; mankind will realize its real potential soon.

FRI., SAT., SUN., MON., TUE. — OCTOBER 16th, 17th, 18th, 19th, 20th:
RULERS — Mercury (God of thieves) & Venus (Goddess of love).

Work, Career and Business: You are close to a new fresh breath of life; just a few more days and her blessings will make your life much easier. Wait for her upcoming white light, then make your opportunities. Do not try to push your business just now. Advertisements, important calls, traveling, and meetings will pay off if you learn to wait for the green light. Use "Moon power" wisely and respect the Universal Law. Knowledge is power; have faith in your abilities.

Partnerships: Mercury rules the mail, telephone and communication in general; expect disturbing mail to reach you. Deal with it now and clean up the situation before the next new Moon of October 20th. A get-together after work could also be a great idea; Mercury will have everyone "gossiping."

Family and Friends: The very last day of the waning Moon will sap your spiritual and physical energy. Help those in need to clean up the mess generated by their karmic experiences. Let no one exhaust your spirit or show frustration with loved ones. Some of your friends need spiritual regeneration, even a helping hand; as usual do so but realize your limits. Use Venus' generosity and show your love to everyone. Avoid spending too much time on the telephone with a depressive person.

Love Affairs: Your sense of perfection will expand with Mars crossing the sign of Virgo; don't be too picky or demanding with those you care for; no one is perfect. However, use your head, not your heart with someone who drinks too much, and realize your limits if you are in a deceiving relationship. You may also use Mars in Virgo to work on yourself, and the great results will stimulate those close to you. Perfect time to apply your will and give up smoking or get rid of a bad habit. With Venus around, the opportunity to find love will be given to you after the New Moon. If you are single and born in December, someone born in August or in June needs to talk to you. A friend born in October has a few thoughts for you.

Travel and Communication: Mars may make you feel like starting a diet, but don't get to concerned with your appearance or your health. Great time to have a medical checkup as the stars will make your physician very detail-oriented, thus helping him in the detection of possible trouble. Get your wheels in action; prepare for traveling under the protection of the upcoming New Moon.

Environment: Recharge your batteries; a trip in the mountain is strongly recommended. The Virgo energy will make you appreciate the beauty of mother nature. Many environmentalists will make serious progress and get the attention they deserve. Sad news from the ocean may reach the media.

Famous Personalities: A new health infomercial will be promoted by a famous person. News of water management is also on the horizon. A notorious religious person could make serious news soon.

Events: We are not yet out of trouble as the Moon is still waning, thus, mother nature may decide to disturb us with bad weather. Negative news may come from the ocean. Be aware of abductions; this type of energy has swiftly taken many children away.

Shopping: With Mars in Virgo, do not poison your mind with imagination and fears. Use your own positive thinking to avoid negativity entering your life or your body. Some may decide to join the local gym or enroll in a weight loss program. Anything to clean around can only be a good thing to buy now.

Note: As always with the Lord of hell in charge of this trend, better think twice before saying or acting on impulse. Expect secrets to be divulged, affairs of sex, and nature's devastative forces at work. The police and blackguards will make the news. More than ever, use diplomacy, as whatever you do now will have very serious repercussions in your life.

October 25th, 1998 — Venus enters Scorpio: With the love planet in the dramatic sign of Scorpio, opportunity to rebuild your partnership (business or emotional) life will be given to you. This trend will allow many souls to see very clearly and do some serious cleanup in the near future. The lucky ones will start a lifetime commitment blessed with love and happiness. If your natal Venus is in good aspect to Pluto, your sensuality will be extreme and sexual relationships will be for the better. Souls born now will be given the opportunity to experience love on the emotional level and much drama is to be experienced there. If Venus is badly affected, "La Femme Fatale" or the "Black Widow" will suffer many disturbing relationships (Elizabeth Taylor is a good example). A full commitment is needed with this position, and the soul will have to learn to love with their head first. Blessed with such a powerful location, Venus in Scorpio will endow the soul with incredible magnetism. Some karmic souls will have to learn to be less emotional and more critical in their natural jealousy. This position makes for one of the most emotional but beautiful and loving partners. Usually artistic talent is present with this position. Those souls are born to experience love on an emotional and dramatic level. Due to the emotional intensity this is a top position for those involved in the artistic field.

October 26th, 1998: Saturn returns in Aries: Saturn, "the teacher," is still going through the fiery sign of Aries and will stay in this sign until March 1st, 1999. Karmic Saturn is also called the "Great Malefic," and its gloomy power brings depression by the sign and house he resides. In the sign of Aries, he may make one overconcerned with his image and personality and could produce a low self-esteem. In any case, if you are feeling Saturn's gloomy energy, you must use your will: the part of God in you is much stronger than any planet. Saturn in Aries rules personal fears and with Neptune (ruler of the Dragon's Tail in Pisces) until October 20th, 1998, you are advised to keep a positive attitude about yourself and rebuild your self-esteem. Saturn is cold and calculated; Mars is fast and aggressive. So, make solid plans, stick to them and respect the Universal Law in all your endeavors. On a more positive note, the structural power of Saturn will provide Aries (Mars' enterprising spirit) with mental progress, solid new-found self-esteem, objectivity, discipline and a reasonable approach to any business venture. A perfect position for those involved in the Army, the Navy or any endeavors involving courage, leadership and discipline.

WED., THU., FRI., SAT., SUN., MON. — OCTOBER 21st, 22nd, 23rd, 24th, 25th, 26th:
RULERS — Venus (fondness), Pluto (regeneration) and Jupiter (belief).

Work, Career and Business: You are now walking on a fine rope, it's windy, and you're high above solid concrete down below! You'd better use all the "savoir faire" you know. A serious wake-up call will come to many unaware skeptics of astrology powers. The possibility to lose it all (and rebuild it all) will be a serious consideration for some karmic souls. You will be able to see exactly what's wrong in your business life soon. The new Moon will help you make all the changes needed.

Partnerships: Secret may surface now. You may learn something valuable about a partner. Keep his/her trust; do not divulge the secret. Money will play an important part of this trend; listen to your intuition in all you do. Venus will help to tone down the stress induced by Pluto.

Family and Friends: Be patient with all the people around you. Do not expect anyone you care about to be diplomatic with you during this trend if Venus (diplomacy) is weak in their chart. Again, do not fall for Pluto's destructive or sarcastic remarks; words of love will pay off in the long run. Be ready for some dramatic news from someone close to you. Whatever happens, be strong; life must go on. Pluto will work for your benefit.

Love Affairs: Passion is in the air. Secret affairs involving sex and passionate love may be divulged to the public, forcing people to take a stand in destroying and rebuilding relationships. This might happen to you too. In any case use tons of diplomacy to save unwanted trouble in your love life. If you are a water sign such as Scorpio, Pisces or Cancer this lunation will touch you directly. Leos must take it easy at home.

Travel and Communication: Expect news pertaining to the police force and the crooks. Nature's destructive forces will be obvious in some parts of the world. Be careful of what you do or say during this trend. Drive carefully, and stay clear from weird strangers and strange places. If you learn about someone else's secret, do not tell, you may be asking for trouble. Your intuition will be accurate; listen to the little voice within.

Environment: Pluto belongs to the Divine family and has a specific regenerative work to do and his impact on earth and its people is needed. As Pluto destroys it all, he also gives the opportunity to rebuild stronger and better. Be ready for all sorts of dramatic news all over. Stay safe; don't try the devil.

Famous Personalities: Some famous people will be called back to God. A famous person's secrets will be made available to the media.

Events: Hopefully with the New Moon, lovely Venus and knowledgeable Jupiter, we can only hope they will stop Pluto from damaging us via dramatic happenings. With the Lord of Hades in Sagittarius (religion/foreigners) we can only expect drama in these areas.

Shopping: With Jupiter with us, a visit to your local church for God's guidance or your favorite psychic/astrologer will do you good. Anything bought now that can be used for metaphysics will bring unusual power to you. Alarms bought now will stop the crooks.

TUE., WED., THU., FRI., SAT. — OCTOBER 27th, 28th, 29th, 30th, 31st:
RULERS — Saturn (glorification), Uranus (amazement) and Neptune (spirituality).

Work, Career and Business: The month will end on a note of surprising but progressive changes. Do not turn down an invitation, as a professional contact could bring people who will positively influence your career. Expect a new beginning concerning your service to the world or your career. Work that you are doing leaves you unsatisfied and is a source of stress; you might be forced to change direction. Many souls are late starters in life and no one should feel depressed about it. Resolve to find a new career that fits your natural talent. The lucky ones can expect a well-deserved promotion. Use Neptune's intuitive power to find your way through the clouds.

Partnerships: Stand strong against opposition; don't let others pressure you into pursuing their opinion instead of your own. Meditate on the possibility to improve and understand where your partnership is going in your life. Did you make the right choices and can you live with them? If not, there won't be a better time to deal with those questions, Uranus' desire for changes and freedom will help you to transform it all. With the waxing Moon upon the world, nothing can really go wrong if you act scrupulously.

Family and Friends: Make the most of this great trend. Some friends may invite you to a gathering or a party soon. Enjoy this opportunity and be ready for lovely surprises. Uranus also makes the children very active and accident-prone. They will be heavy on you; be patient with their young demanding spirits. No one but yourself can bring about joy in your life; just participate with an open heart. Let the children enjoy Uranus' world of miracles, maybe by going to Disneyland or the Zoo. Keep your eyes on everything they do and everywhere they go. Saturn will make it hard to forget your responsibilities on Saturday; enjoy life while you can, tomorrow is another day.

Love Affairs: Expect interesting surprises during these days as many friends will bring some of your dear wishes. With Uranus' touch (surprises) try doing things you would not usually do and go to those places you never visited. Love is around the corner for some willing to go and get it. If you are a fire sign such as Leo, Sagittarius or Aries, your magnetism will be very high and you will be in demand for love.

Travel and Communication: Some lucky souls will travel far and fast or make great plans to visit their past soon. Uranus rules electronics, the future, astrology, psychic phenomena, and UFOs. If you want to see something unusual, talk about it and do it now! Who knows, Uranus may decide to grant one of your important wishes. Keep an eye on your possessions and avoid drinking too much in public places.

Environment: On a sad note, keep in mind that Uranus rules earthquakes and volcanoes. He may also decide to disturb the weather or produce a violent explosion. Let's hope the positive Moon will stop him from getting close to you and those you care about.

Famous Personalities: Be ready as usual for an unusual type of news from some extroverted Celebs. Much will be done for children during this trend.

Events: Under Uranus' surprising power anything weird could happen. The news will be somehow original. Avoid playing in the rain; many people have lost their lives under Uranus' lightning power. The government will make important decisions pertaining to the young generation, computers and education.

Shopping: For this occasion, you may feel like spending time and money on your appearance; great time to shop for new wardrobe items or consult a beautician. Great time to pay a visit to your future and your favorite "spiritual guide." A sense of freedom and brotherhood will be felt all over.

Welcome to Your Day-to-Day Guidance For November 1998

November 2nd, 1998 — Mercury enters Sagittarius: A trend loaded with communication about legal activity, traveling and foreign affairs. Lots of thought will be geared towards finding a better way to deal with other countries. Souls born now will be gifted with a natural ability for learning and teaching, and many will travel far. Many will master foreign languages. The opportunity to acquire knowledge of the law or religions is offered to the soul. Many of them will be born with an aptitude for judicial investigation, philosophical values and some will play an important part in passing it on to the world. Some will be attracted to the professions offering an intellectual aptitude such as teaching and writing, and some will be investing in education for the well-being of animals. Spiritual talents involving the new age will lead these souls towards a position of authority and respect. This position makes for one of the most intellectually advanced or dogmatic signs of the Zodiac. The soul must avoid being righteous with others and may have to endure an overly religious upbringing. Their challenge will be based upon a critical approach to the books and the collected knowledge. However, an opportunity to reach cosmic consciousness and the creator's manifestation is offered to the advanced souls.

Full Moon — November 4th, 1998 in Taurus: This lunation could affect the general aspect of world finance or the stock market negatively. Mars and Pluto are very strong these days and could produce serious confrontations and explosions. Drama is the key word for this trend where financial security will play an important part for all of us. Be prepared for difficult news, drama and some secrets. Nature will be producing devastating forces and destructive weather. Flooding is expected in different parts of the world. The impact will be on finance, secrets including the secret government or the police force. Do not lose faith in the future; we must go on. The stars have a job to do and we must learn from our experiences. Have faith in the future no matter what.

SUN., MON., TUE., WED. — NOVEMBER 1st, 2nd, 3rd, 4th:
RULERS — Neptune (religion), Venus (caring), Mercury (words) and Mars (discord).

Work, Career and Business: You still have a few days in front of you to push forward, then be ready for the full impact of the Full Moon. With the beneficial light of Venus you may just avoid the worst of a decision involving a business situation. Wait patiently for the next New Moon (positive) to restructure or sign important documents. Don't let Mars show his aggressive face to those close to you. Try to be nice with others.

Partnerships: With Mercury's intellectual potential the right words can be used to heal emotional wounds. Just before the Full

Moon, expect interesting news coming your way via telephone or your mailbox. Time to realize the truth about yourself, a situation or a person that you trusted. Make the most of what is left of the waxing Moon, get yourself out of the gloom and do something interesting this weekend. The Dragon's Tail in Aquarius will bring consternation to you soon.

Family and Friends: The family circle could be quite a dramatic place for a while. Again do not let Mars and the Full Moon take over your words or your attitude. Keep emotions in control and be ready for secrets to surface. You can still have a good time, enjoy life and friends, but be aware of what you say or do. Do not lend money to anyone.

Love Affairs: Mars' and Venus' captivating personalities will stimulate sexual activity; your magnetism will improve dramatically. As always with Neptune on the Dragon's Tail in Aquarius, take precautions if you are sexually active. If you're married, plan a romantic dinner with a great French wine and soft music. You have a few more days to enjoy what's left of the good celestial energy; make the most of it. If you are an air sign such as Aquarius, Libra or Gemini, you may feel a strong sense of independence and freedom enveloping you. If you're a Leo, expect some stress in your relationships soon. You may be due for a long-due change where you could experience real love.

Travel and Communication: You may uncover a clandestine relationship or a secret about someone who travels a lot. You may be forced to look inside yourself and see your own strengths or weaknesses. Don't take any chances on the road and avoid flying after the Full Moon. You'd better stay away from anything that moves as this lunation will take many lives. Always plan your trips before the Full Moon and you will save yourself a lot of unwanted trouble. Use the power of Starguide and help those in trouble with it.

Environment: In time of a Full Moon and with ruinous Mars around we can only expect nature's destructive forces. Drama and demise are around the corner; protect yourself at all times. Do a candle ritual if you feel down or if you want to protect someone you care for. Burn white, green and blue candles. Use a nice incense.

Famous Personalities: A serious wake-up call for some. More secrets, more drama, more doom for famous people. Sad news from the rich and famous. This upcoming Full Moon will be devastative for some well-known people. A famous figure will be called close to God, having terminated his work on earth.

Events: The powerful Dragon's Tail will start to exert its power on earth. Religious fanatics will go out of hand. Their own hell-making could come loose; pray for the safety of those you care about as this lunation will be extremely difficult. Stay home and watch a good movie is my best advice; let the drama reach the unaware souls. You will see and appreciate the power of Starguide and the importance of letting others know about my work.

Shopping: Now is the time to buy pesticides and things of this nature. If you want to get rid of something, now is definitely the time. Absolutely no investment in weapons, sharp tools or anything that could explode. Let this nasty energy dissipate; stay safe.

THU., FRI., SAT., SUN., MON. — NOVEMBER 5th, 6th, 7th, 8th, 9th:
RULERS — Mercury (relatives) and the Moon (changes).

Work, Career and Business: Difficult news is to be expected. Work and career matters won't please you much. Serious changes are on the way. Make the most of Mercury's revitalizing energy to plan a form of rebirth in your working life. Be patient; anything weak must give way.

Partnerships: A long-standing partnership could be coming to an end, possibly because you sense that you may do better by yourself, or maybe your partner lost his enterprising spirit. Avoid nurturing depressive thoughts and provide spiritual help for those who have been touched by these difficult changes. Mercury will help you to pass on the right words to those in need.

Family and Friends: Your maternal instincts will show themselves and will be needed by your children. Share your knowledge with them. A friend needs help as they will reflect the full impact of this Full Moon. The subconscious response to the moon's fluctuations upon humans is referred as "lunatic behavior or moodiness" and right now you may realize it for yourself. Expect the beginning or ending of important parts of your life. Expect some surprising news from children; some people close to you need serious attention and plenty of love. Help a close friend deal with a departure.

Love Affairs: Ask yourself about your deep feelings for a person who seems to be moving away from you. An old lover from your past may surprise you soon. An old friend who lives far away may need to communicate with you. Don't expect great news, and provide the help required, as long as you are not being used. Another person from your past will bring you more trouble than anything else. If you were born under an earth sign, such as Taurus, Virgo or Capricorn, don't let the Full Moon depress you. If you are a Scorpio you will be forced to move soon.

Travel and Communication: A business deal that would have required you to travel may be postponed or canceled without much notice. Don't let it get to you and avoid promoting important business just yet. Expect the mail and your telephone to bring you news from the past. Some of us will experience communication problems as telephone appliances, computers or your car may break down.

Environment: The Moon's energy could also make the human race aware of its vulnerability against the shocking destructive forces of nature. It's time for her to stretch herself and restructure her inside.

Famous Personalities: The rich and famous will be planning a meeting for the well-being of many children of the world. Their artistic gifts will benefit many organizations. Some others may make surprising news trying to use Mercury for free publicity. Accidents on the road could take a prominent person.

Events: You will hear about the military performing deeds that will aid the general public and save lives from a disaster area. Thousands of people will be forced to relocate to start a new life.

Shopping: Anything that needs to be replaced in the home or the garden. Avoid signing anything related to real estate endeavors. Do not invest in appliances or a car just now.

TUE., WED., THU., FRI. — NOVEMBER 10th, 11th, 12th, 13th:
RULERS — Mercury (God of thieves) and Venus (Goddess of attachment).

Work, Career and Business: Keep a low profile at work; all the people around you are not exactly aware of the impact of the Moon upon their psyche and could become "lunatic." Keep busy on Tuesday; use the waning Moon to shuffle a few things around you. Not much progression can be had just now. Be patient and endure this tough trend with diligence. Don't get mad if the equipment around you refuses to operate, and be ready for setbacks.

Partnerships: Do not poison your mind with fears; use your own positive thinking to keep negativity from entering your spirit and your body. The future is based upon the creation of positive thoughts and lots of actions. You may feel like joining your local gym or enroll on a weight loss program. Use Venus' gentleness and Mercury's articulation power to communicate your feeling to someone you cherish.

Family and Friends: Family matters will demand much of your attention and could make you feel tired or depressed. Use your will; do not to let her deplete your spirits or show your frustration with loved ones. A child may need some direction and could be impatient with you. A depressed friend also needs spiritual regeneration; as usual, provide help but do not let their problems affect your own spirit. You need to get away and retire away from all the activity in the home. Have an early night and enjoy a great book; tomorrow may bring a surprise.

Love Affairs: Use the sensitive touch of Venus to save yourself from a difficult situation. People are very sensitive and will be easily hurt. If you were born under the sign of Scorpio, a Pisces or a Taurus may induce stress in your life. A Leo friend has better to offer and may present you with an opportunity to develop your inner talents. Venus' diplomatic nature will help you to heal the wounded heart of an old lover. A secret love relationship may be found by the water, and a great trip to Hawaii is in store for some.

Travel and Communication: Mercury rules the mail, telephone and communication in general: during this difficult trend don't expect anything great. Get rid of the extra stuff clogging the house or the garage. Your car may decide to give you trouble and may upset your trip. Take care of it before taking a long journey. Traffic lights or street work may make you late to work; get up a little early as the waning Moon may throw some obstacles your way.

Environment: Do not expect much from nature; bad news may be coming from the sea or the fishing industry. Water, ice, wind — all the elements are there trying to stop you; be careful on the road.

Famous Personalities: Many prominent people will be involved in a lawsuit that could seriously harm their emotional and social standings. Serious drama is ahead for some.

Events: Under the same celestial energy, in September 1996, President Clinton approved federal regulations that declare nicotine an addictive drug; this was a dramatic gesture aimed at curbing teen-age smoking. Expect more important regulation and signing to take place in 1998 too.

Shopping: Great time to do a medical checkup as the stars will make your physician very detail-oriented, helping him detect possible trouble. Stay clear from any psychic; unknowingly they could hurt your psyche. A practical approach to life will pay off for some.

Third
Supernova Window
November/December 1998

From Tuesday November 17th through Tuesday December 15th, 1998.

Specific dates of extreme caution:
November 17th, November 25th, December 5th, December 15th.

November 19th, 1998: Drama, death, police, secret — Concentration of nature's devastative forces at work.

November 25th, 1998: Plane accidents, chain-reaction accident, fires, explosions, earthquakes above 6.3, Electronic problems — Avoid flying on this day.

December 5th & 15th, 1998: Thousands to lose their homes, relocation, secret and drama all over.

Be extremely prudent in driving, and expect chain-reaction accidents. Be prepared for delays, strikes, nature producing awful weather, including hurricanes and tornadoes. The same energy that produced both the Northridge, Los Angeles, and Kobe, Japan, earthquakes is approaching us again. Double-check all your appointments, and if you can, postpone traveling and flying during this Supernova "window." Communication and electricity will be cut off; general loss of power is to be expected. Appliances, computers, telephones, planes, trains, cars — all of these "tools" will be adversely affected by this energy.

They will be stopped in one way or another. The people of the past will make the news, as people from your past will reenter your life. Expect trouble with the post office, education, students, prisoners, newspapers, broadcasting industry and computer viruses may bother us again. As usual NASA, which is not aware of the science of astrology, will waste our tax money with a failed mission due to bad weather and/or electronic malfunctions.

> **Note**: All these malevolent predictions do not have to hurt or touch you as they unfold. Instead, they are printed to prepare you for setbacks and frustrations, thus advising you to be patient, prudent and to synchronize with the will of the cosmos.

November 18th, 1998 — Venus enters Sagittarius: With the love planet in the traveling sign of Sagittarius, an opportunity to find love with a beautiful stranger will be given to you. This trend will allow many souls to find a philosophically oriented mate and enjoy traveling physically and mentally all over the world. Some lucky souls will be given the opportunity to enjoy a very old form of art and may end up at the pyramids of Egypt. If your natal Venus is in good aspect to Jupiter, your sensuality will be stimulated by mental exploration, intelligence and you could find love in learning, traveling or teaching. Souls born now will be given the opportunity to experience love and caring for animals, thus much joy is to be experienced there. If Venus is badly affected, the soul will suffer many disturbing relationships with foreigners or lose a lot of money in gambling. There is a need of freedom with this position and some will have to learn commitment. Blessed with such an intellectual nature, Venus in Sagittarius will offer the soul the opportunity to love with the mind and body. This position makes for one of the most direct and happy partners. Usually artistic talent in teaching and speaking is present with this position. These souls are born to experience love on an intellectual level. Another top position for those involved in the teaching field.

New Moon — November 19th, 1998 in Scorpio: This sign is ruled by Pluto, the planet of death and rebirth. Affairs, finances, health and law enforcement will be on the rise. Expect tragedy of all sorts to take place this month, where all the devil's spirits will be invited to a macabre dance of horror. This will be one of the most difficult lunations where one must realize their limits. This trend will play an important part in your life where judgment from above and below will take place. Health, working life, relationships and the world at large will be affected. Many people and countries may be forced to realize the hard lesson of determination, cruelty, and death. The emphasis is on death and the potential for a rebirth in experiences, strength, and new-found wisdom to perform and live accordingly.

> **Note**: As always with the Lord of hell in charge of this trend, better think twice before saying or acting on impulse. Expect secrets to be divulged, affairs of sex, and nature's devastative forces at work. The police and blackguards will make the news. More than ever use diplomacy, as whatever you do now will have very serious repercussions in your life.

SAT., SUN., MON., TUE., WED., THU. — NOVEMBER 14th, 15th, 16th, 17th, 18th, 19th:
RULERS — Pluto (life and death) and Jupiter (faith).

Work, Career and Business: With the waning Moon and Pluto's deadly touch upon us, keep a low profile and be aware of all you do or say. Some won't be able to stop the upcoming changes and drama. Your intuition about any and all situations will be quite accurate. The future has much better to offer and you should be confident in your dealings. Jupiter, "the Lord of Luck," will make the transition easy and may decide to throw you some luck; listen to your intuition. A serious wake-up call for some where limitations must be accepted. Avoid dealing with money now.

Partnerships: Money will also be on your mind and serious decisions will have to be made soon. Wait for the upcoming New Moon (Nov. 19th) to share new ideas with others. You may take calculated chances now, but you'd better know your limits. As always with Pluto involved, you can only expect to dig into other people's financial or sexual secrets. Surely a great time to get involved with the world of astrology to get some practical direction in your life. The Lord of mysteries may reward you with ultimate light if you take a chance in finding answers in the "forbidden" world. Use diplomacy in all your deals and stay on the right side of the law.

Family and Friends: Emotions and passion are running high these days and Pluto may induce sexual encounters with magnetic strangers. Keep an eye on strangers that may be brought in your home and watch over your children.

Love Affairs: Do not take chances and listen to your intuition wherever you happen to be. If you are married, this is a great trend to stimulate your spouse for some good love-making. Good wine, candle lights, soft music and your imagination are all you need with sexual Pluto involved. Jupiter may decide to send you some news from a faraway friend. Any new relationship started now will be full of sex and passion. Better take precautions if you are a single person and be ready for that "new" relationship to be full of drama. If the weather permits, spend some time in the wild; Jupiter will replenish you with fresh air, fresh spirit and a new approach to life.

Travel and Communication: You may receive news from far away or give presents to a deserving family member or dear friend. You can also expect your telephone to be busy and interesting mail to come your way. Don't try to be in too many places at the same time and if you have to drive, take a little take extra time to get there; don't rush as the police could spoil your day. People from the past will get in touch with you. Be aware on the road; with Pluto absolutely anything nasty can happen to you now.

Environment: Pluto will surely trigger the earth's entrails somewhere in the world and produce dramatic news with the weather. Many human and animal lives have been lost during his dramatic reign. Be ready for the police to make negative news.

Famous Personalities: Pluto will reward those whose lives undergo a metamorphosis, and Jupiter will extend their minds and horizons. Lots of secrets and hidden drama will come to light. A very famous person born in September may go to the other side.

Events: If you are a police officer or a security guard, beware of Pluto. The crooks will be active and deadly. Passion may take over a lost spirit as Pluto will lead him to kill many innocent people. The worst of Pluto's choleric thunders and lightning are about to strike the earth.

Shopping: Invest in anything that can clean or kill pests. Do not invest in anything that could bring danger to those you care for. The Moon will be New soon and a feeling of relief will reach the earth.

FRI., SAT., SUN., MON., TUE., WED. — NOVEMBER 20th, 21st, 22nd, 23rd, 24th, 25th
RULERS — Saturn (governmental changes) and Uranus (freedom).

Work, Career and Business: Following the last few days of destructive Pluto in our lives, Saturn's restructuring power will be a blessing for some organizations and your own business. Expect a new beginning offered to you. Uranus might also throw great surprising developments your way. With the New Moon get active and get what you need; the timing is now right. If the work that you are doing is unsatisfying or a source of stress, with Uranus in charge you can only look for the needed changes. Resolve to find a new career soon and for the lucky ones expect a well-deserved promotion.

Partnerships: Be original; don't let others pressure you into following them instead of your own heart. You will not build anything until you try new grounds. Stressful situations stimulate you to become more independent. Meditate on where you are going in your life and don't be afraid of tomorrow. There is no better time for a new and progressive change. Be nice with others and get active on the social scenery.

Family and Friends: Expect interesting surprises during these days as many will be back with the people of their past. Uranus also makes the children very active and they will drive you a little crazy. Don't be afraid of computers; a study in this area will open many new opportunities. Watch the children carefully, especially close to the water this weekend.

Love Affairs: Friends will call you and with Uranus' touch (surprises) try doing things you would not usually do and go to unusual places on a whim. Visit your future and invest in astrology or the psychic phenomenon. Time for UFOs to materialize in this dense physical world. If you want to see something astonishing go for it now! Uranus may decide to grant one of your important wishes. Love can be found now; get active, do not turn down any invitations. If you are an Aries, an Aquarius friend will surprise you.

Travel and Communication: You may be forced to travel around to visit your past. Do not turn down an invitation, as a professional contact could bring people who will positively influence your career. For this occasion, you may feel like spending some money on your car. Some may get stuck in airports as Uranus may disturb electronic equipment. Many of your plans will be canceled; don't be mad, be patient.

Environment: On a sad note, keep in mind that Uranus rules earthquakes and volcanoes. Let's hope he won't do anything silly now, but he usually does. Flying is fine but the weather will make the trip bumpy. A blackout is high on the list soon.

Famous Personalities: Many famous people will be really active in helping those less fortunate. Beautiful music, great movies and great actors of the past will come alive.

Events: Saturn rules politics, so expect surprising announcements from foreign governments. Under his power in 1997 in Africa, many armed men staged a coup attempt in Sierra Leone. President reportedly flees to Guinea. Armed men launched a coup attempt and said they had taken power in this West African nation. A spokesman, who identified himself as Cpl. Gborie, went on national radio and said that junior army ranks had ousted President Ahmed Tejan Kabbah.

Shopping: Electronic components will fail; you may be forced to invest. You may want to pay a visit to your future and meet with your favorite "spiritual guide." Because of Mercury's retrograde motion, any electronic tools bought now will bring you trouble later.

November 27th, 1998 — Mars enters Libra: Children born during this trend will have a inherent gift in psychology and will fight for justice. A perfect position for those willing to enforce the law. A strong desire to deal and organize with large groups will be offered to the soul. Many will pursue the arts and will gain recognition during the course of their lives. Under too much stress they may suffer back and kidney trouble.

August 23rd, 1998 — Neptune will re-enter Capricorn and will return to Aquarius again in November 28th, 1998. Neptune will remain in the futuristic sign of Aquarius well after the year 2000.

The dogmatic, religious Neptunian energies will melt into the futuristic sign of Aquarius. Then the general spiritual essence of mankind's belief systems will undergo a full rebirth where the dogmatic views of the past will be replaced by a total cosmic consciousness. The true face of God and his celestial manifestation will be divulged to mankind.

THU., FRI., SAT., SUN., MON. — NOVEMBER 26th, 27th, 28th, 29th, 30th:
RULERS — Neptune (imagination), Mars (action) and Mercury (interaction).

Work, Career and Business: Neptune's blurring nature may affect your judgment. Be practical in all your expectations. If a business is not going well, you might be going in the wrong direction. Use all those above-mentioned planets to look for the right one. With the good Moon around, the opportunity might be in your local newspaper; take the time to cruise through it. Communicate your desires to whoever can help.

Partnerships: Come clear with what you mean. Some people could be deceiving you; ask pertinent questions and watch their reaction. Be ready to support depressed partners, but don't let their problems affect your judgment and feelings. A trip related to your business life could prove beneficial. A contract may be offered; sign it before the Full Moon.

Family and Friends: Expect tons of action around you and with Mars cruising above use patience and diplomacy with others. Venus will bring an element of love and joy in the anticipation of Xmas. Mercury will join them and will make us very communicative. Much of your time will be spent organizing trips, or get in touch with your past. This trend will be an interesting one where friends and family members will try to get in touch with you all at the same time. This trio may drive you crazy and you will have your hands full of projects and not enough time to deal with them. The festivities will arrive soon and luckily for us the great blessings of a New Moon will make this Christmas a memorable one.

Love Affairs: Affairs of the heart will progress these days and the weekend could prove to be very interesting. Some teenagers need your attention; if you don't provide it, they could get themselves in trouble. Provide guidance and support to all in need as they are not aware of the stars' impact on their lives. Some will be caught in a love affair of their past and may be deceiving themselves. Neptune will provide lot of care and religious preparation.

Travel and Communication: The strength of Mars combined with the speed of Mercury may bring trouble on the road. Be safe; take the time to do some of your shopping early; give yourself plenty time to deal with everybody you care for. Use precautions and take your time if you have to travel far away to visit people; don't let Mars or Neptune stop you. Most of all, DON'T DRINK AND DRIVE! as Neptune could lead you into serious trouble. The past will become alive; deal with it and enjoy all the planning.

Environment: Keep in mind that Mars is with us and many people will start moving around. He may not care for the early preparation of Xmas time and may decide to throw an earthquake or produce disturbing weather all around. Be patient with everyone.

Famous Personalities: This timing is ideal for meditation and renewing your faith in the universe. Pious rich and famous will prepare all sorts of activities to perform, and will give the checks to charitable organizations. Try your best to participate and provide for those in need.

Events: The last breath of the deceiving Pisces age will be in full action. Religions, dogmas, fears and man-made hell and imaginative stories of the Apocalypse will be soon replaced by a more healthy approach to the future. The new Age of Aquarius will completely transform man's consciousness within the next few years ahead of us. Before this transformation the worst of religious fanaticism must be experienced, producing a form of deceiving religious "madness" all over the world. As we get closer to the year 2000, puritanical America and many of her poisoned children will be indeed victims of the uprising foolishness.

Shopping: Great deals will be found well before the upcoming festivities in the most unexpected places. However, do not let all the advertisers run away with your pocketbook, as you will feel like buying all the best and most glamorous things right now. Be sure to treat yourself to something nice on these days too. The Christmas spirit is already there, but people will be busy and short of patience and tempers. Make sure that you plan a leisurely day to do your shopping where the pull and hurry all around you won't affect your mood. Remember, you know better than the others, so just smile and brighten a sad day. Many of you have realized the value of my work; Starguide is a perfect and valuable present to offer. Contribute a piece of the Universe to those you really care for.

Welcome to Your Day-to-Day Guidance For December 1998

Full Moon — December 3rd, 1998 in Gemini: Dramatic news from foreign countries is to be expected. Let's hope this lunation will not affect the transportation or educational administration negatively. Strikes or problems with students, education or transportation are a high possibility. Combined with Mercury still retrograde, the last thing we need is a strike just before Xmas or some unhappy students to make the news. Much of the established laws will be challenged by groups, and some newspapers or news media leaders will be involved. A serious chain-reaction accident or a famous person from the past is about to make dramatic news. Many people unaware of the stars will have to pay a heavy price for their ignorance and may end up stuck in a congested airport with many canceled flights due to an awful weather development. This lunation will affect communication, sophisticated electronic equipment and may produce an aeronautical disaster in the near future. The winds will blow very hard and rivers will rise.

TUE., WED., THU., FRI., SAT., SUN. — DECEMBER 1st, 2nd, 3rd, 4th, 5th, 6th:
RULERS — Venus (caring), Mercury (contact) and the Moon (variation).

Work, Career and Business: You may find it difficult to concentrate on your duties as your mind will wander about the anticipated good time ahead. The deserving hard-working souls will benefit with well-deserved bonuses or a new opportunity to promote their career soon. Mercury will make you think fast, and action will be everywhere. Be aware of the Full Moon tension and be ready to change many schedules. Wait for the next new Moon to deal with important deals. Contracts signed now will bring you deception.

Partnerships: Some of the people you know will have to move away from you or you may decide yourself to relocate to a better place within the next few days. Expect the beginning or ending of important phases of your life and others' too. Venus will endorse many gatherings with colleagues you have not seen for a long time. Be ready to control your emotions during the Full Moon around the 3rd of December.

Family and Friends: Expect a brother or a sister to pleasantly surprise you. A friend may also decide to show up uninvited and this may affect some of your planning. You may receive an invitation to socialize with some faraway dear friends or family members; use this opportunity to get closer to them. This year, luckily for all of us, the Christmas season will happen in a waxing positive Moon trend and we are all due for a great time. Get together to socialize with some close friends this week end and enjoy the old days. Don't forget the Moon is now full and waning, and a few things may not go your way. A family member needs your advice. Be willing to consider the issue from their point of view; avoid emotional involvement or forcing your opinion on others. Much time will be spent around the children's desires and finding a great Christmas tree soon. Enjoy the warmth and the good food of your mom.

Love Affairs: Don't expect much progress if you are looking for that special person just yet. Some of the people from your past may also become heavy; stand for yourself without guilt. Friends will bring good memories; have fun but don't get caught up in the nostalgia. If you are a Cancer, an older or much younger person will try to steal your heart. Have fun, but don't make any commitment if the person in question was met for the first time in the bad Moon.

Travel and Communication: You will have to run like mad to deal with all the things you must accomplish soon. All this activity will keep you busy and bring you in contact with interesting people. Combined with the Full Moon trend, Mercury will induce all sorts of delays, forcing you to think twice as fast. Slow down; be cautious and prudent in your driving, too. Watch other crazy drivers around the city; they might not have "Moon Power," so don't let them hurt you (or your car). Many will fly to faraway places early and will get caught in bad weather or find themselves stuck in congested airports. Keep in mind that Mercury may decide to twist up some electronic wiring and bring some chaos. Chain-reaction accidents are very high on the list; be careful out there.

Environment: Please refer to the section "Supernova window" and check on the dates I pointed out. Chances are that nature will go berserk soon and you don't want to be a victim. She may demonstrate her power with shocking weather. Thousands of people may be forced to relocate, fleeing disasters, flooding or a bad earthquake. Distressing news from the Middle East could reach the media.

Famous Personalities: A famous person (or their children) will make dramatic news traveling around. Lots of interesting news about many famous or infamous people who made history. The past will turn alive for a while.

Events: Uranus aeronautics, with Mercury retrograde, sophisticated electronics may suffer or fail to function properly. This could produce another dramatic air crash. Not a time to take any risks in the air, unless you made your reservation during a waxing trend. A trend where the beginning or ending of an important portion of your (and other) lives will have to be experienced.

Shopping: Wait for the next New Moon on December 18th to spend money on expensive gifts. You can still find a good deal on a big-ticket item by comparison shopping. If you decide to visit Las Vegas' casinos now, you may encounter stress and will not hit the jackpot. Yes, someone will hit the jackpot in a waning Moon in Vegas, but the money will be spent on paying bills or tax and little will be left. The "lucky" person will be geared by the negative energy to invest the winnings on an "unlucky" bargain and lose it all. Better make all your important plans after the 18th for your own sake. Consider offering *Starguide Moon Power* to those you really care about for Christmas. It is affordable, valuable and if it worked for you all year around it will also work for them. They will probably love you for shedding some light of the universe upon their life.

MON., TUE., WED., THU., FRI. — DECEMBER 7th, 8th, 9th, 10, 11th:

RULERS — The Sun (children/love), Venus (love), Mercury (traveling/communication).

Work, Career and Business: Do not expect much progress these days. The waning Moon (negative) will make sure to obstruct any business venture. Don't take yourself too seriously; set a meeting with coworkers to discuss what could be done to improve the business. Why not forget about your responsibility for a while and smell the roses like everyone else? Enjoy the party after work and let your real feelings show. Another week and the Moon will put a smile on your face (and your affairs).

Partnerships: Old and new friends will be happy to talk to you and will exchange ideas, hopes and wishes with you. The holiday season is getting close; make sure you don't get stuck at the last minute with heavy shopping yet to do. Be aware of what your partner needs and offer the surprise for Christmas. A plan to travel close to the water will make some souls very happy.

Family and Friends: Christmas is really for children of all ages and for those who suffered a hard start in life; this time may bring back sad memories of our own childhood. Don't let this gloomy feeling get to you, and learn to forget whatever dramatic experiences you had to go through. We are on this earth to do a specific work we set for ourselves. Take care of the young, life goes by so fast, let them fully enjoy your love and your care. Don't let the waning Moon bother you with guilt or your difficult past. Do something special that will help you to fight the depressive mood. The children have plenty of ideas; listen to them and enjoy life. Friends may request your help in some area.

Love Affairs: With the Sun (love) in charge, an element of surprise is around you. As usual in time of a waning Moon (negative), don't expect long-lasting love if you fall for someone new. If you are an Aquarius, a Gemini or a Leo needs your spiritual help.

Travel and Communication: The police will begin to plan for the holidays and may stop you if you drive unsafely. Drinking heavily could seriously disturb your plans and should be completely out of the question. You do not want to ruin your or someone else's family for Christmas. Be safe and if you drink with friends on Friday night, take a cab home.

Environment: Hopefully lovely Venus and the magnanimous Sun will stop any drama imparted by the waning Moon. The weather will be difficult; stay clear of lightning. An explosion or a fire could hurt some children; watch over them carefully.

Famous Personalities: Many famous people will shine, helping those born with difficult karmic stars. Great shows will be offered to the public. Don't fall for the promoters of the Apocalypse; they are after your money and their own successful future.

Events: The Supernova negative energy is dissipating fast and the stars will slowly become more tolerant of the earth. We are still in a waning period and some disasters will still happen; be aware and careful in all you do.

Shopping: Use the light of the Sun to regenerate your spirit. Invest in your favorite spiritual healer, psychic or astrologer; it will do you good. Visit your future with faith. Enjoy the fast-approaching festivities. Be wise: those three kings who followed a star to Bethlehem, the birthplace of Jesus Christ were astrologers!

December 12, 1998 — Venus enters Capricorn: Souls born now will have an opportunity to master classical arts and will look for successful people to spend their lives with. They will attract much older partners when young, then much younger as they grow older. The opportunity to mix business, love, wealth and pleasure is offered to the soul. Some will spend quite a long time without love but will strike lucky late in life. Thus if you were born with Venus (love) in Capricorn (rank), you must get active after each and every New Moon period. Avoid criticism and participate in many activities.

> **Note**: As always with the Lord of hell in charge of this trend, better think twice before saying or acting on impulse. Expect secrets to be divulged, affairs of sex, and nature's devastative forces at work. The police and blackguards will make the news. More than ever, use diplomacy as whatever you do now will have very serious repercussions in your life.

SAT., SUN., MON., TUE., WED. — DECEMBER 12th, 13th, 14th, 15th, 16th:
RULERS — Venus (sweetheart) and Pluto (fatal attraction).

Work, Career and Business: With the waning Moon and Pluto in charge, expect dramatic repercussions in your life. Hopefully this energy will not touch you directly, but if it does you will need to be strong and realize the harshness of life. You may also find out your real limits about a business proposition. Time to review all your accomplishments and the reasons for your failures. Accept the upcoming changes with grace. You will be forced out of a situation where you do not belong and you should be thankful for your intuition. Meditate on improving your future and if education is needed to further your progress invest in it.

Partnerships: Money will play an important part in your life now. Be practical in all your expenses; you are advised not to overspend. The lucky souls will receive very expensive presents; some good-hearted people will offer them. As always with Pluto in charge, promises made now won't be kept. Just wait patiently for the next New Moon of December 18th to invest or sign documents. Churches all over will be busy making plans to accommodate many pious souls. Answering to Neptune's power, many will get depressed and will need your support. The Christmas spirit is now getting much stronger and the world will feel compassionate and loving for the victims of Pluto's destructive will.

Family and Friends: Many will travel to foreign religious places and will enjoy the different religious cultures of these people. Expect news from all over as new plans must be set to accommodate visitors. Your family from afar will let you know how much they love and miss you. The friends circle will be extremely busy as we are all enjoying the best of what life has to offer. With Santa Claus' arrival, children get more excited and will be somehow difficult to handle. Pluto will make everyone passionate and restless. A trip out of the house to the shopping center could be a must for some. Be aware of Pluto at all times and use diplomacy at all costs. Don't expect much diplomacy around you as people will become susceptible to your comments. Control emotion and watch what's going on in the house, especially if children are around. A great time is ahead of you if you listen to your intuition. As always, if a stranger is brought to your house, be aware of his motives. Drama is bound to strike a family with a passionate murder. Don't be Pluto's victim.

Love Affairs: A mixture of Pluto and Venus can transform you into a walking magnet. The potential for secret affairs or sexual intercourse is high on the list of things during this trend. The planet of love could make you too friendly or trusting; be aware of mysterious Pluto and his sensual magnetism. Stay clear of alcohol and use your intuition at all times. The Moon is still waning (negative), and trouble may come your way if you fall for unprotected sex.

Travel and Communication: Pluto rules passion, the crooks and the police force. The deadly "Attica" jail riot in September 1971 unfolded under his power. Many guards and inmates were killed by the police. Guards were held hostage for a few days when deadly force was used to end the conflict. Incidentally, the Rodney King dilemma took also place under the same stars. News pertaining to the police force will always appear during his ruling days. It is my aspiration in the future to communicate this knowledge to the police Academy. Pluto's impact upon our courageous police officers is deadly; in the name of ignorance from their superiors, many suffered wasteful death. In the future, when the "ridicule" will be cast aside, the Police Executives will be warning their officers of the impact of the Plutonic impact upon their dangerous endeavors. Astrology one day will be used to point out the criminals. Locating the destructive power of Pluto transpiring in their natal profile, a potential murderer can be identified. Knowledge is power and there is no room for ignorance in the police force.

Environment: Pluto does not care for anything or Christmas for that matter. He will induce drama and could disturb the earth's belly, producing a bad earthquake. As usual with Pluto in charge, be ready for many interesting secrets to surface and remember to keep these to yourself.

Famous Personalities: A famous personality will be called to God and many will miss the soul. A reminder of our own mortality and the signature of Pluto's short passage upon our world.

Events: Pluto stirs man's animal tendencies and the infinite forces of good and evil constantly teasing each other. If you are a Police officer and on duty now, don't take chances.

Note: Controlled by the planet of death and drama, the higher suicide rate is to be found within the police force.

Shopping: Only second-hand shopping or well advertised sales will give you the best deals in town. Better wait for the New Moon (December 18th) for valuable items. Do not invest in dangerous toys for your children; with Pluto signature, they could get hurt. Give old toys to unfortunate children.

New Moon — December 18th, 1998

THU., FRI., SAT., SUN., MON. — DECEMBER 17th, 18th, 19th, 20th, 21st:
RULERS: Jupiter (foreign affairs) and Saturn (dominance):

Work, Career and Business: Jupiter's positive energy will help to restore faith and new opportunities in your life. You could use this trend to gather your thoughts and get close to God in your local church or in nature and enjoy the wildness. Keep your notion of life clean; avoid poisoning your future with a negative attitude. Pray for the world, for the children of the future. Many of those restorative thoughts are needed, then slowly but surely a healing process will take place. With the New Moon upon us you may begin to see the light. Signing important documents is OK, and valuable opportunities are on the way. Be ready for the beginning or ending of important parts of your life.

Partnerships: A new business partner wants to share a great plan with you; it probably is! Don't rush. Listen to your intuition before and add your own creative force in the process. A foreigner could also enter the scenery and the meeting could positively affect your future. Avoid tensions this weekend about a specific project or trip. Nothing can really stop you if you mean business. Keep a positive attitude.

Family and Friends: Friends will be active and many will be requesting your presence. Just before Christmas, one should not refuse invitations as many wishes will be granted by the waxing Moon and your great friends. You may plan to throw your own party with some good friends this weekend. Keep your eyes open for an older person with good deal or kind words to offer. Kids sense that they are the center of attention; be patient with their demands. If Mom is faraway, she may call you; don't dwell on the past and avoid gossiping. Be happy. Don't let the Christmas preparations upset you, all will be fine.

Love Affairs: Socialize with friends on Saturday or Sunday night. You will feel positive away from home with the people around you. They will enjoy your company and one of your wishes may come true. Avoid impulsive actions where romance is concerned and drive carefully on your way back home during the late hours. Do not fall victim to Saturn's gloomy power; forget about your responsibility, go out, meet new people and expect a lot. If you're born in January or in September you could find love. The future has better to offer, so put a big smile on your face and be confident. Progressive changes ahead; be patient and participate in life. If you are single and born in April, a Leo or a Libra could be strongly attracted to you.

Travel and Communication: Saturn rules old people and parts of your past. Take care of the old people you love. Make this upcoming holiday season a good one, as they might not be around for the next one. Some will plan to travel to faraway places this weekend, some just around town to meet their future. Be aware of early celebration as people could drink too much and drive dangerously. Stay safe and watch the road.

Events: Jupiter may decide to entertain us with some gospel music or religious performances. Many great souls will be busy preparing food for the homeless. Under Saturn's power, people challenge governmental structure. For instance, in June, 1997 many Taliban fighters asserted authority in northern Afghanistan. Warlord Dostum flees to Turkey. Taliban fighters moved swiftly Sunday to assert their authority over this northern stronghold, whose capture nearly completed a three-year campaign to unite Afghanistan under the white flag of the radical Islamic army.

Famous Personalities: The rich and famous will also busy themselves to alleviate pain in the world.

Events: A political person may make surprising news. Be ready for startling news from a foreign land soon. Mexico or a Spanish-speaking country needs help.

Shopping: Invest in traveling or a foreign language and you will have a very rewarding great time ahead of you. Use Jupiter's philosophical values to improve your consciousness, or plan to start an important study.

New Moon — December 18th, 1998 in Sagittarius. This sign is ruled by Jupiter, the planet of codification of thought. Affairs of religion, foreigners, and the formation of new laws will be on the rise. Expect news coming from foreign powers, forcing many governments to take secret drastic action. This trend will play an important part on the religious front and could directly affect the Pope. Many people and countries may be forced to realize the hard lesson of religious freedom as dramatic changes are taking place. The emphasis is on abortion rights, foreigners, religious values and the potential for a rebirth in a newfound wisdom to perform and live accordingly with the rest of the world. Don't fall for the Apocalyptic promoters.

TUE., WED., THU., FRI., SAT. — DECEMBER 22nd, 23nd, 24th, 25th, 26th:
RULERS: Neptune (religion, make-believe) and Mars (action):

Merry Christmas to all my wonderful readers.

Work, Career and Business: The New Moon is still with us and her beneficial white robe will provide all we need. Do not expect much to be accomplished as we will find it hard to concentrate on tasks. Time to socialize with co-workers as Saturn's children (CEOs) will be out in public places and many of them can further your career wishes. The month is about to finish on a note of serious changes and interesting development. A business trip or an invitation may lead you to many good contacts. You will have time to play and mix business and pleasure.

Family and Friends: Many will be enjoying foreign places and the different cultures of these people. Expect news from brothers and sisters from afar and let yourself be immersed in the great Holiday season. Children are very excited and will be enjoying the festivities. The friends and family circle will be extremely busy as we are all enjoying the best of what life has to offer. People will race to the Churches all over responding to Neptune's religious power. Many of God's houses will be crowded and you should get there on time. Combined with the New Moon and Neptune, the Christmas spirit of love will receive its full support from the stars, thus making it a pious and wonderful one. Please try to participate in volunteer work to provide love and help to the needy. Merry Xmas from both Brigitte and me to all; may the future bring you all you need and more.

Love Affairs: As usual with Mars in charge, avoid impatience and be aware around water or boating. With Neptune with us, control your emotions and your imagination. The Moon is waxing (positive); any surprises ahead of you should be of a positive nature. Many will find love, and this new relationship may lead you to a rewarding future.

Travel and Communication: Your telephone and your mail will bring you all sorts of news and invitations. The lucky ones will enjoy a faraway trip close to those they love. Expect news from your brother or sister; get in touch with some of your friends for a good chat. Remember, Neptune is also part of the festivities and you must not overindulge in eating or drinking. A quiet walk by the sea will bring your spirit high and stimulate your faith. Many lonely people will feel the depressive power of Neptune, and some older souls may call on you for help. With Mars' desire for action and Neptune's stressful imagination, many evangelists will hard-headedly spray the gospel words, and "repent, hell, and the end of times" will be their favorite topic. The only changes ahead of us are our consciousness and a new faith based upon the understanding of God's celestial tools.

Environment: Neptune may bring disturbing news from the Middle East or the ocean. Let's hope the New Moon will stop anything drastic. The weather could prove to be very difficult in some places. Be aware around water.

Famous Personalities: A fantastic time is to be expected from the efforts of many gifted artists efforts to bring love, joy and faith to the world. Some of their nasty secrets will become public.

Events: Some abortion activists will bring their conviction and trouble around with them.

Shopping: These days belong to the children and all toys bought now will bring great joy to them. Invest in anything that can be used around water or any survival gear.

SUN., MON., TUE., WED., THU. — DECEMBER 27th, 28th 29th, 30th, 31st:
RULERS: Venus (sweeping love) and Mercury (twin):

Work, Career and Business: You need to take some time to bring the routine back into your life. Reach out to new people and expand the various social networks while the Moon is still on your side. Work hard to reach your goals; business started now will have the potential to bring financial security to all parties involved. Time to ask for favor, even a loan from your bank manager. Money and security will play an important part of this trend and you might find yourself investing in a good deal. You should be confident of the outcome.

Partnerships: The year 1997 will end on a sweet note. Candlelight, soft music, courtship and social gatherings are on the agenda for many lovers. The soft Venus energy will tone down the militant attitude of the people around you. You may also use her diplomatic gift to apologize for your mistakes. Push forward, and reach out to new people and expand the various social networks in your life. Use finesse in all you do; you can't miss. Under Venus' blessings, you must keep in mind that whatever is offered with true love will bring luck to the giver. Let your partner know about your deep feelings and offer flowers to those you care about.

Family and Friends: You are a bit tired with all the running you had to do lately. You will be still in demand by friends; do not turn down an invitation as some of your wishes are around the corner. Communication is the key; don't be shy, everybody will listen to your comments. Avoid falling into useless gossiping over the telephone; only "Ma Bell" will benefit from that! You may hear good news about brothers or sisters. The children are finally happy and enjoy much of their time playing with their toys. Take valuable pictures. Use Mercury's power of expression to reach your goals.

Love Affairs: Presents you have received make you very happy. Promote words of love, and nurture the feelings of those you care about. You may discover that a relationship is growing towards romance and you need to be confident in your partner. A situation with another person may force some to make a decision; use your intuition and keep a cool head. The lessons of the past should be remembered. If you are single and born in May, a Pisces or a Capricorn will be strongly attracted to you.

Travel and Communication: Interesting news is on the way and your telephone will get busy these days. Now is the time to plan or do some traveling. Avoid the impulsive Mercurial need for speed on your way back home. You might have to deal with high winds and snow. Take care of your wheels and take enough rest before taking your journey. Flying is fine.

Environment: Nature may get out of hand around the 29th, with a bad earthquake. A monetary scandal could make the news. A famous personality will pay a heavy price for a selfish act.

Events: The broadcasting, transportation and educational industry will undergo some progressive changes. Strikes are high on the list. The educational department or transportation industry may impose their demand for changes.

Shopping: A camera purchased now will bring you great joy. Time to invest in a new car or invest in expensive items for the office. Whatever you do, Use Mercury's bargaining power aggressively. A pet bought now will bring great joy to the owner. Don't be afraid to use your communication powers. Be happy and have faith in your future.

The greatness of the Universe is unknown, but the magnetic forces that guide and move all the planets in our galaxy are known; this Divine source of power can be used to guide and bring man a life filled with happiness, peace and harmony.

— Dr. Turi

Chapter 8
Solar and Lunar Eclipses

Note: There are three types of lunar eclipses distributed as follows:

A = an APULSE, a penumbral eclipse where the Moon enters only the penumbra (shadow) of the Earth.

P = a PARTIAL eclipse where the Moon enters the umbra without being totally immersed in it.

T = a TOTAL eclipse, where the Moon is entirely immersed within the umbra.

There are six types of Solar eclipses distributed as follows:

P = a PARTIAL eclipse where the Moon does not completely cover the sun.

T = a TOTAL eclipse where the Moon completely covers the Sun.

A = an ANNULAR eclipse where the Moon will not entirely hide the Sun so a narrow ring of light will surround the dark New Moon.

AT = an ANNULATOR = TOTAL eclipse, total for part of its path, annular for the rest.

A non C = a rare ANNULAR eclipse where the central line does not touch the Earth's surface.

T non C = a rare TOTAL eclipse where the central lines does not touch the Earth's surface

On the evening news, you'll only hear about eclipses when they occur someplace interesting, usually in your own back yard about once every twenty years. In fact, solar and lunar eclipses occur in pairs every six months or so in what we call "Eclipse Seasons." Sometimes you get a bonus: two lunars and a solar, or two solars and a lunar in the space of a single month. Solar eclipses can range in intensity from the moon's just clipping the sun to the dramatic total eclipse. A lunar eclipse can range from an imperceptible darkening of the lunar disk, to complete disappearance. Unlike solar eclipses, a lunar eclipse is generally visible to half the planet. The importance of eclipses in modern astrology has long been known, but is still not clearly understood. Later on, I will try to put some light using Divine Astrology for future Eclipses and predictions.

The final total solar eclipse of the millennium, in 1999, is a once-in-a-lifetime chance for those living in Europe to witness this incredible astronomical phenomenon. On Wednesday, August 11, 1999, a total eclipse of the Sun will be visible from the Isles of Sicily, the Cornish mainland, Alderney in the Channel Islands, and much of mainland Europe. Incidentally, since 1927 the United Kingdom's mainland population has not seen a total eclipse. This is truly a lifetime opportunity and should not to be missed. The chances of clear skies are not excellent, especially in UK (I lived there for nearly 15 years.) Thus this is the last chance for many people living today to observe a total eclipse in the British Isles before the 23rd of September 2090. The European countries will not see such an event again until 2081. This event will be extraordinary in itself and should not be missed; if you can afford it go to Europe and enjoy this celestial show.

Future Eclipses: Here is a comprehensive list of the total and annular eclipses occurring between now (Jan. 1998) and the year 2010, plus UK eclipses up to 2151. This will depict how scarce total eclipses visible from dry land are, and how important the upcoming eclipse of August 1999 really is.

Thursday, February 26, 1998 — On my birthday and on a New Moon! What a present from the Gods!

Prediction: Be ready for incredible surprises, perhaps extraordinary things that many thought hitherto impossible.

Thursday, February 26, 1998 — a total eclipse of the Sun will be visible from within a narrow window that crosses the Western Hemisphere. The path of the Moon's umbral shadow starts in the Pacific, proceeding through northern South America and the Caribbean Sea, and ends at sunset off the Atlantic coast of Africa. A partial eclipse will be seen within the much broader path of the Moon's penumbral shadow, which includes parts of the United States and eastern Canada, Mexico, Central America and the northern half of South America. The area of partial eclipse reaches as far as Portugal, and parts of Spain and Iceland, but just stops short of the south-west corner of Ireland at sunset. The maximum duration is 4 minutes 8 seconds, and the path width at maximum is 151 kilometers.

August 22, 1998 — The track crosses Australia, and southeast into the Pacific.

February 16, 1999 — The track goes from the south of South Africa, across the Indian Ocean and Australia. Be ready for nature's incredible forces to enter in action. On both of those eclipses expect volcanic eruptions and extra large earthquakes. This phenomenal seismic activity will mark the beginning of an inner restructure of the earth's entrails.

Astro Weather Service (A.W.S.)

A.W.S. Supernova Windows with 1998 Worldwide Weather Predictions

There will be three major SUPERNOVA negative windows in 1998 — each destructive "window" is operational for three to four weeks, so caution is strongly advised during this period. Heavy loss of lives due to nature's devastating forces, aeronautical disasters and structural damage is to be expected.

> **Note**: A Supernova Window is a concentration of negative celestial energy coming from certain planets and distant stars. Everything on this dense physical world is in direct relationship with other Celestial bodies. Thus, the repercussion of such an intense field coming from outer space to the earth will transform into a mighty "wave." Sir Isaac Newton said that "For every action (physical or spiritual) there will be an opposite and equal reaction." These circumstances often disturb the regular orderly magnetic fields of the globe and induce more stress on our planet's faults. This phenomenon also disturbs sophisticated electronics, produces aeronautical disasters, blackouts and a variety of nature's forces such as tornadoes, volcanic eruptions, large earthquakes, typhoons, hurricanes, tsunamis, etc. I have also noticed that, in time of a Supernova window, the inborn navigational system of whales gets obstructed, resulting in incomprehensible beaching or mass suicide.

Chapter 9
1998 Supernova Windows

Note: 1997 Last Supernova Window

December 1997: Fourth Supernova Window
Thursday December 4th through Wednesday December 31st, 1997.

Specific dates of extreme caution:
Dec. 4th — Dec. 16th — Dec. 25th — Dec. 31st.

December 16th, 1997 — Chain-reaction accident in Los Angeles, large earthquakes in Mexico / Japan / Ring of fire / Thousands forced to relocate / Nature's devastative forces at work / Loss of power / extreme cold and flooding. Avoid flying.

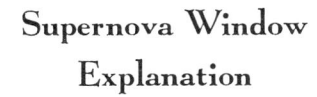

Supernova Window Explanation

Concentration of negative celestial energy approaching.

Be extremely prudent in driving, and expect chain-reaction accidents. Be prepared for delays, strikes and nature producing dreadful weather. An increase in large-earthquake activity, volcanic eruptions, hurricanes and tornadoes will plague the world. The same mighty seismic force that produced both the Northridge, Los Angeles, and Kobe, Japan, earthquakes is approaching us again. Double-check all your appointments, and if you can, postpone traveling and flying during any Supernova "window." You may have to travel anyhow, but double your attention on the road and do not trust anyone. Communication and electricity could be cut off; a general loss of power (blackout or brownout) is also expected. Appliances, computers, telephones, planes, trains, cars — all of our human "tools" will be affected by this energy.

Many moving or electronic parts will be stopped in one way or another. The people of the past will make the news, and some folks from your own past will re-enter your life. Expect trouble with the post office, education, students, prisoner escapes or riots, newspapers, broadcasting industry strikes and computer viruses may bother us again. Be prudent as many unexpected "detours" or "broken" street lights will induce more danger on the road. Watch for the many broken-down cars on the side of the highway, and slow down to avoid speeding tickets. As usual NASA, which is not aware of the old science of Divine Astrology, will waste our tax money with a failed mission due to bad weather and/or loss of very expensive pieces of electronics due to various malfunctions.

All these malevolent predictions do not have to hurt or touch you as they unfold. Instead, they are printed to prepare you for setbacks and frustrations, thus advising you to be patient, to be prudent and to synchronize with the steadfast will of the cosmos.

Knowledge is power and there is no room for ignorance or excuses in the stars. Thus, the opportunity to plan in advance in both the physical and the spiritual worlds is given to you in *Starguide*. During any "Supernova Window" in 1998, I strongly advise you to be patient, to be prudent and to understand that this timing is to look back at your life and fix any of the problems that you may have experienced. Now is the time to send out those apologies, and take care of any niggling little matter before it grows larger. Get together with people whom you have not seen in a long while and catch up. This is the cosmos' way of saying slow down and smell the roses before they have all gone.

In the stormy game of life, to be victorious is to reject defeat

— Bradley

First Supernova Window: March 1998 / April 1998.
From Tuesday March 24th through Sunday, April 26th, 1998.

Specific dates of extreme caution:
March 24th, April 3rd, April 13th, April 21st and April 26th.

March 24th, 1998 — Violent weather in parts of the US and many other parts of the world with the potential to produce volcanic eruptions, earthquakes, floods, tornadoes, hurricanes and aeronautical disasters. High seismic activity. Earthquakes above normal in Japan and California.

April 13th & 21st, 1998 — Violent weather in parts of the U.S. and many other parts of the world, producing earthquakes, flooding, tornadoes, hurricanes and aeronautical disasters — Quake activity well above normal in Japan and California.

Second Supernova Window: July/August 1998.
From Tuesday July 21st, through Thursday, August 27th, 1998.

Specific dates of extreme caution:
July 21st, July 31st, August 7th, August 13th, August 18th.

July 21st & 31st, 1998 — Large quakes, tornadoes, loss of power, electronic disturbances/aeronautical and sea accidents.

August 7th, 13th & 18th, 1998 — Thousands of people to relocate — Concentration of natural destructive forces and a succession of earthquakes, hurricanes, flooding and tornadoes.

Third Supernova Window: November/December 1998.
Tuesday November 17th through Tuesday December 15th, 1998.

Specific dates of extreme caution:
November 17th, November 25th, December 5th, December 15th.

November 17th, 1998: Drama, death, police, secret — Concentration of nature's devastative forces at work.

November 25th, 1998: Plane accidents, chain-reaction accidents, fires, explosions, earthquakes above 6.3, electronic problems — Avoid flying on this day.

December 5th & 15th, 1998: Thousands to lose their homes, relocation, secrets and drama all over.

Chapter 10
Back in Time

This section is a reminder of a small fraction of the most obvious predictions made over the years by Dr. Turi in previous Moon Power publications.

Memo: Printed in the 1993 Starguide: "Some new lung and respiratory diseases will plague the masses and will force local government to take serious health measures."

Note: The *Phoenix Gazette* reported on June 3rd 1993. Mysterious respiratory illness, "What is it that's killing our Indian people? What?"

Memo: *Printed in the 1995 Starguide* — "Be aware of the Full Moon (Jan. 16th); expect the beginning or ending of an important part of your life. Keep your eyes (and ears) open and realize the drama or changes affecting others too. Time to control emotions, provide spiritual help and be ready for the worst. Only faith, strength and courage can help you now! Pray to God for the souls of the poor victims. Nothing is made to last forever and that is part of life."

Note: Jan. 16th, 1995 the city of Kobe in Japan experienced a 7.2 earthquake killing more than 5000.

Memo: Printed in the *1996 Starguide*: "Bill Cosby will have to suffer problems with his children. The loss of a family member will affect him terribly!"

Note: The only son of entertainer Bill Cosby was found shot to death in the early hours of January 16, 1997 lying next to his car, which was parked along a major freeway in the affluent Bel Air area of Los Angeles.

Memo: Printed in the 1996 Starguide: "President Clinton — Born August 19, 1946. Trouble will be coming from his knees and later on his heart as he gets older."

Note: President Clinton injured his knee after falling at Greg Norman's Florida estate.

Memo: "One hundred churches will be burned down" and "1996 will be the worst year for fires since 1948." Printed in *Fate* magazine Jan. 1st, 1995 edition.

Note: 1. A long series of church fires plagued the media in 1996.
2. Interior Secretary Bruce Babbitt said the cost of fighting the fires, which have raged for two months, was about $1 million a day, not counting property damage. Nearly 5.3 million acres have been consumed by flames in 1996, the West's worst fire season in more than 25 years.

Memo: "Prominent Army/Navy figures lost"

Note: 1. Israeli Prime Minister and Former Army Chief of Staff Yitzhak Rabin was assassinated.

2. Plane carrying U.S. Commerce Secretary crashes in Balkans. Rescue teams search for survivors. Search and rescue teams were combing the Adriatic Sea Wednesday for survivors of a plane that crashed with U.S. Commerce Secretary Ron Brown and 33 other passengers aboard.

3. May 16, 1996 — Navy's top officer dies of gunshot, apparently self-inflicted. The nation's top Navy officer, Adm. Jeremy Michael Boorda, died Thursday from an apparently self-inflicted gunshot wound hours after learning *Newsweek* magazine was raising questions about the legitimacy of some of his combat medals.

Memo: "New mind diseases and come-back of meningitis"

Note: March 21, 1996 — The concern stems from new scientific research that reveals likely links between "mad cow disease" — known as BSE — and its fatal human equivalent, CJD, Creutzfeldt-Jakob Disease. The disease attacks brain matter and literally riddles the brain with holes, like a sponge.

Memo: The following predictions were made April 7th, 1996; printed September 1996 in the *1997 Starguide* — "1997 will be a wet year; a year of water and wind."

Note: 1. Driving rain continues across most of the state as Arkansas awakens to devastating damage inflicted March 8th, 1997 by tornadoes and relentless storms. In all, at least 24 people were killed in the state as winds ripped through Little Rock and smaller towns, such as Arkadelphia. Through the week, the combination of thunderstorms, tornadoes and flooding is blamed for more than 50 deaths in Ohio, Kentucky, Tennessee and Mississippi and the destruction of tens of millions of dollars worth of property. **Ohio River** *rises to its highest levels in 33 years with crests 15 or more feet above flood stage at various places. Flooding forces thousands from their homes in Tennessee, Kentucky, Ohio and West Virginia.*

2. North Dakota floods break 100-year record — Homes evacuated as waters rise April 17, 1997 to 22 feet above flood stage — "A real problem." **Fargo, North Dakota** — *Police pounded on the doors of homes in south Fargo early Thursday morning to evacuate people in the way of the worst flood this city has seen in 100 years. "I've been here 22 years, been through lots of floods, and we've never had an evacuation like this," Lt. John Sanderson said.*

3. Windy storm buffets New England with snow and rain. **April 19, 1997** — A windy storm system blew through New England with a mixture of snow and rain, and thunderstorms developed along the coast of the Gulf of Mexico. Wind gusted to as high as 97 mph at Falmouth, Massachusetts and many other states by afternoon.

4. Red River still rising. — The flood could be the worst seen in Manitoba since 1852. **April 30th, 1997** — WINNIPEG, Manitoba — Thousands of Winnipeg residents fled their homes Wednesday as Red River flood waters seeped through a 16-foot (5-meter) earthen dike. This year's

flood should cover twice the area flooded in 1950, inundating up to 800 square miles (2,072 sq. km). More than 28,000 Canadians and 50,000 Americans have been forced from their homes by the rise of the Red River.

Memo: The following predictions were made April 7th, 1996; printed September 1996 in the *1997 Starguide* "WED. — MARCH 26th; RULERS — Pluto (hidden things brought to light)"

Attention: Pluto is back with us — Expect dramatic happenings all over, control is a must. The Lord of Hades doesn't forget and doesn't forgive! Be aware, don't be his victim.

Environment: Avoid places overloaded with turbulent, crazy people. Pluto likes accidents and panic. As always, especially in a waning Moon (negative) expect dramatic and destructive news to plague the media. Earthquake, mass murderer, vicious killers, rapists and the worst of society will be active, led by the Lord of Hades.

Events: This energy has the awful power for unity in discord. A form of death in any form, the beginning of becoming born again is to be experienced soon. People around you will become their true selves and during this transforming cycle a new you may be rediscovered. All changes MUST BE accepted and some of us must be ready for the ugliest time of their life. Pluto rules the police force and all of those dramatic stories.

Serious increase in drug consumption by underage children: Starting Jan. 1st, 1997, Neptune's subtle power will begin its karmic work upon this world. Using Divine Astrology — Neptune will be operational as of January 1st, 1997 and will stay with us until October 25th, 1998. Neptune raises drug and alcohol consumption, which promotes greater incidence of sexually transmitted diseases and elevated suicides. A negative Neptune rules fanaticism, illusion and desperation. Combined with the illusive power of Neptune, fueling this feeling of despair upon the masses will bring many young victims to the abuses of drugs, hopelessness and suicide.

> **Note**: March 26th, 1997 — Rancho Santa Fe, CA — The bodies of 39 victims of a mass suicide were transported to the San Diego Medical Examiner's Office where officials hope to determine the cause of the mysterious deaths.

Memo: The following predictions were made April 7th, 1996; printed September 1996 in the 1997 Starguide — "MON. — JUNE 2nd: RULERS — Mars (instigator of disputes and accidents)."

Family and Friends: Use tons of diplomacy with your friends and loved ones as patience is not Mars' quality. A great time is to be expected as the New Moon will shine on all of us. Enjoy the love and good food provided by those souls that really care. Spend some time with the children; teach them love and harmony as Mars may make them play rough. Be aware around water.

> **Note**: Water slide collapses, kills one, injures 32 — An amusement park water slide collapsed Monday June 2nd, 1997 after a group of high school seniors on a graduation outing ignored a lifeguard's warning and went down together. One student was killed and 32 were injured, six critically.

Chapter 11
Earthquake Predictions

A magnitude 3.5 earthquake causes slight damage, a 4 causes moderate damage, a 5 considerable damage and a 6 severe damage. Any reading over a 7 is considered a major earthquake. My windows posted on the California earthquakes group on the Internet are designed to point out probabilities for earthquakes above 6. Often people ask me, Dr. Turi, when and where an earthquake will take place. Well, it is much easier for me to predict WHEN a major earthquake will occur than WHERE one will occur. It's like someone asking me not only when a plane will crash, but also where. To do so is very difficult indeed and as the years go by I hope to be able to be more precise in my premonition in predictive astrology. However, I surely agree with Mr. Halloran's theory that there are different types of faults; the latest one in Los Angeles was an upthrusting mountain-building fault. Earthquakes tend to occur when diurnal tidal forces are able to release the accumulated strain on a fault. Hard planetary aspects appear able to increase the strain on a fault. Perhaps the computer-aided Astrogeologists of the future will be able to do the kind of micro-mapping and analysis needed to predict which faults are most susceptible to increased strain. As for the timing, Divine astrology technique to predict earthquakes seems to be more accurate than all the latest computerized electronic equipment combined together!

Note: Divine Astrology requires a specific housing system. Thanks to Mr. Halloran's electronic genius and his help in introducing my formula to my students via his software. (1-800 SEA-GOAT.)

Note to my faithful supporters: Please bear with me if I sound repetitive in some parts of this book. However, with every passing year, more and more new subscribers purchase *Moon Power*. I was very surprised to learn that some of you bought several copies at a time (between 4 and 30!) for Christmas gifts. However, nothing could work better for a new reader to be able to see the record that *Moon Power Starguide* has set forth. I thank you for your continued support from the bottom of my heart.

Sample 1:
IDL: 81706 3427.004 400
Received: by /c=us/admd=telemail/prmd= nasa/;
converted (1A5-Text; ate: 22 Nov. 1995 10:00:53 -00
from ///private//nel@pl.nasa.gov
to "drturi@goodnet.com>"
Subject: request for 1996 Top Universal Predictions.
Content length 603 —
Newsgroups — sci.geo.geology, ca.earthquakes, hkbu, geo. maps
WEEKLY — USGS Quake report 9/28-10/4/95 CA.
Seismology Institute -WWW -INTERNET —
Message -ID: DG1t4Hv@goodnet.com

Kudos to you, Dr. Turi!
I surf the Internet periodically for predictions on forthcoming events, specifically all relating to earthquake activities. You hit the 11/22/95 Egypt/Israel/Saudi Arabia 7.2 quake smack dab on the head, per your earlier prediction. Congratulations again! Keep up the good work.

Appreciatively,///E-Mail<///private///nell@ccmail.jpl.nasa. com>

Sample 2:
WWW -INTERNET — USGS —
Message -ID: G1t4Hv@goodnet.com
sender news@goodnet.com (News Administrator)
Dr. Turi drturi @goodnet.com>
Newsgroups— sci.geo,sci.geo.geology,
            ca.earthquakes,hkbu,geog .maps
WEEKLY USGS Quake Report 9/28 — 10/4/95 CA.
Seismology Institute — in article DG1t4H.v @goodnet.com>
DATE — Oct 6h, 1995 drturi@goodnet.com says..

POSTED (Oct, 6th. 1995) — From Dr. Turi
Dear Sirs: — On Oct. 8th and Oct. 9th a very unusual seismic activity will be noticeable and will produce many quakes above 6.1. More information is available pertaining to my method if requested. <drturi@goodnet.com> Respectfully — Dr. Turi

SUBJECT: RE: Weekly USGS Quake Report
Results — Full proofs of predictions:
Oct. 8th: a 7.0 EARTHQUAKE HIT SUMATRA
          (INDONESIAN ISLANDS)
Oct. 9th: a 7.6 EARTHQUAKE HIT MEXICO.

Sample of a post placed on the Internet for April 23rd and April 30th, 1997

MEMO — From: drturi@pacbell.net (drturi)
Newsgroups: sci.geo.geology,ca.earthquakes
Subject: S-R-E large quakes coming April 23rd -30th.
Date: 19 Apr 1997 16:55:58 GMT
Organization: Dr. Turi

Expect SRE "Sudden Release of Energy" on those dates such as explosions/volcano eruptions/blackouts/drama/police/death — April 23rd and April 30th, 1997.

> **Note**: A window is operational a few hours before and after the given dates.

Results:
1. April 29, 1997 MEXICO CITY — The Popocatepetl volcano erupts near Mexico City.
2. May 1st, 1997 — VOLCANO, Hawaii (AP) — Lava is again pouring from Kilauea in an area at Hawaii Volcanoes National Park where visitors willing to hike a couple miles can see clearly, geologists say.

Explosions:
1. April 23, 1997 — MOSCOW — A bomb ripped through a railway station in southern Russia on Wednesday April 23rd night, killing two people and wounding some 20 others.
2. April 30, 1997 — Explosion at Albanian weapons depot kills 20.
3. Surprise Liberation — Police and explosion — April 23rd, 1997 — Peru, Japan relieved by hostage rescue — Peru 14 rebels, 3 others die.

Earthquakes:
Those two windows will produce a Sudden Release of Energy THAT WILL SURPRISE MANY with nature's devastative forces producing quakes well above 6.5. Remember, a posted "window" is always operational a few hours before or after the given day.

RESULTS — Within the window!

Santa Cruz Islands.(8.0Mb)   Tonga islands (6.5 Mb)
97/04/22 09:31:26 10.97N 61.17W 33.0 6.5Ms A TRINIDAD
97/04/23 03:47:18 13.54S 166.02E 33.0 6.1Ms B VANUATU ISLANDS
97/04/23 19:44:28 14.22N 144.58E 100.2 6.3Mb A MARIANA ISLANDS
97/05/01 11:37:34 18.87N 107.26W 33.0 6.7Ms A OFF COAST OF JALISCO, MEX

Next windows May 21st and May 28th
(MAKE NOTES PLEASE!)
Sincerely — Dr. Turi

Our greatest glory is not in never falling but in rising every time we fall

— Hadley

Update 5/23/97 — Nature was quiet for a while then on the window of May 21st window series of or above 6.0 quakes took place as anticipated.

> **NOTE** — A window is always operational a few hours before and after the given date!

Results:
DATE-(UTC)-TIME LAT LON DEP MAG Q COMMENTS
yy/mm/dd hh:mm:ss deg. deg. km
97/05/21 14:10:28 20.44S 169.11E 80.2 6.4Ms A VANUATU ISLANDS
997/05/21 22:51:28 23.18N 80.02E 33.0 6.1Mb A SOUTHERN INDIA
97/05/22 07:50:47 18.41N 101.52W 33.0 6.0Ms A GUERRERO, MEXICO
Sample of a post placed on the Internet for April 23rd and April 30th, 1997

All I have asked for is a fair scientific investigation of my work for the sole purpose of promoting man's cosmic consciousness, saving time, money and the lives of many people.

— Dr. Turi

Stars there they stand shining in order like a living hymn written in light for those blessed with a clear mind.
— Nathaniel Parker Willis

Chapter 12
Celebrity Predictions

Increase in celebrity divorces: 75% of all actors/actress/entertainers who have appeared in movies will have sought an emotional or business-like divorce before the end of 1998. Loss of eminent actors, singers and painters is also high on my list. Due to the Dragon's Tail in Pisces (drugs, alcohol) many of those listed below will be forced to a full restructure. The following names will be directly affected by the Dragon's Tail and should be cautious in all they say, sign or do.

Stress/drama in partnerships is foreseen for some famous names below: Michael Douglas — Gloria Estefan — Lily Tomlin — Raquel Welch — Larry Hagman.

Stress/drama in the area of Work and Health is foreseen for some famous names below: Tony Braxton — Bill Wyman — Tracy Nelson — Maria Maples — Dale Evans.

Stress/drama in the area of Children and Love is foreseen for some famous names below: Tracy Nelson — Roseanne — Julia Roberts — Richard Burton — Prince Charles.

Stress/drama in the area of Family Members is foreseen for some famous names below: Don Johnson — Janine Turner — Amy Grant — Gerard Depardieu — Rush Limbaugh.

Stress/drama in the area of Career is foreseen for some famous names below: Art Bell — Will Smith — Juliette Lewis — Jo Piscopo — Marky Mark.

Noticeable career growth is foreseen for some famous names below: Larry King — Tonia Harding — Ken Griffey Jr. — Meg Ryan — Sally Field.

Children and Love are foreseen for some famous names below: Jennie Garth — Andy Garcia — Shannen Doherty — Connan O'Brien — Julian Lennon.

Great Contracts or Marriage are foreseen for some famous names below: Michael Jordan — Greena Davis — Laura Dern — Christie Brinkley — Zsa Zsa Gabor.

Fabio — Sharon Stone — Glenn Close — Elizabeth Taylor and Jon Bon Jovi will experience a dramatic year, where health or serious deception could play an important part of their mischief.

Man is superior to the stars if he lives in the power of superior wisdom. Such a person being the master over heaven and earth by means of his will is a magus and magic is not sorcery but supreme wisdom
— Paracelcus

Chapter 13

1998 World Predictions

Anticipate the Incredible!

America and Japan are both born (corporation dates used) with a Dragon's Head and Dragon's Tail in Leo/Aquarius axis. While the South of France, parts of Italy and Spain have a strong Leo impact. Thus much is to be expected in terms of "explosive news" with those countries in 1998 and 1999. When the Dragon's Tail moves into Aquarius in October 1998, Uranus will unleash a form of sudden release of devastative energy. Thus be ready for the incredible to take place then. Volcanic eruptions, earthquakes and explosions are very high on the list and will increase in 1998, 1999 as ordered by Uranus, responding to a higher order imposed by God through his celestial planetary plan and purpose.

Incidentally, Japan is ruled by Uranus and these small islands, have more earthquake activity and volcanic eruptions than anywhere else in the world. Uranus also rules computers and indicates the aptitude of Japanese people in the production of high-tech products. One of the "explosive peculiarities" of Uranus is being used in the construction of atomic weaponry with the use of Uranus' element, "Uranium." Thus, unfortunately, Japan has also experienced the worst of Uranus' manifestations: two terrible atomic blasts killing thousands of people in an dreadful explosion and the terrible Kobe earthquake that killed over 5000 people. On a more positive note, Uranus also rules group activity and brotherhood, and all the world could learn from Japan's emphasis on team work. Tremendous electronic tools and new discoveries will be brought to the human race. Children born during this period will have sparkling genius qualities and a strong sense of independence. The plan is set and nothing can be done to alter the will of God through the stars. At the end the impact of the Dragon's Tail in Aquarius will translate into a full rebirth of the earth and man's psyche. Thousands upon thousands of souls will perish in the process but there no such a thing as dead really. Just a rebirth to a much higher plane, for somewhere the soul is given the opportunity to co-create with the creative forces of God and the Universes in time and space.

Neptune in Capricorn: Neptune is quietly located in the down-to-earth sign of Capricorn until January 1998. He will then enter the sign of Aquarius and will stay in this sign until August 1998. After this date Neptune will move back into the sign of Capricorn until November 1998 and then will reside in the futuristic sign of Aquarius until the end of the millennium. When badly asserted, Neptune is known to be the planet of illusion. Thus as all planets are both positive and negative, Neptune will visit a form of positive (arts) or negative (deception) energy upon the world at large. In the practical sign of Capricorn (structure), Neptune's creative energy is being used to the maximum. A wave of "new" evangelists will take to the bullhorn, using the "last days" of the Apocalypse, making fortunes in deceiving the uninformed, God-fearing religious masses.

Later on when "Poseidon" enters the electronic sign of Aquarius, artists of all orders will invest in an incredible imaginative source and produce incredible stories. Those Neptunian (dogmas) and Uranian (UFOs) tales will transform into incredible movies. Again my premonition for such a development was written in your 1996 "Moon power" and took place in 1997 with the "Mars invasion" buster. As anticipated, an incredible work was performed by both the actors and the electronics genius of movie producers in Hollywood, California. Some will let their imagination (or past lives' pious residues) get loose and re-create either religious legends or a form of the end of the world. It again, in the sign of Capricorn and Aquarius 1998, will promote a serious increase in creativity and a solid restructure within the cinematographic industry.

Pluto in Sagittarius: Pluto moved from Scorpio to Sagittarius on November 11th, 1995. Constrained to face the horrible consequences of his own destructive power and pay the heavy consequences of mass destruction, man turns to religion for comfort. In Sagittarius (religion) Pluto (regeneration) will promote a disturbing wave of religious fanaticism that will plague the world. In the US, the impact of Pluto in Sagittarius has already spoken, with some religious fanatics committing serious crimes, and many will have to pay the ultimate price for their destructive behavior. Some Middle Eastern residents have also shocked the world, and will keep spawning suicidal bomb attacks on major European and US cities. The "contract" they sign with their manipulators, before blowing themselves surrounded by the highest possible number of innocent victims, promises "the martyrs" twenty or more virgins after an immediate entrance to paradise!

Ignorance is evil; when you control someone's source of information or education, chances are that you will control that person's entire life.

— Dr. Turi

After the painful passage of Pluto (expiration) in Sagittarius (codification of thoughts), the world will be ready for wiser, new age and religious leaders. Those well-adjusted souls will teach all the higher expressions of all the religions of the past. They will introduce a new image of a God free of fear, full of love and attention. Those futuristic religious leaders will combine their teachings with a more comprehensive scientific understanding of the manifestation of the Creator throughout the Universe.

Chapter 14

1998 Dragon's Head and Tail Universal Predictions

It takes approximately two years for the Dragon to pass through a sign of the zodiac. On the Universal world's horoscope, the Dragon's head (progress) will bring about positive changes pertaining to nature, health and general service. On January 25th, 1997 the Dragon's Head entered the critical, health oriented sign of Virgo and will stay in this sign until October 20th, 1998. The Dragon's Tail will reside for the same period of time in the dreamy sign of Pisces. In 1996, the nasty Dragon's Tail was in the sign of Aries and produced many of the worst major pieces of news in 1996, such as war, explosions, accidents, heat waves, large quakes and a very destructive fire season. Thus, many of the predictions for 1998 will be similar to 1997 due to the two-year length spent by the Dragon in a zodiacal sign. On Tuesday October 20th, 1998 the powerful Dragon will enter the sign of Leo. It will stay in this sign until Sunday April 9th, 2000. The upcoming predictions for the dawning of the age of Aquarius are somehow incredible and will be totally different from those presented this year. The 1999 "Moon Power" issue will be available to the public in September 1998; don't miss this copy.

Since 1996, the mighty Dragon has moved away from the fiery red planet Mars and got closer to the intellectual energy of Mercury and the deceiving power of Neptune. This 1997/1998 trend promises to be interestingly speedy and wet; years with "more water, more wind and more victims of spiritual delusion." The complex abortion dilemma, religion, suicide, drugs and alcohol use by children run high on the list for 1998.

Dragon's Head in Virgo: The persistent power of the Dragon's Head is still going through the businesslike sign of Virgo. This impact will force the working masses to experience more restructure where work, health and security are concerned. Much effort and shaping will be directed towards the workers, and significant improvements will still be made towards personal health insurance. New security measures and affordable plans for the working class will be available and imposed on major businesses and corporations. Social Security will still undergo a full and positive restructure, and the changes will bring more help to some impoverished groups. Many modernistic buildings and new technology will be needed, and many office workers will find good rewards and better working conditions. New services and special agencies will flourish in the process. Thus Uncle Sam's administration will see a serious growth and more employment security. The Dragon's Head in Virgo (health) will further important medical discoveries, and new affordable methods involving laser surgery will be available to a good portion of the population. More environmental agencies will be born from the Dragon's Head in the perfectionist Virgo's desire to protect the remainder of the rain forest and all natural landscapes.

Greenpeace will still captivate much of the news in 1998, and many new members will join and expand its power to a significant level. Much education will be directed toward the young generation, and attention will be given to the fragile remaining wilderness left in the world. Enhanced laws will be imposed on those who continue to dump toxic waste in our bodies of water or cut down the rain forest without regard for local regulations or wildlife. Recycling will be enhanced in many states and will be reinforced by a new form of "environmental police." Serious punishment is awaiting large companies, especially those unwilling to compromise with waste dumping. Smoke generating factories will also undergo a serious restructure to stop the depletion of the protective ozone layer. More and tougher laws will be passed against the cigarette and alcohol manufacturers and advertisements will be seriously controlled by the government. As predicted for 1997 in your 1996 *Moon Power,* many new governmental legislatures will put well-established tobacco companies out of business. In addition to training programs, diets and exercise equipment, more people will turn to homeopathic medicine and enjoy out-of-doors activities to regenerate themselves.

As we progress through 1998, the "Health Generation's" (see Pluto in Virgo) disposition will become more obvious in their subconscious desire to promote the "Virgin/Virgo" purity principle (see Pluto in Virgo.) With the powerful Dragon's Head impact in the "perfectionist" sign of Virgo, expect the health and the "hypercritical attitude of the Virgin" to be increasing until October 20th, 1998. At it worst, this celestial energy will breed many "puritans" and make them prone to exaggeration with health and environmental matters.

Dragon's Tail in Pisces: The Dragon's Tail's inauspicious energy in the sign of Pisces will keep disturbing the world until October 20th, 1998. This sign is ruled by the deceiving planet of Neptune and has produced a form of hysteria in 1997 with the predicted March 26th, 1997 "mass suicide dilemma" (see page 87, *1997 Moon Power*) that took place in Rancho Santa Fe, California. Neptune brings forth uncontrolled imagination, fears, religious frenzy, dogmas and suicides. His legacy in 1998 must be kept in check constantly. On a negative note, Neptune rules the subconscious, the past, illusion, deception and devout followers of dogmas (or UFOs) ready to die for their spiritual purpose. More disturbing news of this nature is to be expected this year too as Neptune's jurisdiction is still upon us until October. On a positive note, this planet regulates real psychic phenomena, intuition, creativity, spirituality and the higher fields of music. The Church authority will try hard to keep or bring new followers to the dying religious dogmas. As predicted, the power of the Dragon's Tail (decay) in Pisces (religion) spoke in 1997 when Pope John Paul II made a choice for sainthood. VATICAN CITY — Under a Neptune trend (deception) for Saturday May the 3rd, 1997 (see *Moon Power 1997* page 104) he draws attention to a long neglected and often despised group in Europe, beatifying a Gypsy for the first time in the history of the Roman Catholic Church. Beatification is the last step before possible canonization or sainthood. Responding to the real God's celestial order (the stars), ignorant Catholic leaders are trying to change their approach in a desperate gesture to gain more followers and more money to survive. Only the plain truth will survive the powerful Dragon, and their deceiving teachings will fade away with time.

General impact on the population: The Dragon's Tail in Pisces is still about to bring another thick cloud of deception upon mankind and many unaware people will fall for Neptune's deceiving pull. Weird elements in our society will be again active on many fronts. This includes the promoters of the "Apocalypse" using either dogmatic religious or "Frantic New Agers" convictions to die with UFOs. This doesn't take away the reality of extraterrestrials and we, Brigitte and I, surely know something about it.

Many souls will end up poisoned with fears, looking for salvation and forgiveness, and will join cults and other manipulative organizations out of naiveté. The only purpose of those religious organizations or their "guru" leaders is to gain attention and financial support. Consciously or not, your chosen "savior" is welcoming such "spiritually depraved" victims. For some of these people a very serious karmic time is ahead of them, where critical thinking will be born out of financial, spiritual, sexual abuses, castration and finally death. Neptune is very strong in nature and like the treacherous quicksand zones, once in his sands, it is extremely difficult to escape. This generally leads to a confusing, slow and suffocating end. Sometimes, if you're lucky and scream loud enough, a saving hand is available (ask and you shall receive). But time is of the essence with Neptune; the longer you stay in his puddle, the deeper you go! The David Koresh, Applewhite dreadful dilemmas are solid examples of Neptune's deceptive powers. Unless one is aware of Neptune's tricky waters, the price of ignorance will be heavy. Many souls will feel the urge to spiritually educate themselves. The lucky ones will invest in the understanding of the dynamics of our Universe (God's real tools) other karmic souls will be reborn somewhere else.

I am inclined to exaggeration with the negativity coming from the nebulous planet, principally because of the location of the Dragon's Tail in 1997 and 1998. However, like all the other celestial bodies, each planet can be used either positively or negatively once its energy is clearly understood. This is where Divine Astrology and "Moon Power" truly applies and gives you real information. Knowledge is power. Another way to characterize Neptune's illusive powers is when you are sitting inside a movie theater — In the darkness of the room (the subconscious), you are forced to enter someone else's world of imagination (constructive or destructive). There, the purpose of Neptune is to make you forget reality and deceive you. His depressive energy will sap many peoples desire for life, and many of his victims will end up homeless or from desperation or rejection will commit suicide. Thus the use of chemicals, drugs and alcohol to "forget" reality is one of Neptune's best tools to get control over your sanity. Under his command in 1998, expect another increase in demand for drugs and alcohol. Because of the strength of Neptune's illusive tentacles grabbing our children at school, the battle against his vices must become a priority right away. However, in 1998, with the health-oriented Dragon's Head in Virgo, much progress will be accomplished for those who are willing to explore the human experience with a critical thinking process. Keep in mind that I teach Divine Astrology with a complete course by mail. Your diploma will follow the sixteen 90-minute audio tapes/video. The Golden key of knowledge and the understanding of what it means to be human is available; if you "ask you shall receive" the knowledge.

As in 1997, so in 1998, be cautious, as doctors and hospitals including chemists will be prone to make serious mistakes in their processional assessment of drug prescriptions. Many organizations will be sued and their medical licenses taken away. Due to the incredible pull of Neptune, drug and alcohol consumption will rise and more and more people will commit crimes and illogical acts.

Caution: if you happen to be born with the Dragon's Tail in Pisces or if the Tail is located in your sixth house of health, you are strongly cautioned to stay clear from any chemicals, and this includes doctors' prescriptions. (See Dragon's Head/Tail tables). Thousands will be incarcerated and asylums, like jails, will be overloaded with hopeless people. In 1998, expect also many jail riots where corruption, drugs and murder will reign. On a more positive note, Neptune can also be used positively to enter the intuitional domain of psychics, reach the fourth dimension and hear the angels' songs or produce fantastic works of art and entertainment. As in 1997, 1998 will induce new laws pertaining to alcoholic beverages or cigarette products. This will affect the markets and their investors.

Entertainment: Due to new developments of high-tech in film production, many of Hollywood's producers will save time and money. This phenomenon will leave some actors worrying about cheaper contracts and future big-screen appearances. These changes will induce rejections and lead some actors to the abuse of drugs, alcohol abuse and a general sense of lack of self-esteem. Sadly, some young actors will be lost to depression and suicide. As in 1997, in 1998 actors and actresses born in March, October, April and June will be directly affected in the areas of health and career. Last year, as predicted in *1996 Starguide,* Elizabeth Taylor went through a brain surgery; let's hope for a better fate for the great actress in 1998. Also, famous Pisces singer Bob Dylan was afflicted and suffered the Tail on his sign. Luckily for them, those great souls beat the Tail and went back to normal business.

Combined with the pull of Neptune (depression) this year will be a high suicidal period for many. Interesting movies based on the Apocalyptic times, UFOs and religion will be released and may intensify the mass' subconscious fear of the near end of time. Movie producers and directors are not fully aware of the impact of their products upon the subconscious of the young generation. Combined with the illusive power of Neptune, fueling the feeling of despair will bring many young victims, as predicted for 1997 with the maniacs of the Haven's Gate followers, to the abuses of drugs, hopelessness and suicide. This prediction is well documented and was printed in the *1997 Moon Power* by my publisher The Book Tree, Inc. a year earlier.

Environment: On the physical plane, 1998 will bring about devastative oil spills when Neptune (Ruler of the Oceans) will war with the Dragon's Tail. See Astro Weather Service "Supernova Windows" section. 1998 will be one of the worst years since World War II for high-sea accidents due to difficult weather patterns taking place during the windows. Flooding will plague the world at large with some parts of the coastline being so flooded as to become islands. Again, this is not the prediction for the "Apocalyptic times," just mother earth responding to Neptune sitting on the nasty Dragon's Tail who in turn responds to the Divine celestial order imposed by God upon the earth. Specific dates for those disasters will be in the "Day-To-Day Guidance for 1998" section. There is a strong possibility for a serious sea accident in 1998 and tons of poisonous chemicals and thousands of gallons of oil may be spilled into the oceans. This will contaminate the coastline and poison much of the marine life. Many vessels will not reach their destination and many will be lost at sea. As for mother earth (as she did many times before!), don't panic, she is well able to take care of herself and any manmade disasters, and with time, she will restore herself.

Foreign Affairs: The Middle East is directly affected by Neptune, and religious fanaticism is the worst trait of this planet. In 1998, the Dragon's Tail will directly affect this specific part of the world. Much of the prominent religious variety and belief systems were initiated in this part of the world. Neptune rules oil, and most of the world production is also from this hazardous area. Thus, a mixture of oil and religious war is imminent and could start from this unstable area of the globe from 1998 on. A holy terrorist-oriented war against the West is right now in progress and will get worse as the months of 1998 unfold. Extremist groups will keep organizing terrorist attacks on more government buildings in many European and US cities. This chain of destructive behavior will produce serious "secret" consideration of retaliation by the Allied forces. In the process, eminent Middle East, US or European leaders will be assassinated, fueling more and more trouble on many foreign soils. Along with many natural disasters such as the (predicted) 11/22/95 Egypt/Israel/Saudi Arabia 7.2 quake, the Middle East will captivate much of the world's attention in 1998 in terms of natural and manmade disasters.

As experienced and predicted for 1996, Saddam Hussein and other Arab leaders will also have to pay a heavy price for some of their political decisions in 1998 too. A full embargo on oil sales will be again imposed by other countries. A strong shortage of oil and its accompanying rising prices will have a devastating impact on both the economy of many dependent countries and the Middle East itself.

> **Note**: This section was written long before the chain of bloody bombing extremist terrorist attacks on the population of Israel and the assassination attempt on one of Saddam Hussein's family members.

However, the upside to an oil shortage is in the use of other environmentally safe energy agents. Many scientists will work much harder and before the end of this century, new technology, especially cold fusion energy will take over from polluting petroleum products.

Religion: The years 1997 and 1998 predispose for the death of the Pope and/or Mother Teresa, indeed a very negative year for any and all denominations. She received in June 1997 the higher form of respect from the nation. Note, the great Lady was born under the sign of Leo, and this sunny sign brought fame to the soul. No matter what the endeavor is. Astrophilosophy, during the day all the planets shy away from the powerful light of the Sun. Thus, in respect for her undeniable work, her Sun sign in Leo (eminence/love) is a major contribution for her being literally thrown in the limelight of fame and success. She really seemed bored at the meeting and couldn't give a damn about all this attention. Remember, she is a clergyman (woman — that's changing soon too!), precisely a nun and she particularly needs privacy, away from the celebrity lights.

Interestingly enough, Mother Teresa's 8th house (corporate money) is in the sign of Pisces which rules the Vatican and Christianity. Pisces is also the sign of total service, unselfishness and pure love, and wherever this sign resides, the soul is bound to attract a form of manipulation, even deception. The desperate Vatican agenda needs her work and the money she brings to their secret bank accounts all over the world. I guess they can afford to send her around the globe (at her old age) to sell Christianity. I sincerely believe the church authorities should leave her alone and let her die in peace. However, Leo is a bright and intelligent sign, so she has a good idea of what's really going on behind her angel's work and the Vatican. Incidentally, President Clinton, Madonna (another nun!) and Michael Jackson are also born in August. (Makes you think about the power of the stars, doesn't it?) My book "The Power of the Dragon" will shed some real light to those willing to expand their cosmic consciousness.

As induced by Uranus (new Age) the battle has started against the dogmas and deception. A form of war between a defiant congregation and a determined church hierarchy and the new Age leaders will take place. Many "old skeletons" will be revived and stories about men and women being abused, decades ago, by their ministers will plague the media. The potential ramification of those cases will seriously affect the "image" and the financial aspect of those religious denominations. Much of the faithful followers' financial support will be cut dramatically short and many devoted souls will be "born again" somewhere else! Combined with increasing criminal church burnings (predicted also for 1996 in *Fate* magazine), and many expensive legal battles, the cost will be too much for some religious groupings to survive in the long run.

1998 — Interior Religious War: Dozens of people will die by suicide or be killed for their religious convictions. This sensationalism may lead to many more churches burning down. All denominations are at a serious risk from 1998 on, including Baptist, Episcopalian, Unitarian or Presbyterian Union, with responsibility claimed by persons or groups claiming a certain political or religious conviction for doing so. The operation of deceiving Neptune will affect the relationship between the Christian Coalition versus the liberal party and later with ethical confrontations with Muslim and Christian religions right here in the US. Most of the Middle East, ruled by illusive Neptune, will undergo a strong holy rebirth and a deceiving sense of immortality. Many will gladly accept death as a liberation for paradise and will be proud in doing so. The Revolutionary Guards, Shi'ite extremists, will also commit suicidal bomb attacks, in Europe and the US.

Anti-Abortionist Activity: The possibility for anti-abortion clinics to be a target and burnt is high on the list for the US. This prediction took place in 1997 when abortion clinics were set on fire by a fanatic soul.

Violent Ethnic Clashes in Germany: There will be also the possibility of a number of minority people killed by some white supremacist groups, as a result of street fighting and deliberately lit fires.

Morocco/Algeria/Iran/Iraq — Civil War threats and terrorist activity will also get worse: This prediction, sadly enough, also came true as thousands of Algerian souls lost their lives in the conflict. Annual casualties attributed to civil war will be much higher in 1998 than 1997. More people will be killed in Western Europe and the U.S. as a result of terrorist activity (explosions/murders) attributed to Middle Eastern extremists in 1998 than in 1997. Danger coming from terrorist acts using homemade chemical agents, as seen in Japan, is also high on the list in the US and Europe.

Middle East leaders' assassinations: Again a possibility in 1998 — An increase in terrorist activity in the Middle East region will lead to the assassination of one of these men: Arafat, Saddam Hussein, Chimon Peres, Hafez Assad. Poisoning could be one of the reasons.

Japan, Russia and China: A terrible energy will affect the children of these countries within the next few years. Many will lose their precious lives in search of freedom.

Russia, England and the US: An increase in psychedelic drugs and music will plague the media, producing a high level of suicides. Those born in January and all the water signs such as Pisces, Cancer and Scorpio will be particularly affected and must practice positive thinking at all times. Any study will be a good outlet to stop the spiritual decaying process. Spiritual regeneration is the key.

Middle East: Oil shortage/fires/terrorism/war: March 1998, in response to terrorist attacks on their and foreign soils, Europe, Japan and the US will consider a multinational plan to retaliate. Control of oil production, sales and stability of the region will prevail, but not without heavy loss of life and diplomatic failure.

Major Riots in France, Germany, UK, China, Russia and US: Reports on CNN of police confrontations with protesters and rioters is high on the list in 1998. In Germany, US, France, and England, more youth will die as a result of riots.

A serious increase in drug consumption by underage children: Starting Jan. 1st, 1997, Neptune's subtle power will begin its karmic work upon this world. Using Divine Astrology — Neptune will be operational as of January 1st, 1997 and will stay with us until October 25th, 1998. Neptune raises drug and alcohol consumption, which promotes greater chances of sexually transmitted diseases and boosts any form of suicides. A negative Neptune rules fanaticism, illusion and desperation. An alarming number of suicides is foreseen in 1998.

His impact upon the world will bring about a serious increase in general homelessness and depression and will promote a serious increase in hopelessness. The government will have to take drastic measures to "save" families, destitute children and fight more vigorously in the "war" against drugs, cults, alcohol and gang-related issues. In great contrast to this, expect greater advances in the arts and creativity for those children who are properly motivated. Also, expect children to become more involved in teaching each other the vital lesson of tolerance.

Water Pollution: Many cities will suffer flooding, and other underdeveloped countries such as Mexico will suffer an increase in dysentery and many will die due to poisoned water consumption. On March 10th, 1997 I was invited on Channel 8, KLAS by news anchor Charlotte Evans. There I made a specific prediction about the police force and my concern with the water situation. The very next day following the show, all television channels and radio programs announced a general breakdown of the water sanitation system. The city residents were solicited and advised to save water until the problem could be fixed. A few days earlier, the police force made a serious mistake by jailing a nine-year-old without notifying the concerned parents. He was caught leaving marks on fresh cement on the city property and sent to jail. This "narrative" went all the way up to CNN and made national news. Amazed listeners called the TV station and a fantastic letter of endorsement came to my mailbox a few days later. Be aware: bad water means also the possibility for intestinal disease, or a new virus may plague the world. However, cures for and prevention of more common intestinal disorders will be brought about.

Dr. Turi is available to do your city astrological forecast. Call (619) 275-5853 for information.

New Bacterial Diseases: A new bacterial disease may plague the world. It may be from Africa and may bring a form of panic to the population. It will affect the skin, the digestive tract and/or the brain. Hopefully, the powerful Dragon's Head location in Virgo (health) will see to defeat the infection.

Prison Riots: in 1998, expect many inmates and guards to lose their precious lives in a prison riot. Conditions, overcrowded jails and despair will produce a serious increase in suicides. An explosion of murders due to drug trafficking in jail will come to light.

Loss of a Large Vessel at Sea: Neptune rules the ocean, so many people will lose their lives at sea. A replica of the "Titanic" experience could also be experienced during one of the four "Supernova" windows — see 1998 Starguide "Moon Power" for the possible dates of those predicted calamities.

Sports Predictions: 1998 will see lots of boat racing accidents in the US and Australia.

Loss of Prominent Water Sport Driver: An increase in accidental deaths will be produced by water-related accidents (or dam failures) worldwide, and many prominent figures will lose their lives. Serious fires and explosions are also high on my list with oil rigs and other vessels.

Increase in Fires and Fxplosions in Oil Refineries: The total estimated damage (as claimed by insurance companies) due to fires and explosions in some oil refineries.

Oil Strikes/Gas Price Increases: In 1998 you can expect corruption, scandals and confrontation between union workers and oil company CEOs. There will be a Congressional investigation of the activities of at least three major oil companies due to their high level of oil spills and ocean contamination.

General/Admiral Rank Naval Figure Scandals/Suicide: The unauthorized use of military aircraft, as well as sex and monetary scandals, is to be expected in 1998. This prediction took place in June 7, 1997 WASHINGTON when Secretary of Defense William Cohen announced that three panels will be set up to review military training, privacy issues and the "clarity" of its policy on adultery.

"Accidental death of high-ranking Navy officers or a rise in drug/alcohol consumption, even sailor suicides will worry the Navy. An accident with a nuclear submarine is also to be expected." (See Supernova windows).

> **Note**: Dr. Turi accurately predicted the suicide "loss of the Chief of US Navy" in his 1995 Starguide.

Merger of Top US, French and Japanese Automobile Manufacturers to Produce Electric Cars: 1998. The US and Japanese automobile manufacturers (each with sales up) will merge. (Both shedding their previous names.) The reasoning given will be that it will help fight off the uprising oil market, save the environment and bring high prices down.

Merging of Top US Oil Companies: 1998, major oil companies will have to merge to survive. Some other companies will also merge directly with Japan and European countries.

Oil Company Workers Strike — Accidents/Insurance Strikes: 1998, the company currently called "Exxon" will lay off some of its workers and will be forced to merge with another oil company to survive the impact of an impending strike. Many serious construction accidents will also happen, especially around cranes and bridges on rigs, taking the lives of ill-fated workers.

Increase in Flooding Leading to a Dam Failure: Work will be needed to rebuild part of the country destroyed by natural disasters and a dam failure. Las Vegas and other large dikes area are high on the list. (see Supernova windows).

Upsurge in Anti-Pollution Groups: Many peaceful marches in different US cities will try to bring attention to the rapid destruction of nature.

Major Overhaul of Fishing Practice: This prediction took place in 1997. Again, in 1998 a Supreme Court decision will rule that some parts of the world oceans must be left unfished long enough to replenish the diminishing fish population. It will be deemed illegal for a fishing vessel to be seen in those waters. Supervision will require taxpayers to help support this expensive endeavor. All international communities will be forced to participate.

POSITIVE IMPACT OF THE DRAGON'S HEAD

Breakthrough in Microbiology: Fame and fortune for some researchers and medical scientists.

Breakthrough in Plants, Flowers and Cloning: A new way of handling the blooming and growth of plants, vegetables and flowers.

Serious progress in Saving the Remainder of the Rain Forest: Peaceful marches will pay off for many groups. Important documentation will be signed to save the ocean, some animal species and earth itself.

A strong Comeback of Homeopathic Medicine: More and more people will turn to natural medicine and vegetarianism.

Investment/Financial: Considerable progress is to be expected in the textile industry and clothing design.

Stock Market: A serious blow to the cigarette industry as predicted in your 1996 "Moon Power" took place in 1997. There is a possible crash of the stock market in March and September 1998.

By the end of 1998, the healing process will slowly take place as the desperate cry for help will get much too loud for many of earth's caring souls to ignore.

As in 1997, the ultimate challenge for the human race in 1998 will be to perceive our spiritual strengths and the physical boundaries of mother nature.

You are a child of the Universe and there are reasons for you to be. One is to find all the answers that God has enslaved everyone of us to search for and the other one is to appreciate his creation and manifestation throughout the Universe.

— Dr. Turi

Chapter 15

Astro-Profile of Marshall Applewhite

> **Note**: In the 1996 issue of "Moon Power," I used O. J. and Nicole Simpson's astrological configurations to depict their respective fates. In this case (and others like it), it is important to realize that, when dealing with a group, all the stars of all the "actors" are involved and will produce events of an extraordinary nature, such as the infamous April 26th, 1997 Rancho Santa Fe "Mass suicide." With this basic understanding, using Divine Astrology, I will attempt to clarify the fate of cult leader Marshall Applewhite. As a rule, the stars and fate of any leader (cults/corporations/governments/etc.) fall upon all his followers or his countrymen. Thus, the awful fate of people like Hitler, David Koresh, Applewhite and many others are propagated and experienced by those who put them in power. The importance and awareness of this fact should be carefully noted for the benefit of future generations.

The Life of Heaven's Gate Cult Leader Marshall Applewhite

Applewhite: From great accomplishments to a mad cult leader.

Apparently, the change came after a near-death experience in 1972. The adolescent life of Marshall Applewhite offered no evidence to the common scientists about the tragic end in store for him and 38 of his followers years later at a mansion in Rancho Santa Fe, California. His acquaintances called him Herff, and his own sister, Louise Winant, recalls him as amusing and happy as could be, also an overachiever with plenty to show for his hard work.

"He was generally the head of everything, she said. He was a born leader and possessed a very charismatic personality. He could get people to believe in anything he proclaimed."

"He was totally comic at times and took great pleasure in acting for all of us. He knew how to do something he called an elephant walk that would always get the entire family laughing."

Applewhite also had great musical talents. He was born in 1931, and was the son of a Presbyterian minister who spent his life starting new churches. He kept moving from place to place in Texas about every three years. As a teenager, Applewhite wanted to become a priest and stand in the pulpit too. However, his real talents were musical. "He was blessed with a beautiful voice." He had sung in a few operas and had also taught music at the University of St. Thomas in Houston. He was just a very loving, wonderful brother." she said. Throughout his 30s, in the 1960s, Applewhite lived an ordinary life. He played starring roles in stage musicals in Colorado and Texas. He got himself a good position then and became the choir director at St. Mark's Episcopal Church in Houston. In addition to teaching at the university, he also sang 15 roles with the Houston Grand Opera. He finally married and had two beautiful children. Sadly enough for Applewhite, Venus (the arts) is the ruler of his Dragon's Tail in Libra and no matter how much efforts you invest on the Dragon's Tail, one will face serious difficulties and will not be rewarded easily.

Suddenly, in 1972 he left his family at a time when he felt that his life was falling apart. Incidentally, the negative Dragon's Tail of the year 1972 was in Leo in his 4th house (home area) and forced him into a full restructure of his base of operations. He met the 44-year-old nurse who would change him forever — Bonnie Lu Nettles. It is reported that Nettles told him he could be "used mightily."

Again, Applewhite's inherent Dragon's Tail (negative) was located in the sign of Libra (partners), so he was attracted to many wrong partners. In this case, the partner changed his life and led him to a full commitment to his Tail or group endeavors. Uneducated in the power of the Dragon and his weaknesses, he, like many other innocent souls, paid the ultimate price of ignorance.

As Applewhite has described events, he was at the hospital visiting a friend when he met Nettles. His sister tells a different story. "He was living in Houston at the time, and he had some trouble with his heart and ended up in the hospital and, according to the nurses, had a near-death experience," she says. "One of the nurses convinced him that it was for a very special reason and that he could be used mightily in a group that she knew about. She began seeing him and talking him more into joining this group. She certainly played an important part of his future and I would be much interested in getting her birthdate. She could easily have been a Venus' soul, reflecting his fated Libra Dragon's Tail. Then they become sort of co-leaders for a while, but he always considered her the senior leader." Applewhite and Nettles would live together in what he termed a sexless union until she died in 1985. They changed their names, first to Bo and Peep, then to Ti and Do.

The press reported that in 1974, they were arrested in Harlingen, Texas, and charged with stealing credit cards and a car. They explained that the items belonged to the husband of a member of their group. Soon after the arrest, Applewhite and Nettles cut off all ties with their families. Again, anything involving others (especially a husband and wife) is directly related to his Dragon's Tail located in the sign of Libra. This sign traditionally rules the 7th house of marriage and partnerships.

"He came to see us in Dallas, where we were living at the time, to tell us that he was going off with this group and we would not hear from him again," she said. "And we, of course, tried to talk him out of it. I told him that this wasn't him, but he said, 'You don't know the real me.'" Sadly enough, Applewhite did not know himself either and he was already drawn into his Dragon's Tail (group) endeavors. In an amateur video recorded a few years back in Arizona, Applewhite outlined the reactions of family members of people who join his group. "It seems to always cause all of the people in the periphery of your life to turn against you — think that you've lost your marbles, you've gotten duped by someone who has a spell on you and will lead you down a crooked path," he said. In this statement, right here, his own subconscious is trying hard to make him aware of his own hazardous Dragon's Tail path, but he and his followers did not catch the hidden message and paid the ultimate price later on. By 1975, the duo claimed to be space aliens: Applewhite and Nettles made news in 1975 when they convinced a group of 20 people from Waldport, Oregon, to leave their homes and move to eastern Colorado, where they would meet with a spaceship. They claimed to be space aliens in contact with aliens from a heavenly kingdom. By then, the rest of his chart, especially Uranus (UFOs/electronics) in his 12th house (deception) came into the picture of his life.

When the ship didn't come, the group stopped its public activities. It didn't resurface until 1993, when it bought an ad in USA Today saying that the earth's present civilization was about to be "recycled" and "spaded under." Then in October 1996, Applewhite rented a big house near San Diego, California. He told the owner his group was made up of Christian-based angels sent to Earth, affiliated with other groups in Arizona and New Mexico. Of course, less than six months later, all those "angels" would be gone. "I don't think he needed to have a following," says Bebe Kok, a former Applewhite student. "I think he was the kind of person who truly believed and had a lot of charisma. And so other people followed him." Obviously, Applewhite's charisma came from his powerful Pluto (persuasion power) located in his 3rd house (the mind) and made his speech very magnetic (as well as dangerous).

Dragon's Tail Aries — Head Libra
Marshall Applewhite profile
Born Sunday, May 17, 1931   Time Zone: 00:00 {UT}

PLANET	POSITION	DIGNITIES
Sun	25Tau08	1st House – Self (wealth/beauty)
Moon	17Tau37	1st House – Self (feminine/wealthy home)
Mercury	04Tau01	1st House – Self (intellectual/business sense/wealth)
Venus	25Ari04	12th House – Subconscious (secret affairs/homosexuality/deception)
Mars	17Leo36	4th House – Home (danger/death/regimentation/war)
Jupiter	17Can26	3rd House – Mind (teacher/philosopher/religious/righteousness)
Saturn	3Cap07	9th House – Study (educational structure/honor/manipulation)
Uranus	17Ari32	12th House – Subconscious (madness/irrationality/new age/pilot)
Neptune	03Vir00	5th house – Love (children/drugs/alcohol/partners/deception)
Pluto	19Can05	3rd house – Mind (control/fanaticism/mental obsession/death)
Personality	27Tau46	1st House – Self (beautiful/wealthy/feminine)
Midheaven	27Aqu46	10th House – Career (original/group oriented/UFO/new-age)
Dragon's Head	13Ari52	Fate – The soul has lost all true personality. The purpose of his incarnation is to find himself and learn independence. Once the self has been discovered (for good or for worse!) a position of leadership is usually experienced.
Dragon's Tail	13Libr52	Karma – The soul must learn to stand for himself and will attract only wrong partners (marriage, love, business) until he has found his true self.

RULER OF CHART: Venus

Astrological Interpretation of Marshall Applewhite:

Sun in Taurus: With his soul's purpose located in the attractive, steadfast sign of Taurus, the soul was given an opportunity to experience not only wealth (Merrill-Lynch financial corporation) but also love and the best of what life had to offer. Sadly enough due to a lack of information, fear, ignorance or specific circumstances, many souls do not fulfill their specific purpose on earth.

Moon in Taurus: The location of the Moon in the sign of Taurus indicates a strong desire for a beautiful home base. "Do," aka Marshall Applewhite, rented an extremely expensive property in "snobby" Rancho Santa Fe. A constant conflict between wealth and army-like spareness for spiritual growth is obvious with the choice of his "home" base.

Mercury in Taurus: Once more the practical financial orientation induced by his natal Mercury (the mind) in Taurus (wealth) produced an evident conflict with his visceral desire to "escape" the reality of this dense physical world and his stars' purpose to enjoy the best of it. The confusion and stress the cult leader experienced internally finally came to an end when he ordered the dramatic mass suicide.

Venus In Aries: Venus regulates love matters and made him a magnetic person. However, the planet of love inhabits his subconscious area of life. This house is traditionally ruled by dreamy Pisces and brought heavy guilt and misconception to his sexual nature. A heavy chart of this nature brings about sexual diversity and perversion and explains castrations. Furthermore, fueled by guilt, a strong desire to end sexual activity and commit spiritually to a "wedding" with a godly figure is often the result. Indeed a very deceiving position for the planet of passion that usually is a marker for homosexuality, heavy guilt and secret sexual love affairs. Thus in matters of love, Applewhite was very private and extremely deceiving to himself (and others).

Mars in Leo: Mars is well-known for his warlike attitude to the wise astrologer. Incidentally, like another religious fanatic cult leader, David Koresh, Applewhite was also born with the planet of war (fire/danger/explosion/weapons) in his fourth house (home). Also, the sign of Leo (the king) is found regulating the leader's base of operation. Thus a majestic home in distinguished Rancho Santa Fe, California became the "manifesto" of his Taurus Sun/Moon and Leo on the 4th. Combined with Mars (Army-like) desires, this is a solid indication of a need for order, command and power over the rest of the residents. Mars is also seen as a malefic planet and indicates where danger, even death may enter the scenery of one's life.

Jupiter in Cancer: The Lord of religious philosophy and teaching is strongly affecting Applewhite's third house of communication. Thus, a strong desire to educate himself with a form of codification of thoughts (bible) was always present. Traditionally, Cancer rules the 4th house (household) and this suggests an inflexible philosophy from and about home life, connected with the fast-approaching apocalyptic times. Jupiter also rules foreign lands, publication, publishing, so the "Heaven's Gate" site was a perfect means to reach via the World Wide Web the "forbidden" world, right from the privacy of the cult leader's home.

Saturn in Capricorn: The great tower builders, Saturn traditionally rules the 10th house of career. Accidentally, when Saturn's structural power is located in the 9th house of learning, teaching and preaching, the soul subconsciously aims for a position of honor. On a negative note, this affliction engenders evangelists, religious fanatics, cult leaders, where their specific belief system is based upon their rigid, self-created religious codification. In the case of Marshall Applewhite he endeavored for many years to achieve intellectual recognition and public standing. Divine Astrology sees and recognizes Capricorn (the goat) as the head of the "Devil" or the principle of manipulation. In this case, because of the particular cerebral department involving this area of the human experience, mental exploration and "egghead" manipulation for status took place. The Saturn stratagem principle convincingly transformed Applewhite onto a fanatical "higher level" deceiving teacher and a disturbed cult leader.

Uranus in Aries: Uranus is a cerebral planet regulating the next 2000 years of the human karmic experiences. This highly original planet also governs the new age phenomenon, UFOs, computers, and anything related to the incredible future not yet experienced. The "eccentric" release of energy planet was located in Applewhite's twelfth house furthering much of his deceiving subconscious motivations. Incidentally, Pisces (the fish) was also subconsciously (or perhaps consciously) chosen and used by Christianity (another belief system) to represent a form of "martyrdom."

Those archaic teachings (including those of the cult leader) are based upon purity, chastity, deprivation, self-inflicted pain, castration, humility with death as a final act to own a place in the "Heaven's Gate" or the kingdom of God. In this case, Uranus' power (the future) became out of control and got mixed with the recipient of his subconscious 12th house (religion). This deadly mixture involving Uranus (the future/UFOs) and Neptune (the past/dogmas) simply produced a disaster to all the parties involved. Sadly, unless one has a solid understanding of the dynamics of the universe, the subtle motivations of the cult leader responsible for the mass suicide will not be adequately understood.

Neptune in Virgo: To make the situation worse, in this case, illusive Neptune (ruler of Pisces) happens to be located in the prudish sign of Virgo (Puritanism/Virgin Mary) in his 5th house of love and romance. This house is also the house of speculation, creativity and joy created in specific endeavors. Neptune rules music, and combined with structural Saturn (classical), we can see why he was a gifted musician and once taught music. Incidentally, Neptune also regulates religion, imagination, drugs, alcohol and testifies to his "creativity" in the use of chemical mixtures to further his "prudish" purpose. His desire for purity, organization, chastity led also some members of his group to make a "commitment" against physical temptations and choose castration!

Pluto in Cancer: Indeed Pluto is a mighty influence. This planet is called in Greek mythology "The Lord of Hades" or the planet of death. Casually, Applewhite and Hitler shared the same awful position of Pluto (fanaticism) in their respective 3rd house (the mind). Furthermore, Jupiter (religion/righteousness/teachings) is also there and dangerously close to the planet of expiration. Pluto regulates reincarnation and the process of life and death itself. Thus, with such a placement in the (upper story) there is no surprise to me to realize the deadly motivations and lethal repercussion produced by both luminaries. Divine Astrology simply describes Marshall Applewhite's celestial identity as a radical, with a mental recipe for control, obsession, fanaticism and ultimately death.

When the old science of Astropsychology is accepted as a valuable discipline in all our colleges and universities, much of the mystery behind incomprehensible acts will be brought to light. Then, for people like Marshall Applewhite, Hitler, David Koresh and so many others, their ill-fated incarnations will not be allowed to overshadow the lives of other lost lambs.

Knowledge is power; there is no room for ignorance in the human experience. Wisdom conveys truth and veracity brings freedom from man's madness.

— Dr. Turi

The greatness of the Universe is unknown, but the magnetic forces that guide and move all the planets in our galaxy are known; this Divine source of power can be used to guide and bring man a life filled with happiness, peace and harmony.
— Dr. Turi

Chapter 16

Interviews with Dr. Turi:

During the course of my career I have been asked many questions. The following is a collection of questions and answers most commonly ask, plus my own thoughts pertaining to my books and general metaphysics.

Section I.

1. **What is *Moon Power Starguide 1998*?** *Starguide* is a direct link between the earth and the heavens simply translated for your convenience and day-to-day guidance. There is no room for ignorance in life; if you break any law, physical or spiritual, you'll have to pay the price.

2. **Is *Starguide* general or personal?** I prefer my own forecast. *Starguide* is not only very personal, it is also very objective. Your personal forecast, those you care for, and the entire world's fate for the current year is in it. May I add that if you were a fish in the ocean, would you be the only one to respond to the moon's fluctuations and rise with the tide? I don't think so."

3. **Yeah, but what about the rest of the book, it seems pretty general!** That question is often asked; my answer to you is also a question, "Did God create the stars, the Sun and the Moon only for you?" You are a child of the universe, a part of the human race and this involves an incredible complexity of spiritual and physical laws and structures called a macrocosm. Cosmic consciousness as a whole is the key.

4. **Yes, but what if in 1998 I want to know about me precisely?** Then you would have to commit yourself to a Full Life Reading in my office. You can only get what you pay for; this means a 35¢ newspaper horoscope, a $2.50 magazine forecast, a $25.00 reading at your local psychic fair, or you decide to invest with a professional and get valuable results. This

involves a minimum of 90 minutes of taped information based upon your celestial make up or your horoscope. If you can't make it physically, do not worry; 90-minute tapes are sent all over the world. You do not have to be present for me to enter the intuitional domain of your stars. No matter what you choose to do, *Starguide Moon Power* is an affordable and practical choice.

5. **Some astrologers use the Tropical Zodiac; what do you use?** I use it too, but I also benefit more with a different system called a *Monthly Housing System*. I created it a few years ago. This system has proven to be unarguable and gave me specific dates for my predictions. With all the respect I owe my astrologer colleagues out there, if the integrity of the ancient art is to be reestablished to the scientific world, one must have solid proofs. The work must be well documented, especially if it involves the news! My predictions have been printed in well-known magazines such as *Fate, Perceptions, Leading Edge* and many others in the US, Canada and *Magazin 2000*, Germany. My predictions were written in my books, at least a year earlier, and specific dates were broadcast on many televised programs for destructive earthquakes such as the January 16th, 1995 quake that killed over five thousand people in Kobe, Japan. Printed predictions of many major breaking news items such as the Rancho Santa Fe mass suicide, the Rodney King beating, the O. J. Simpson dilemma, the death of Bill Cosby's son, the mad cow disease and so much more must be available upon request. I can, and my predictions are very specific.

6. **How did you came to such a precision in predictive astrology?** Well, after my UFO experiences I felt compelled to literally "swallow" all of Nostradamus' work. Born and raised in Provence, France like him, I had the advantage of speaking the same language. Thus in my research, I realize that the Seer used a very different access to the stars. It took me nearly 20 years to re-kindle his 16th-century Divine Astrology forgotten formula.

7. **Other astrologers request the exact time of birth, you don't; why not?** Nostradamus did not have a watch! He is still seen

as the most accurate astrologer of all time, isn't he? One must investigate the Universal Mind with a telescope (intuition), not a microscope. I leave this scientific approach to the stars to the astronomers.

8. **Yes, but, for example in your book, you never wrote that 39 people were to commit suicide in California on March 26th?** Really? If you read closely, I mean between the lines, you may see that the drama was fully predicted. Astrology is classified as a pseudoscience, so one must realize its limits. In *Moon Power* I give "windows of probabilities" and I know from previous experience that in some of those windows, something dramatic will happen; it always does. That's why on page 87 of *1997 Moon Power*, I specifically made a note for those days. Here are a few sentences collected from this page pertaining to this drama. Notice also that I explained the energy pretty clearly and glasses are not needed to read between the lines. i.e.:

> **1997 *Moon Power* memo for Wednesday — March 26th:**
> **RULERS** — Pluto (hidden things brought to light): Attention: Pluto is back with us! Expect dramatic happenings all over; control is a must. The Lord of Hades doesn't forget and doesn't forgive! Be aware, don't be his victim.
>
> **Environment**: Avoid places overloaded with turbulent, crazy people. Pluto likes accidents and panic. As always, especially in a waning Moon (negative) expect dramatic and destructive news to plague the media. Earthquake, mass murderers, vicious killers, rapists and the worst of society will be active, led by the Lord of Hades.
>
> **Events**: This energy has the awful power for unity in discord. A form of death in any form, the beginning of becoming born again is to be experienced soon. People around you will become their true selves and during this transforming cycle a new you may be rediscovered. All changes MUST BE accepted and some of us must be ready for the ugliest time of their lives. Pluto rules the police force and all of those dramatic stories.

1997 Universal Predictions (page 230): Serious increase in drug consumption by underage children: Starting Jan. 1st, 1997, Neptune's subtle power will begin its karmic work upon this world. Using Divine Astrology — Neptune will be operational as of January 1st, 1997 and will stay with us until October 25th, 1998. Neptune raises drug and alcohol consumption, which promotes greater incidence of sexually transmitted diseases and elevates suicides. A negative Neptune rules fanaticism, illusion and desperation. Combined with the illusive power of Neptune, fueling this feeling of despair upon the masses will bring many young victims to the abuses of drugs, hopelessness and suicide.

9. **Is there a specific way to read your work?** Not really! Sometimes the energy will affect man's computer (his brain) and disturb his common sense and his spiritual nature. His natal program (horoscope) may also be fatalistically affected by the general stars' trends directed to the earth. This happens to be the case in the drift forecast for March 26th, 1997. Simply explained, because of his heavily afflicted celestial identity combined with his own ignorance, Applewhite lost his marbles and became another victim of the stars.

10. **What about his followers?** Well, a magnet will not attract a piece of wood; usually like attracts like! Somewhere, somehow, this crowd was doomed and in some way they magnetized each other in the drama of their own life on earth. Obviously, like their leader, those victims were spiritually lost and had to find a way and sacrifice themselves to regenerate in some weird activities. Some souls choose one of the numerous religions or a specific Deity as an excuse to die; in this particular case, Heaven's Gate chose UFOs. Nowadays the choice is pretty much yours!

11. **What about your earthquake and volcanic eruption predictions?** You see, the energy from the stars in our solar system does affect the earth and will "disturb" her entrails (faults). We are part of a much bigger scheme, and all celestial bodies (including the earth) are interacting with each

other. This phenomenon is not yet understood by scientists, geologists and seismologists alike. Nevertheless, on the physical level, it will translate into an earthquake or a volcano eruption. Often following a powerful quake there are signs of an increase of volcanic eruption. The following is some feedback from the Internet, when a few days earlier, I predicted "an unusual high seismic activity."

From:Private11
To: Dr.Turi@worldnet.att.net (drturi) —
Subject: Swarms at Mammoth
Date: Tue, 30 Jul 96 14:49:37 +0000
Subj: Mammoth Mountain 7/30/96 -

>Dear Dr. Turi: Over 65 EQ's near Mammoth mountain since 7/30 am and it's only 10:30 EST thus far. This is an enormous swarm — larger than I have seen since monitoring this area.

Another sample:
>To Dr. Private//@climate.gsfc.nasa.gov

> You should be watching my next window for July 24th and July 30th, especially in Hawaii! (I see an island, water and fire!). Please make a note. — Respectfully,
>Dr. Turi

Subject: Re: Hawaii swarm!
Date: 1996/07/24 (observe the dates!)
Newsgroups:ca.earthquakes,sci.geo.
earthquakes,sci.geo.geology

>Could we have a professional commentary on the Hawaii swarm we're seeing tonight?
>There is currently an earthquake swarm going on beneath Loihi Seamount about 25 miles off the southeast coast of the Big Island.

Dr. Turi -today's NYTs had an article >that Loihi is currently erupting.

12. **Do you consider yourself a professional psychic?** Let make sure we understand each other here; I consider myself as a professional astrologer and also a gifted psychic. Yes.

13. **Do you participate at psychic fairs, hold seminars, or teach?** No more. I used to participate at psychic fairs but I never felt right doing so. Yes, I hosted many seminars and taught at many different associations of Astrologers. I also spoke for various New Age, UFO groups and single associations. I also taught at an international gathering of top surgeons in La Jolla, California, discussing and watching videos on the later discovery on Cancer reconstructive surgery. There I explained the relationships between depression, the moon and woman's breast cancer to "Who is Who" in the international world of medicine.

14. **Have you written, or are you planning to write other books?** Yes, I write constantly. I am in my fourth year of producing the yearly *Moon Power Starguide*, first published by Horus House Press, Inc. and then The Book Tree, Inc. in conjunction with Truth Seeker Co., Inc. My two new books *The Power of the Dragon* and *The Power Within* will be released soon. I also write for magazines and newspapers in Europe, South America and the US.

15. **How long have you actually been working as a psychic?** I started counseling people back in 1976 when I was a student at the Royal School of Music in London. The urge to do so started after my second UFO experience that took place when my sister Noelle and I got lost in the French Alps.

16. **In which area of psychic ability do you consider yourself strongest?** Spiritual regeneration or regenerating someone's subconscious in time and space. Some of my counseling has also helped people physically and spiritually.

Section II.

1. **Do you have memories of your birth or womb state? How have these affected you?** No! It's only after the cutting of the umbilical cord that the spirit enters the physical body. Once the Doctor cuts the umbilical cord or "kills" you from your mother's warm uterine life, you become an independent spirit and receive your celestial karmic legacy (astrological chart).

2. **What do you mean?** The amount of work a soul performs during his past lives becomes an investment for future incarnations. Thus, if you worked really hard for many past lives as a musician, you will inherit impressive symphonic gifts. At an early age, Mozart and Beethoven were already loaded with such gifts and displayed their musical genius in creating incredible classical compositions.

3. **Do you have recurring dreams?** Yes, every night for years, since I was about 5 years old all the way up to the tender age of 12 years old. I am tied down on a large rock table in a cave. It's cold; I can see the snow picks and eagles flying outside of the cave. All my family members are against the cave walls; they are silently watching me. A moment later, two Chinese soldiers come in the cave and plunge their long knives in my upper body. I wake up screaming. Later on in my life I made a connection to this dream. Just before my birth in 1950, the Chinese invaded Tibet and killed all the elite monks!

4. **When did you first know you were able to "see" things others couldn't?** Soon after my first UFO abductions when I was somewhere between five and seven years old. All my family thought I was mentally disturbed when the morning after I innocently reported the frightening "monkeys with big eyes."

5. **What were some of your first experiences?** Before the ET nightly visitations I used to watch myself sleeping or rising all the way up to the bedroom roof; this is commonly called

"astral projection." I used to fly right through the window and all over the little village where I was born. The feeling was just incredible, but nobody could relate to my nocturnal experiences.

6. **Were you frightened, or did you just take them in stride?** No, I was not afraid at all; I actually enjoyed the deliverance from the weight of my body. I was amazed and kept asking everyone if, like me, they could fly too. The UFO abductions were of a very different nature and came later. They were very shocking to me, mostly because I could not move a muscle when those entities materialized in front of me.

7. **Were there other psychics in your family?** Yes. Both my mother and grandmother were gifted and quietly practiced their psychic work. However only my mother practiced her "Supreme Wisdom" gifts and many times she reported to her children the visitations of our deceased father.

8. **How did your family react to your abilities, and how did this affect you?** Apart from Mom, nobody else in my family really reacted positively, understood or supported my psychic experiences. I quickly realized that I was to deal with all this alone and learned to keep it for myself.

9. **What nationality are you, and do you think that your heritage affects your ability?** I am French; I was born in the southern part of France; and no, my heritage has nothing to do with my inner gifts!

10. **Where were you born? Do you think that your place of birth affected your abilities? In what way?** Like notorious Nostradamus, I was born in Provence. Again, there is no reason for me to believe that either France or Nostradamus' birthplace, la Provence, has anything to do with my psychic aptitudes. The stars' pattern above your head at birth determines the spiritual (or physical) gifts you inherited from previous past lives. Thus vibrating at such a high level of consciousness, I am not surprised to deal every day with the Sun, the Moon and the stars.

Section III.

1. **How has your psychic ability affected your relationships with others?** Knowledge is power; there is no room for ignorance in life, especially in terms of relationships. My psychic ability had greatly helped me to pick the right partner and after eight years of marriage we are still in love. Once I get the date of birth of someone, that person becomes an open book to me. Thus I know all the strengths and weakness of that person and I know how far I can go to deal and involve myself with his world. Your stars are like a painting; sometimes the colors do not match those you're involved with in terms of love, business, etc. The wisdom produced by the stars saves me much time, heartache and money.

2. **How does your family feel about you and your gift?** They love me and respect my gift, especially when it brought me notoriety and wealth.

3. **Did they understand you when you were a child? Did they encourage or discourage your psychic ability?** As mentioned earlier, they failed to understand not only my sensitive nature but what was happening to me. They did not do anything to support or discourage my psychic ability, mostly because nobody then was interested or knew of such a thing. Because of the hardship we all endured after the death of my father, much of our thoughts and attention were given to deal with real life.

4. **When you decided to claim your gift, what strength did you gain, what did you lose?** I was never really aware of my gift early in life; I thought everyone could "fly." I never really claimed anything; my psychic aptitude has been a part of me since I was born. It's like being born with beautiful eyes, they are a part of you, they belong to you. However, it's only after a succession of UFO experiences in my early 40s that I really felt a strong urge to educate myself in metaphysics and focused mostly on astrology.

5. **Were you trained as a psychic? Did you study with any certain people or groups?** Yes, I self-taught myself and did a lot of home study with the Progressive Universal Life Church in Sacramento, California. In March 1991, I graduated and got my Doctorate in Metaphysics. Much of the knowledge gained did not do much to further my natural aptitude until I mastered the science of astrology. Anyone can be trained to become a psychic, but the result is based upon your celestial identity and your inner gifts. It's like a runner: you can train anyone to be a professional runner, but the ones born with longer legs will be naturally faster and will win the race. Nostradamus mentions in his letter to his son Cezar, "These Centuries were born out of my nocturnal prophetic calculations, and from my instinctive nature, when seated near the bronze tripod, like the Delphic Oracle, God's messengers of fire came to me, and with the gift of judicious Astrology, I could foresee the moments and hours of events."

6. **What is your formal education? School, college, etc.?** I was thrown out of school at the age of 14 because of an Attention Deficit Disorder (ADD) problem. However, I managed to get my CED, CAP and an FPA in engineering ASME section 9; I graduated from the Royal School of Music with honors and got a pilot's license. There is a big difference between formal education and intelligence. I always thought of a battle for IQs between a parrot and myself and the "scientists" doing the testing. Because the parrot will be able to remember and repeat a full book word for word, he will graduate and get higher IQ marks than me! I have no memory and can barely remember my own telephone number, so "the educated" would fail me. To me, in my line of work, this "disorder" acts as another gift of protection. Imagine if after an intense week of astrological readings, as I usually do in Las Vegas, I could remember everybody's problems and take it all home. I would lose my sanity real fast! The educational system nowadays stinks; there are no books yet written to teach the teachers about the unforgiving will of the Cosmos reacting throughout the Divine bequest of the Creator within his celestial manifestation.

7. **Are you upset with education?** You bet: none of those teachers out there is aware of the position of Mercury (the learning principle) in his or all his students' celestial identities. Thus, they do not understand why Paul is gifted in math while John can't stand it. However, John is loaded with creativity, while Paul cannot draw a straight line or carry a tune. Looking past the physical manifestation they would realize that the difference between Paul and John is pretty obvious. John was born with a Mercury (his intellectual potential) in Pisces which rules the intangible, the arts, imagination and the spiritual world, while Paul's Mercury (education) is located in the down-to-earth Capricorn rational element. The proof of that is seen by looking at the educational system nowadays and the students' gigantic dropout rate.

Section IV.

1. **What abilities do you use to help people?** Like Nostradamus I also use my nocturnal prophetic calculations, and I draw on my instinctive nature, or 25 years of experience involving my knowledge of the stars and their relationships with the body and the mind of all my clients.

2. **How do you keep your abilities "tuned up"?** They never shut down — it's a curse! I regenerate in my work, the more I do it the better it feels and the more accurate I become. In my case, the ADD becomes a gift and allows me to forget immediately, not only my client's face, but all the trouble or stress he/she may have poisoned me with. Thus, I take nothing home and can read 10 hours straight for a full week without feeling exhausted.

3. **Have you been formally tested for psychic ability?** I am tested every day by thousands of people reading my daily guidance all over the world. The waves of incoming faxes, letters and telephone calls tell me I do not need to do so. My well-documented predictions of the Kobe earthquake, the California mass suicide, the 100 church burnings printed

in *Fate* magazine January 1st, 1995, the O.J. Simpson dilemma on 91X, radio station San Diego, the death of Bill Cosby's son Ennis, certified mail from the White House and NASA from the WWW, etc., etc., proves me right.

4. Do you think that psychic ability can be truly tested? Why or why not? Yes, it can. If I predict something using my psychic power and it is well documented before unfolding, then it works. Anyone pretending to possess psychic ability should be tested. It should be mandatory, especially when a service is offered to people. There is just one hair between Divine information and pure imagination; only the legitimate psychics should be allowed to deal with the fragile psyches of their clients.

5. What sort of problems do you help people with most often? You name it, but career, love, money and health are common questions asked. Some need spiritual support when they experience the painful loss of a loved one. Some invest all their possessions in a business venture and need to know all about the partners involved. Some are seriously ill, even mentally disturbed psychotics, and try to deal with sexual urges, depressions, loneliness, past lives residues, killing, and various psychological problems.

6. Do people benefit from your work? How? Obviously — if not, I could not make a living as an astrologer. The caring, understanding and direction I give them allows them to "recharge" their shattered spiritual batteries. Most of my counseling is extremely practical and after the two-hour taped meeting the magic touch is there to stay. Many of them honestly tell me that they listen to our work on a daily basis and it gives them the support they need to keep going. The solid direction I offer my clients is based upon the respect of some forgotten universal rules and the rebuilding of their self-esteem. Regularly, many of them, as they leave my office, will leave something behind them. Sometime it's a jacket, a book, a wallet, a checkbook. Once a client of mine left without his enormous boom box that he brought to tape the session. It's simply a subconscious desire to stay where the healing took place. Thus their higher selves make them forget something, to come back again. This won't happen if they go to the dentist!

7. **Do you use your formal education in conjunction with your abilities?** Again, like all other real Prophets or competent psychics and astrologers, most of my abilities are inborn; I mostly use my intuition in conjunction with my formal education.

Section V.

1. **As you understand them, please explain what is meant by the following:**

   a. **Magic, black or white.** There is such a misconception pertaining to magic. Paracelcus said: "Man is superior to the stars if he lives in the power of superior wisdom. Such a person, being the master over heaven and earth, by means of his will, is a magus and magic is not sorcery but supreme wisdom." However, one may decide to use the white power "magic" to do harm to others; then it becomes "black magic." Any standard dictionary interprets magic as "the pretended art of producing effects or controlling events by charms, spells and rituals supposed to govern certain natural and supernatural forces." Again, both words "pretended" and "supposed" are used to represent the skeptical attitude adopted by the "educated."

   b. **Rituals or ritual healing or magic? Do you use them in your work?** We all use rituals on a daily basis; the majority of untutored people use prayers; this pious behavior is nothing less than a religious "ritual." The Indians use different and more perplexing rituals than the common person and many disappeared civilizations all over the world such as the Incas, the Sumerians, the Atlantis, etc., used an even more complicated variety of "rituals." Yes, I do use "rituals" by suggesting specific physical and spiritual cleansing techniques based upon the laws of Nature. I also teach the Universal Law and a specific candle ritual to celebrate the New Moon ceremony on her honor and blessings upon the earth.

c. **What is the relationship between the physical/spiritual body and the Moon?** Our bodies are vulnerable to EMF (from AC wiring) because the AC frequencies (harmonics of 60Hz) are so close to the frequency nerve cells use to communicate with each other. This frequency is also similar to the frequency (10Hz) that emanates from the earth herself. This frequency "celestial energy" changes in intensity from distant stars (suns) planets and our very close satellite, the moon (gravity/magnetism). The earth is a spinning magnetic field with a core of iron, and our bodies and earth herself have evolved in relationship to that "subtle but real" outside stimulus or harmonic.

d. **Hypnosis. Do you use it, are you Board Certified?** No, I do not use hypnosis, mostly because I am aware of the damage that can be inflicted on the mind of the patient, especially in conjunction with drugs such as Sodium Pentothol. Some souls were born with a Neptune (illusion) in hard aspect with Saturn (fears/depression) or the Moon (emotion) in opposition to Pluto (death) or malefic Saturn in hard aspect with any planets. Thus a natural negative reaction, not only to drugs (prescribed or not) but to any suggestions that may be a challenge to the subject's belief system or his "reality" would be seriously detrimental. More damage is often inflicted by the physician upon the patient's fragile psyche after many hypnotic sessions, especially if the "perpetrator" has not cosmic consciousness or lacks awareness of the working of the universal mind (astrology.)

e. **Native ceremonies from ancient cultures?** Divine Astrology and all its implications reflect the legacy left to us by many ancient cultures. In my judgment, Astrology is primarily a pure art where a mathematical task does apply but must not blur or eliminate the intuition. Astrology, as practiced today, is mostly financially oriented. You will find it in the daily horoscopes generated by prominent people with a inborn business mind. Those "astrology" enterprises are to be found mostly in major newspapers and magazine publications all over. This type and many other "900" psychic "famous" endeavors have seriously hurt the integrity of the old discipline and take away real information from the gullible consumers.

f. Sorcery. Do you use sorcery; is it effective in helping people? The subconscious fear behind the word sorcery is a caution to anyone who dares to tread in the forbidden world of spirits. Someone who understands and uses sorcery for any higher purpose possesses Supreme Wisdom. Only those gifted at birth with an incommensurable Pluto will be attracted and able to deal safely with the unforgiving world of the spirits. Sorcery properly practiced can thoroughly free someone from a low astral entity invasion or a disturbing thought form.

g. Spells, curses or hexes. What are they, and do you use them? There is a formidable variety of positive or negative spells, curses or hexes to choose from, and these are readily available for those interested in using black or white magic. However, beware of fostering magic negativity as "for every action there will be an equal reaction." Karma will always find a way to reach you if you willingly decide to hurt anyone. Yes, I do use positive spells on a regular basis.

h. Removal of spells, curses or hexes. What method do you use? It is seriously advised to understand the forces that you're dealing with before attempting to do any ethereal removals, especially when curses are involved. Protection should be the number one concern to the practitioners of witchcraft. Those malefic forces could see you as a target and could literally invade you. Specific incantation, invocation of higher protective spirits, amulets, talismans, combined with protective circles of candles and incense rituals are some of the protections used by the magician. Timing your removal conjuration under a positive trend is also strongly advised.

i. **Why do you think that rituals have powers?** Because they do interact with the laws of relativity since everything in both the spiritual and physical worlds is connected. The incantations have stimulated my thoughts, my faith and my supraconscious in time and space. Thus, some of my clients and I have experienced the solid results of many of my magical rituals.

j. **What is a talisman?** A talisman is an object made of a specific substance, usually metal or wood. The most effective talismans can be produced by a learned Divine Astrophile. Mostly because astrological wisdom becomes the essential element to "time" and induce the specific celestial energy into the matter. Thus if you were born with a weak Venus you will experience problems in love matters. By making a talisman with copper (Venus metal) during the Venus hours or when Venus is rising above the ecliptic, you can "collect" enough Venusian energy to enhance your personal magnetism and stimulate your fifth house or the seat of attraction between human beings. These talismans, rituals and charms are designed to stimulate faith and both the celestial and physical laws to attract a specific wish. Also, when done efficiently, a "money ritual" will elevate the expectation thoughts and activate the faith grounds. This process will in turn arouse the supraconscious subtle forces to bring about wealth. Again, a strong knowledge of the mechanics of the universe and the perfect timing of all rituals becomes a major contribution to the success of the operation. A full knowledge of the physical and spiritual conception of the stars and their relationships with color, sound and metal is indispensable if you intend to become a proficient magician. I teach this marvelous wisdom.

k. **Do you think that any of the above are truly psychic ability, or do you place them in a different category, as**

religion or superstition? I am firmly convinced of all of the above mentioned topics to be truly psychic in nature. What cannot be seen, conceived or understood just yet by the scientific community doesn't mean it cannot be a possible reality. I had many unarguable proofs and experienced such phenomena myself. I am also aware of a number of psychotic problems facing many disturbed people nowadays. In many cases, they do reflect an early form of induced religious or superstitious poisoning that allows the psychic invasion in question. Combined with a regular use of drugs, alcohol or medicinal narcotics (including Prozac), the situation gets rapidly worse. Under such a stress, slowly but surely, the physical brain deteriorates and the mental sanity worsens. Then the physical and spiritual vibrations of both the body and the mind are altered to a slower pitch. Deprived of his protective higher vibrations, the etheric body becomes an attractive recipient for lower entities scourging the astral plane. I unconditionally believe that their inner fears become the consequential ingredient that allows any form of possession or madness.

1. **Have you ever crossed an energy threshold while working? What happened?** Being ultrasensitive by nature, I feel energy everywhere I go. Sometimes when visiting people I can feel their thought process bouncing back from the inside of their living quarters. Often, positive or negative thoughts are generated by others, and they reach the privacy of people's homes and I strongly react to them. Most often I counsel people to see, enter or touch their future house at a specific time of the month. I also teach them the importance of doing a candle ritual to negate the built-up energy generated by the previous owners. Someone might have been very sick or depressed and loaded the house with an undesirable energy. In some cases, a person might have been killed there, and the awful thought form is still very strong. Sometimes the owner of a young soul cannot let go of his earthly property and still hangs around, producing a haunted house. There are many good

reasons for the new owners to be aware of the energy. The impact in their lives can be disastrous and a *cleansing* becomes a necessity for their own spiritual well-being. In New Jersey, my wife Brigitte worked hard to cleanse an old house. A light green candle turned completely black in one of the rooms where a child died years ago. The lost soul was finally allowed to *go home* after the incantations.

2. **What is your purpose in this lifetime?** That is a sensitive question to me, mostly because it means so much for me to do something valuable for the children of tomorrow. Most of the knowledge of the stars (the real face of God) was taken away from us around the 15th century. Politically oriented churches at this time were not exactly interested in passing on wisdom, mostly because knowledge brings power and power leads to freedom. Keep in mind that back then, pen and paper were also expensive if available. Thus the rich and the monks got the education. Educating their countrymen was a serious task and somehow impossible. Thus, they changed the complexity of astrology (which had been around forever) into ten intelligible commandments. This was good for them at that time. The point is that we've grown and we need much more today. But I am confident with the help of the new ruler of the world Uranus, *the new age* Neptune, (religion/dogmas) is slowly but surely fading away. Reinstating the old science of astrology in all our colleges and universities all around the world is my goal. Renegotiating God's celestial tools is a must; doing so will bring forth the golden truth and a constant wind of spiritual regeneration, faith and love to the world.

Chapter 17

In the News

FRANCE AND ASTROLOGY

In France, the land of Nostradamus, astrology continues to make news. Former French president Francois Mitterrand recently dropped a bombshell by suggesting that astrology be included in the curriculum of the Sorbonne, the French university. The director of the Sorbonne, attempting to be at once funny and sarcastic, responded, "Sure, astrology will be admitted — over my dead body!" But interest in astrology has captivated French citizens. Books, newspaper columns, and feature articles are everywhere. The French, renewing their interest in the legendary Nostradamus, have made it crystal clear that they will never permit astrology to be dead and buried.

As if outgoing President Mitterrand had not created enough furor, the new French president, Jacques Chirac, took the French people into his confidence. He confided, "I ran for this office twice before and was defeated. I won't try to fool you; I was discouraged. Well, the third time was a charm — I won, as you know, on the third try, and for that I am grateful!" It was then that astrology once more came into the picture. Jacques Chirac disclosed that an astrologer had predicted he would twice be defeated but would run again and win on the third try.

RUSSIA AND ASTROLOGY

Astrology is booming in popularity, not only in France but also in Russia —Boris Yeltsin, an Aquarian, reportedly consults a committee of astrologers. Yeltsin wants to keep up to date on his horoscope. He has survived accusations of being an alcoholic, and is now attempting to survive charges that he is a fanatic who consults psychics and astrologers. But whatever Yeltsin's personal convictions, the Russian people themselves have embraced astrology. Recordings, newspaper features and columns, and books are popular, and wherever you go, you hear this greeting "What's your sign, Ivan?" Visitors to Russia should be forewarned: "Don't deprive a citizen of his vodka or his horoscope!" During 1997, tragedy could befall a member of the Yeltsin family. Yeltsin will be pulled in two directions simultaneously. His popularity may wane as accusations fly, and if he manages to survive it will be a miracle.

Yeltsin's weight could create a problem requiring a doctor's care or even hospitalization. May could be his most difficult month. More than ever, Yeltsin will need information provided by his planetary configurations.

Selected excerpts from: *Sydney Omarr's Astrological Guide for you in 1997.*

Every man who observes the stars diligently will uncover their subtle secrets. Having earned the golden key of wisdom he will understand the real meaning of being human. He will then be ready to lead others towards cosmic consciousness, peace and happiness.

— Dr. Turi

End of Your 1998 Starguide Universal Predictions

Chapter 18

Closing Thoughts

Today's date is June 7th, 1997.

Dear Clients and Friends:

I would like to sincerely thank you for your patronage and wish all of you a very successful New Year. It has been my privilege, with *Starguide,* to escort many of you through 1998. Please help me promote the cosmic consciousness of everyone you care about. Communicate my work and help those in need to find guidance, comfort, direction and assistance in the celestial order. I hope you found in *Starguide* the pathway to the stars and the realization of God's ultimate will throughout the Universe.

Walk in peace with the blessings of the stars.

> God bless you all,
>
> — Dr. Turi

He is wise who understands that the stars are luminaries, created as signs. He who conquers the stars will hold the golden keys to God's mysterious universe.

— Nostradamus

Chapter 19

About Dr. Turi's Practice

Dr. Turi uses tools that he created with the help of his higher self. One is a canvas art work measuring 15 feet long and 7 feet tall, and it helps you visualize your life in a whole new way. In the Doctor's presence, you will feel the warm field of his aura and you will be amazed while looking at his mystical tarot tables. Your reading will be accurate and very original. You will be taught at least two extremely important Universal laws that will stay with you for the rest of your life. Most of all, you will notice a genuine healing compassion in his teachings, and you will leave his office feeling fully rejuvenated. A better understanding of how to handle your particular lesson in life will be the result of the meeting. You will be informed of your subconscious fears and prepared to overcome them. You will realize your personal strengths and how to apply them right away to promote your life. A session with Dr. Turi feels like a magic wand healing your most troubled areas. Dr. Turi uses both Oriental and Occidental Astrology for your benefit. This information will help you to understand the tremendous impact of your natal Dragon's Head or Tail. This rare oriental teaching can be a major contribution to your success or failure in life. He will explain your past-life residue (and karmic debts) responsible for your deepest fears.

Each and every house commanding your destiny will be explained, using his mystical art work. A session with Dr. Turi will be the most rewarding experience you will ever have. You will sit throughout the astrological session, wondering how this man could have such intimate knowledge about your personal life. Dr. Turi will choose one of his custom-made tarot tables and will exercise the old French Tarot De Marseille to reach the deepest part of your soul. Any amount of negative energies created by your own subtle subconscious thoughts will be explained and cleared away. Dr. Turi is a genuine spiritual healer, and after clearing your "blocks" he will guide and enlighten the path to your immediate journey. A word of caution: Dr. Turi is well aware of the power of the supraconscious and your own subconscious as you become very vulnerable to suggestions, and as a practiced surgeon will not leave any of his psychic sponges in your subconscious.

Nostradamus was "Un Medecin Et Astrophile Du Roy." I've done numerous lectures and introduced the Seer's life with my slide show all over, and I am constantly promoting his great teachings. I am faithfully lecturing for different associations of Astrologers in the United States and for many UFO organizations. Many students of Divine Astrology have successfully learned the intuitive interpretations of the stars. Those "Astrophiles" have graduated and are happily promoting the integrity of the old science promoting their new career. In any case if you happen to be interested in my classes by mail (audio/video), contact my office at (619) 275-5853 for information. I've noticed that the Divine method seems to be easily assimilated by students.

On the other hand, the modern method and its complexity seems to attract those born mathematicians. Thus the difference of learning, reasoning and assimilation between the location of a Mercury (mental power) in an intuitive (water), intellectual (air), dramatic (fire) or practical (earth) element. Divine Astrology is an art and will attract those born with a powerful intuition. Those souls are more readily able to enter the archetypal realm of consciousness, and can understand the divine intuitional message breathing within the symbolic essence found in each sign of the Zodiac. However, properly trained, anyone, regardless of the natal Mercury location by house or sign, can master the intuitive science of Divine Astrology.

As mentioned many times in my lectures, cheap newspaper personalized horoscopes rob the people of real information and hurt the integrity of the old science. On the other hand, the Divine method makes you aware of the big scheme and your participation in it. You are a child of the Universe, a microcosm, part of a macrocosm, and the stars never intended to shine on a single person. The enlightened but mighty impact of the stars on your psyche and fate is related to everyone around you. Focusing on your horoscope's Sun sign and interpretations only is a big mistake, just as focusing on a single tree and missing the entire forest is. The true impact of astrology, as a whole, has much more to offer in terms of accuracy and guidance. This technique is just remarkable and took me many years to rekindle and is available to those interested. Because of the therapeutic values, and concentration of information involving this ancient art, the Full Life Reading session must be taped, if you are to recall all of it. I also caution my clients to never listen to the recording while driving, considering that a certain degree of mental hypnosis may occur while listening. Listen to your intuition, and learn to recognize the sincere, learned person by using also your rational thoughts. There is only one hair between Divine guidance and pure imagination.

You are a child of the Universe and there are reasons for you to be. One is to find all the answers that God has enslaved everyone of us to search for and the other one is to appreciate his creation and manifestation throughout the Universe.

Chapter 20
Dr. Turi — Services Offered

Dr. Turi, M.D.S — Astrophile, Author.
Tel: (619) 275-5853
Fax: (619) 275-4416 *51
WWW site — http://www.dawn21.com/Pages/DrTuri.shtml
Universal Predictions visit — http://www.newage.com.au/library/turi1.html

Dr. Turi regular Radio programs:

PREMIERE RADIO NETWORKS
Live & on the net on Jeff Rense worldwide radio show:
Listen to "Sightings On The Radio" <www.sightings.com>

Lou Epson Nationwide radio show from KNPX 840 AM, Las Vegas, NV
Joyce Isaacs — KVET 1300 AM — Austin, TX

Books order — www.thebooktree.com
http://www2.truthseeker.com/ft/index.html

Dr. Turi specializes in the business of Divine Astrology and offers you its unique method of work and service. The highly qualified and certified astrological work performed by Dr. Turi offers you the unconditional guarantee of quality. Astropsychology taped readings (90 minutes) are sent all over the world. This is the opportunity to experience and be amazed by Dr. Turi's incredible extrasensory talents. Satisfaction unconditionally guaranteed. Prior to your Full Life Reading, for channeling purposes, Dr. Turi insists that you call him first at (619) 275-5853. Thank you.

- Dr. Turi also deals with the issues of private life as well as business activities.
- Determine the suitability for your joint activities of your business partners or your office workers, the present and future ones.

- Foretell the efficiency of the specific contracts as well as the availability of perspective for proceeding with those already in force.
- Foretell the compatibility degrees of the partners both socially and intimately.
- Hiring the best suitable candidate for a specific job.
- Foretell the condition of the individual physical data along with the further determination of the most probable disease characteristic of the given person.
- Determine the exact date of the commencement of the medical treatment or operation.
- Compile an individual horoscope to reveal the most critical negative and positive vital.
- The complete confidentiality of application is guaranteed by Dr. Turi
- A contract is to be concluded for specific orders. The scopes, time of performance and fees are to be stipulated in the contract. It is essential for Dr. Turi to have at his disposal a date of birth of a private person or a legal entity.
- Based on the astrological chart, Dr. Turi can assist you or another entity to choose a partner whom he would be pleased with due to his own innate emotional attraction. This is the subconscious ideal image that a man or a woman is constantly seeking for an emotional or financial fulfillment.
- The quality of work is guaranteed by Dr. Turi. A client's exact date of birth is an indispensable datum in Dr. Turi's astrological work

Full Life Reading: $200.00 This detailed reading will be used throughout your existence. I will explain (using Divine Astrology) the significance of all the planets in your horoscope and thoroughly clarify all the vital departments of your life. In addition to adding new insight to your personality, this tape uncovers unique information based on the location of your natal Dragon's Head and Tail and the teaching of the implacable Universal Law. Keep in mind that I do not practice the Astrology you know, read, practice or have studied. My work is totally unique and does not resemble any previous psychic readings or astrological work you may have experienced. All readings are taped on top quality cassette tape. All your questions will be answered and the right direction/ guidance for a successful career or specific problem will be offered. The second part of your reading is the psychic cleansing and reading of your own supraconscious forces in time and space. All areas of your future and past life residue will be covered. Your satisfaction is fully guaranteed. — Tapes of private Full Life Readings are sent all over the world (you don't have to be present). Be amazed — Try me on the telephone first! (619) 275-4416.

Astro-Carto-Graphy: $200.00 — Map your future, don't relocate without it! Find out where and what the best of your stars have to offer you. You may be just a few hundred miles from a splendid Venus (love) Sun (fame) Jupiter (study) Mercury (writing) line. You might be right now living and striving without any hope of success under a nefarious planet like Saturn (depression) or Neptune (drugs). Take a chance for yourself and make your own reality; learn where those wonderful lines are waiting for you. Don't buy a house without checking it out as you might not be able to keep it for long. Avoid financial stress (Saturn lines); avoid locations where you are prone to lose your home because of nature's devastative forces (Uranus lines). Avoid fires (Mars lines); instead, let me direct you towards happiness (Jupiter) wealth (Venus) health power and fame (Sun). Call now for information, do not hesitate, your house is your biggest and the most important investment you will have to make — Call me for info first — Dr. Turi (619) 275-4416. Work available by mail. World Wide Map and booklet will be also mailed to you.

Divine Astrology Course: $1500 — Learn the incredible Nostradamus 16th Century method offered by Dr. Turi. If you are afraid of mathematics or the complicated Astrology as practiced today, you are the right candidate for Divine Astrology. Give yourself the chance of a lifetime in learning Real Astrology. Use the same tools used by Nostradamus. 16 weeks intense course, 2 exams — 75% of correct answers minimum to earn Diploma. The class includes the French Astro-Tarot tuition — Learn to read the cards correctly using the French Divine-Astro-Tarot method. You will be more accurate in your readings than the most renowned psychic you know. Understand how to tab on the Supraconscious in time and space for an impressive guidance. Using Nostradamus 16th century Divine Astrology method, learn to interpret the real value behind the symbolic power of the Tarot De Marseille cards. This procedure is a part of the Divine Astrology tuition and can only be executed accurately with the full knowledge of the stars. Large discount and easy payment plan is offered to students taking the course by mail with audio and video tapes. Call for information — Dr. Turi (619) 275-5853.

Prospective Students of Divine Astrology

In today's troubled times, man has sought answers to complex problems in medicine, politics, philosophy, science, religion and many other disciplines, all the while pondering the heavens and looking toward the stars as if to find answers but not seeing, as did the ancients, that the key to many of life's mysteries was in front of his very eyes. As man has turned his vision toward the stars, in space travel and technology, we have seen an unprecedented interest in astrology, a virtual renaissance of the oldest science in the world. Still, it is ironic that the explosion of modern technology and centuries of religious dogma have produced more questions, death and trauma than answers.

It is no wonder then that man's thirst for a more meaningful way of life has once again captured his interest in Divine Astrology. Sadly enough, astrology has been debased and maligned in modern times as a result of misunderstanding and commercial distortion. Thus the old science has been deprived of its true spiritual values and reduced to a confusion of mathematical jargon or a spot on the comedy page of the newspaper. Through education and renewed interest in Divine Astrology, future generations of new scientists will join in a common search for truth and wisdom. Then, as it once was, the old science will be back in our colleges and Universities and accepted as an esteemed discipline. We all are related "genetically" to our family members, we may even look like mom or dad; however, within the concept of the interstellar mind, we are total strangers to each other. You will not think or do things the way your mom, sister, brother or your dad does them. You were born with unique gifts that will help to guide you through life to a greater understanding of what it means to be human. The secret and key to the Creator's mysterious universe are available to you if you but "ask and you will receive" the answers you seek. The Divine Astrology method is free of confusing mathematics and the less you know about astrology the easier it will be for me to teach you and guide you to cosmic consciousness. This study will stimulate your mental exploration and regenerate your spirit while allowing you to enter a subtle but very real dimension.

Knowledge is power, and understanding the ultimate will of the cosmos can only help you achieve all that you desire. Once you invest time in Divine Astrology, new doors will be opened to you as more and more people and children need direction in this perplexing age. You are not only building a new career in metaphysics right from your home, but also securing yourself financially with another social security that can really support you and your family during the retirement part of your life. For every action there will be a reaction, thus for your investment and moment spent in learning, you will have to teach and gain the financial rewards of the decision you're about to make.

These classes are available by mail and include audio, video and study guide materials. There is one video on the basics of Divine Astrology attached to the tuition. More video programs are available upon your request. Fourteen 90-minute audio tapes that cover every single aspect of Divine Astrology with innumerable examples from which to learn.

Four 90 minute audio tapes that teach all the cabalistic secrets of the Astro-Tarot so that answers may be reached quickly and with stunning accuracy. Two exams that need to be passed with 75% accuracy or better. For those of you who have a computer, there is a special monthly housing system option software available. I created this specifically for all the future students of Divine Astrology. It is easy to install and operate and will be offered to pupils at discounted prices from Halloran Software Inc. Some of the students we have are masters in computing and can help you directly on-line if you encounter any problem.

There is no pressure to keep up with anyone; you can learn at your own pace. There is no need to find hours in your busy schedule to sit and learn; you can listen as you commute to work or as you relax from a busy day with the children. I am even working on setting up a support group on the Internet so that students can converse with each other as well as with me to better understand the sea of information you will be learning. Advanced students are ready to communicate with you on the net once you're started. People from all walks of life have earned their diplomas from this course with amazing results. Remember, no one but yourself is in charge of your destiny and for every action there is an equal reaction.

Be the one to understand the motivations of yourself and your fellow man as you walk the maze of life. As I lead you to the door of understanding, hope, success and security I would like you to be able to open it with ease so I offer all of this for $1000.00 or four payments of $250.00 which is a large saving over attending in person which would cost you $1,600.00. I want this information to be affordable so that all may attain their true rewards in this and every lifetime to come. Knowledge is power and this tuition will lead you to all the freedom you're looking for.

Ask and you shall receive the Divine tools of the great designer. Be a promoter of light, a New Age teacher and help me to reach all the children of the world.

— Dr. Turi

Attention all Radio and Television Hosts Reps: If you are an individual with a radio or television program and would like to assure your audience an incredible time, please call or fax

Truth Seeker Co., Inc.
P. O. Box 28550
San Diego, CA 92198
E-Mail: medmktg@cts.com
Tel: 800-321-9054 ext. 207
Fax: 619/676-0433 Attn: Nicole

> **Note**: Dr. Turi benefited from California Cities Board of Directors financial support to produce videos of their respective city's astrological profile, and he is the only astrologer in the world to have done so! The last city he explored for KLAS-TV Channel 8 was Las Vegas, Nevada. Let him explore your own city! Call the Truth Seeker Co., Inc. at 1-800-321-9054 ext. 207 for information.

Lectures, Workshop and Slide Presentations Topics:
- Nostradamus Slide Presentation
- UFOs Slide Presentation
- Astro-Carto-Graphy Works Wonders!
- Astropsychology
- The Power of the Dragon
- Fighting Depression
- Moon Power
- Building Self-Esteem

Lecture — Thought Power: Have you ever wanted to possess something badly? a piece of jewelry? clothes? a car? a computer? a situation? a job? a person? etc. Success is based upon a mixture of self-esteem, enthusiasm and full dedication. To bring about those wishes, depend on your awareness and utilization of your own superconscious in time and space. Your future is nothing else than the reincarnation of your own positive thoughts. I will disclose the mind's secrets and show you how any of your deepest wishes can be granted. Anything and everything that you need, even better health, is fully available and right there in front of you. Anything can become your reality if you understand and correctly use the dynamics of the Universal mind.

Workshop — The Power Within: The potential to make all your dreams a reality will be offered to the audience. Realize the importance of your own thought process and how it molds your future. See how *The Power Within* can be used to heal people and its real potential for miracles. Realize the importance of our common "thought links" prevailing faith and the subtle process taking place behind all the world changes. Several examples will be given to the attendance to prompt your own *Power Within*. An in-depth study of the subconscious mechanism involved will be revealed as Dr. Turi will work with you to expand your consciousness, offering you the golden key of knowledge. If you have an interest or a degree in psychology, do not miss this workshop. This workshop will change the way you think about it all. The golden key of wisdom can change one's life, simply because knowledge is power. With this comes the possibility for each and every one of us to reach for the best with the realization of your spiritual conception. Conventional disciplines fall short in the explanation, let alone the complexity, of the workings of our mind. The purpose of this workshop is to enhance the possibility for you to understand what it means to be human and achieve peace of mind, faith, love, emotional and financial security. Thus, a genuine chance to experience true happiness. In the long run, this workshop will undeniably help you to discover the mechanics of your supraconscious in time and space and ascend to your own *Power Within*.

Please do not hesitate to contact Dr. Turi directly at (619) 275-4416 or (619) 275-5853 if you need more information.

He is wise who understands that the stars are luminaries, created as signs. He who conquers the stars will hold the golden keys to God's mysterious universe

— Nostradamus

Synopsis — Dr. Turi's books

Moon Power Starguide 1998 — Universal Guidance and Predictions

This book is the articulated link between earth and heaven. It is a yearly 258 pages of day-to-day guidance and Universal predictions. It is produced using Nostradamus' unique 16th-century Divine Astrology method (like the Seer, Dr. Turi was born in Provence, France and rekindled his old method of divination). Many major pieces of news have been accurately predicted in previous *Starguides* well before unfolding. For example, as the Rancho Santa Fe mass suicide dilemma was fully predicted for March 26th, 1997. *Fate* magazine also printed Dr. Turi's prediction with the one hundred church burnings dilemma. *Starguide* is educational, reliable, unique in qualifications and a genuine tool for those needing legitimate predictions. Included in ***Moon Power Starguide 1998*** you will find incredible material such as the Power of Pluto Upon Generations, Famous People's Predictions, Gang Generation, the Universal Law, the Fate Of The World, Mystical Dragon etc. *Starguide* genuinely helps the reader to respect God's Universal Laws, sign important documents in the right period, get married on the right date, start a business on a specific cycle and become successful in business matters. For those in search for affection, ***Moon Power Starguide 1998*** will guide them in finding real love when the stars are exalted. Accurate Universal Predictions for the world, weather patterns, earthquakes, tornadoes, volcanoes and major breaking news have been unarguably predicted. While glancing at horoscopes of everyone you care about for the current year you recognize the ultimate will of the cosmos. Most of all, ***Moon Power Starguide 1998*** offers fascinating material and an accurate guidance for each sign of the Zodiac.

The Power Of The Dragon

A 250-page masterpiece of incredible information. There is more power to be found on the Dragon alone than the entire mathematical complexity involving a person's astrological chart. The accumulation of all the soul's past lives residue, his sins and virtues are stored on the mighty Dragon's Tail. While the real celestial identity involving the soul's strengths and weaknesses hides on his sharp tail, the true fate lies on his fiery head. Most importantly, its location and awareness, by house and sign, is a major contribution to success or failure in one's life. Pushed by their respective natal Dragons, this work includes many samples of famous and infamous people and their fated endeavors. A challenging relationship between conventional psychology, psychiatry and Astropsychology's indisputable overtaking wisdom is efficiently demonstrated to the reader. The impact of the Dragon upon different countries and its repercussion upon the masses involving future, present and past generations is fully illustrated. In summation, this book holds the genuine key of wisdom in what the ancient occidental and oriental astrology knew as *The Power of the Dragon*. This reference work is especially designed to reach the professionals and beginners alike in re-exploring the therapeutic values found in the old science of astrology. The reader will advance his own cosmic consciousness and will benefit tremendously in his perception of ***The Power Of The Dragon.*** Like his notorious predecessor, Nostradamus, Dr. Turi was born and raised in Provence, France. After many years of arduous work, he successfully rekindled the Seer's Divine Astrology method. Television anchors in cities such as Phoenix, Tucson AZ; Las Vegas NV; Manhattan, N.Y.; San Francisco, San Diego,

Oceanside, Carlsbad CA; Seattle WA; and Denver CO invited Dr. Turi to broadcast information pertaining to the "Dragon" flying above their respective cities.

The Power Within
Dr. Turi's most incredible and latest book (in progress). This work explains in great detail the mechanism involving the reincarnation of your inner thoughts creating your own future. Many solid examples are used to demonstrate the incredible *Power Within* we all possess and how to use it to bring about all your wishes. This book contests the traditional psychology and psychiatric formula in the explanation of what it means to be human. Indeed, a book that has an incredible potential in furthering the new consciousness experienced by humankind at the dawning of the millennium.